Editor's Note

Jonathan Wilson, Editor

There are times when being a football journalist is tiring. It's not the late nights, the long hours and the ceaseless travelling - although by the end of the season that is beginning to wear you down — so much as the relentless anger you have to deal with. Hooliganism may have fallen away but football is a terribly angry sport.

Maybe it's always been that way and it's just that social media has revealed it, but it's a terrifying thought that so many should go around waiting to be outraged, desperate to find evidence of disrespect, that so many should believe in the most absurd conspiracy theories, that so many should seemingly spend so much time sitting around waiting for the opportunity to be unpleasant. I used to think *Eastenders* was ridiculous because I couldn't believe nastiness was a default setting; maybe I was naïve.

It's almost impossible to write anything about football without annoying somebody. The most banal observation will cause offence. You'll be at a game, something will happen 30 yards away, you'll tweet about it, and you'll find yourself abused for reporting something you saw clearly, something backed up by replays. Often you'll draw fire from both sides of an argument, that you're somehow simultaneously both too tough and not tough enough on biting/ bad tackles/ diving/ racism (delete as applicable). And, of course, the most objectionable aspect of that last sentence is that something as serious as racism has somehow become another football issue, and as such tends to be debated on partisan grounds.

But actually the most grating thing is the kneejerk snideness. Earlier this season, after Barcelona had beaten AC Milan 4-0 in the last 16 of the Champions League to overturn a 2-0 first-leg deficit, I wrote a piece for the *Guardian* reflecting on the away goals rule and whether a) it was ever fair and b) even if it were, whether it has become counterproductive. It's an issue of regulation, it's not about fundamental beliefs or one team over another: it's hard to imagine people getting too worked up over it.

The following night, Arsenal — to general surprise — won 2-0 in Munich, to go out of the Champions League against Bayern on away goals, having lost the first leg 3-1. Not surprisingly, a lot of Arsenal fans then retweeted the piece, as did the US journalist Grant Wahl. I then got a reply from an American sneering that I'd only made an issue of it because it involved a Premier League club. He obviously hadn't read the piece: if he had, it would have been clear it had been written about Barcelona. But even if he had, and even if I had questioned the validity of the away goals rule on the back of the Arsenal game, so what? I am a British journalist and the piece was in a British paper: it's hardly outrageous that it should discuss an issue when it became relevant to a team based in Britain.

This obsession not with the contents of a piece but with its existence is bizarre.

Somebody may not be interested in a piece on the away goals rule, which is fine; nothing compels them to read it. Somebody may not like carrots but they wouldn't email the farmer to tell him not to grow them. But somebody actually went to the effort of composing a tweet to complain that I'd written a piece he'd hadn't read. As a rule, you try to ignore such people but occasionally the drip-drip of attrition gets the better of you. So I called him out on it. He sneered back (it seemed to be his natural mode) that of course he hadn't read it as it was in the *Guardian*. So he was complaining about a piece he hadn't read on a website he doesn't read. Still, he ended with a smiley face, so it was all alright.

It's a minor issue, obviously. All that story tells you is that there's one bloke in the US who for about five minutes of his life acted like a prick. It happens. But it seems to happen an awful lot. There is a strange culture of entitlement around football. An opposing player goes to take a throw-in and you're in the front row. What's the natural reaction? Is it a) to think, "Look! I'm six feet from Full-Back X"? b) to ponder that Full-Back X looks a lot thinner in real life? Or c) to hurl abuse at Full-Back X while making wanker gestures? For far too many people it's c). Full-Back X has, after all, had the temerity to come near them wearing the shirt of an opposing team so he had it coming.

A similar reasoning seems to motivate those who discover a journalist disagrees with them and respond with abuse and accusations of bias. How could it be? How could somebody possibly think differently to me? They must be an idiot/ wilfully drumming up controversy/ in the pay of somebody. This reached an apogee for me when Tottenham's game against Southampton in May was delayed for 30 minutes because large numbers of fans had been held up getting to the game by a chemical spill on the M25. Pretty much everybody in the press room at White Hart Lane reacted in the same way: an irritated shrug at half an hour added to the day, but an acceptance that it was probably the right decision. But my Twitter feed filled up with people expressing disbelief, furious that their sitting on their sofas watching television had been inconvenienced by people who had paid for tickets actually trying to get to a match. I confess it was something of a watershed moment, the first time I realised that there is a world of television consumers who actually see themselves as more important than people who attend the game in person, who actually thought their cable subscription outweighed safety concerns on the Seven Sisters Road. Again, in and of itself it's a minor issue; what's worrying is the trend it represents.

The self-entitlement is also manifested in the willingness of so many on Twitter and in comments sections to pass judgement on others. The media as a whole, of course, can be guilty of this and does have an annoying tendency to go after low-hanging fruit. This is where the familiar "lazy journalism" jibe does have currency, less in terms of the hours put in than the intellectual energy expended. It's easier to follow the familiar templates of previous stories than to work out what is actually going on and apply perspective.

Twitter and comments sections should be a boon, a way for people with a shared interest to interact. It's a positive when journalists are called to account

for a mistake or a misjudgement or if
they are forced to defend their opinions.
But that's not the way it's working.
What's happening is a grim attritional
process that means most journalists give
comments sections at most a cursory
glance. Worthwhile criticism is lost amid
the idiocy and the abuse.

But actually the situation is worse than
that and extends far beyond the confines
of social media reaction to journalism.
That is just a symptom of a wider
malaise. Football, the one global sport,
something that should be a great unifier,
has come to be dominated by the angry
and the self-entitled. It's terribly sad.

June 2013

Contents

The Blizzard, Issue Nine

8

Iran

"The alley games are dying out,
traffic and construction eliminating
the small, safe places where you
could play."

The Vacant Lot

The search for a kickabout in Iran is complicated by religion and gender politics

By Gwendolyn Oxenham

Ali has only been in the United States a year but he speaks perfect English. "Satellite TV — *Friends*, Chandler, Monica — that's how we all learn English," he explains matter-of-factly, running his hands through long wavy hair. "Now, onto the football!" He scribbles Farsi soccer terms and the phonetic equivalents into my notebook. "You must look for a *dough-lay-year*. It is a ball special to Iran. Children buy 25c rubber balls from drugstores and rip them open, stuffing them inside each other so the rubber gets thicker and the ball gets heavier." He draws a picture of a ball next to the word. Then he writes out a list of phonetic sentences that we can use later: "Do you know where we can find soccer?" "Can I play with you guys?" "Is it ok if she plays too?"

When I tell my mom we're going to Iran, she says, "No, you are not." Luke's grandma says, "Turkey's a beautiful country — why don't you go there?" And Luke's aunt tells me over the dinner table, "You know, over there, they stone women for adultery. When you try to play, what do you think they will do to you?"

Three friends and I had come up with a plan to travel the world playing and filming pick-up games and writing about the experience. Luke and I played, Ryan and Ferg filmed. Ali had heard the four of us wanted to go to Iran and got in touch with Luke via Facebook. We never really expected to be able to go. We made a few phone calls just to see — just to rule it out so we wouldn't always wonder if we could've gone to Iran. The first two tour groups that came up after we Googled "Iran +travel+ agency" told us "no" right away. They could take us to museums, to the Towers of Silence and the Zoroastrian Fire Temple but they could not let us wander the streets filming pick-up games. For that, we would need a press visa. Rick Steves — travel writer and TV personality extraordinaire — barely got approved for one. There was no way the Iranian government would give them to four kids who'd only made school documentaries about ferret-lover clubs and college sports teams.

The last company we called wasn't really a company. It was just a guy, an anthropology professor in San Francisco who helped people get to Iran because he wanted them to know the country the way he did.

Jerry said "sure, sure" and "of course" as I explained our film and what we wanted to do. "Well, you know," he sniffed, "the people of Iran love their football." And yes, we would have to go with a tour guide, and yes, we had to have a set itinerary approved by the government...

but one does not always have to follow the itinerary. "I will call Ahmadreza — he is the head of an Iranian tour company. I will see…"

A month later we land in the Tehran Imam Khomeini International Airport. Ahmadreza, as it turns out, has a son who considers himself Manchester United's number one fan. A series of emails with the subject line "The Sports Enthusiasts" ended in a visa and the implicit understanding that these four Americans were coming to look for soccer. There would be the appearance of a tour and we would be assigned a guide. "Everything depends on who you get as your guide," Jerry said. "Not only must you trust him but he must trust you."

Like every other female on the flight, I'd wrapped my hair in a scarf 15 minutes before touchdown. (Ferg and I had watched How-to-Wear-Hijab videos on YouTube.) Over jeans, I'm wearing a long-sleeve shirtdress I bought at Target. Ferg is wearing a fitted, navy-blue trench coat. We feel rather impressed with ourselves by how much we've managed to look like everyone else. This is important to us — we always want to belong.

Standing in line at customs, I'm nervous. When it's my turn in front of the glass booth to face the customs officer, I smile up at him even though this is exactly what I told myself not to do: *Persian Odysseys*, the book I'd read on Iranian customs, said women aren't supposed to make eye contact with strangers. I quickly look down at my feet… until he begins to speak and then I forget again and look right into his surprisingly apologetic face. "I am very sorry but we must take your fingerprints," he says. "It

is stupid, I know, but your country does it to us, so we must do it to you."

Before we left, I imagined our guide — the man who'd be helping us skirt Iranian law — as a roguish rule-breaker, provocative grin and stance. He'd grab our bags from the carousel with an authoritative, casual swoop. A buzzed head, old faded t-shirt, you'd be able to see right away that he was a player, good on the field.

But the man standing before us, with four roses and a clipboard, is thin and rather frail-looking. His shoulders are narrow. He's wearing a Tommy Hilfiger polo shirt and jeans, and to be honest, he looks like somebody who'd scare easily. He has wavy brown hair, big green eyes, a big nose, and expensive glasses. I smile at him, feeling guilty for my disappointment. He waltzes towards us, bent slightly forward, arms crossed in front of his chest, fingers grasping the sides of his arms. His chin moves side to side as he talks, an involuntary no: "Welcome to Iran. I am Atef."

Atef leads us over to a man standing on the curb. "This will be our driver, Saeed." Ryan and Luke shake his hand and Ferg and I wave. Saeed has the kind of face you trust: grey eyebrows and moustache, brown eyes, bashful smile. He hurries off to retrieve his taxi and we wave goodbye to the adventure-tour Americans. Then Atef asks, "So, what would you like to do while you are here?"

I study his face, looking for football, for some awareness that that is why we are here. I'm thinking of the San Fran professor, how he repeatedly urged us to follow the unspoken way of doing things in Iran. Maybe what Atef wants is a conversational commitment to an itinerary none of us intend to follow. "Football," I say, casually, quickly, lobbing out the word.

"Football?" he says with a half-laugh, a polite sort of bluff — unsure, it seems, if the American is making a joke that doesn't translate.

Atef knows nothing about the football.

Ryan, Ferg, and Luke turn and look at me. I am the one who set this up; I am the one whose fault it will be if we spend the week inside museums.

"Ahmadreza, Ahmadreza," I say. "The head of the tour company—he knows about the football."

"Ahmadreza? I do not know any Ahmadreza."

I pull out the chart of phone numbers we'd made for ourselves and point to his name, hoping I'm just butchering the pronunciation so badly he can't recognise it. He shakes his head and looks up at me. "I do not think this person exists."

Our taxi is a slime green VW van with big rectangular windows. There's great light, coming in on all sides, reflecting off the white vinyl seats. Over the past three years, the four of us have reversed down main highways in Trinidad and Peru, wrecked a taxi in China and hydroplaned during a violent storm across a mud road in the Amazon, but we've never seen anything like the scene on the streets of

Tehran. It's a kind of communal dance — an old woman walks into the centre of the road and holds up her hand with the authority of a traffic cop, cars screeching to a halt in front of her; motorcycles cant like sailboats in high wind as they zoom in between the taxis; wide boulevards converge upon each other, old Peugeots all going in different directions. Tehran has fourteen million people and it feels like they're all out on the street.

Drivers move at the same speed as those on foot and everyone talks to each other, screaming over the loud sounds of construction. There are tall buildings the same colour as the heavy smog that blocks the view of the Alborz Mountains. I stare out at the women who pass by, some clad in the full chador, some wearing skimpy, brightly-colored scarves that seem provocative, accessories to brightly-colored faces, rouge streaked across cheeks, thick liner defining red lips. I see some of the thinnest, most aggressively plucked eyebrows I've seen in my life. Even more startling are the bandaged noses that keep passing by. Luke, keeper of a wide collection of random facts, told me Iran was the nose job capital of the world but I hadn't really believed him. But the bandaged noses, which, according to Luke, are status symbols for the wealthy, are as frequent as the police who plug up the street. I see a female officer in a long robe usher a woman wearing high heels into the back of a green and white squad car. "That's the Morality Police," Atef tells us. The Morality Police is the arm of the Islamic Revolutionary Guard Corps, which patrol the streets, enforcing the Islamic code of behavior, cracking down on Western-style clothing and hairdos. But the Tehran youth, like youth everywhere, risk the crackdowns, attempting to get away with as much as they can.

I brace my knees against the seat in front of me. *Lonely Planet* warned that visible signs of Iranian football fever were almost non-existent — this is because the government puts the fields behind brick walls. So every time we drive by a wall I sit up very straight and try to see, annoyed that we might be zooming past games, people I'll never know playing behind walls I can't get behind.

Iranians have a reputation for being the most courteous people in the world, never wanting to disappoint a guest, never wanting to tell you no; maybe this is why Atef decides he's willing to let us look for games. It helps that Saeed was a player. From the driver's seat he speaks in fast, enthusiastic Farsi that Atef thinly translates: "Saeed grew up playing in the streets. He loves football."

Saeed tells us that nowadays, the alley games are dying out, traffic and construction eliminating the small, safe places where you could play. Nearly every country we go to we hear this — people frowning, voices thickly nostalgic, speaking of old ways and games that disappear. But there are still fields, and after 20 years of driving the city, he knows where to find them.

On the first field he shows us there are some young kids practising. This is not the kind of soccer we look for but we get out and watch anyway. The boys wear their shorts very high, shirts tucked in, and for some reason this makes them look innocent, swaddled. Saeed frowns,

knowing this isn't what we're after. We follow him inside a great brick building.

Men, presumably dads, stand in the entrance, watching young boys dribble soccer balls around cones. The cavernous ceilings echo the sound of feet drumming against wooden floor. One of the onlookers — he reminds me of Jack Arnold, Kevin's dad from the *Wonder Years* — looks at us with interest and then speaks to Atef, who does not translate the conversation.

Mr Arnold comes and stands beside me. "My English is no good," he says shyly, waving his hands. "But it is an honour to have you in our gym."

"Thank you," I say, my mind racing with possibility. I struggle to come up with the Farsi word Ali had taught us for pickup. Cringing, knowing my pronunciation will be terrible, I ask, "Do you know where we can find *goal-coo-chick*?"

His head jerks back in surprise. "No, no one plays on the street anymore — we scoop them off the streets and teach them here." He says this with a frown, like he's feeling a little embarrassed, even though he's never been embarrassed of this before. He doesn't like not being able to help us. He stands there, eyebrows furrowed, trying to think if there is anything he has forgotten. "There is a game — in Southern Tehran, around midnight. Unbelievable stuff, tricks you haven't seen anywhere."

"It is too late," Atef's voice says from behind me. "As your host, I cannot permit you to go there."

Once Atef has walked away, the man scratches behind his ear and we stand together in silence. Then he says, "Of all the gyms in all the world, I find it incredible that you have walked into ours." It sounds like *Casablanca* and gin joints and fate. I lean my head against the brick wall of the gym and think about that. Probably, I'll never see him again, and probably, this meeting changes nothing. I don't like it when you can only know someone for 10 minutes.

As we leave the gym, I catch the end of a conversation between Ryan and Ferg and one of the dads. "You come to my home, I will give you special alcohol," he tells them. He glances around and whispers, "Iran is the largest prison on earth... please tell the world."

Our next stop is a synthetic field in the center of Tehran. Luke doesn't want me to play. We've been having this fight for the past two weeks and he continues it now. "They've already come to a decision on this," he says. "Are you going to try change national policy this week?"

"But they haven't come to a decision — it's against the law for women to wear toenail polish, but women still do wear toenail polish."

"It's against the law for you to play — it's illegal."

He's right; it's against the law. But there's a giant fissure between the government's laws and people's actions and beliefs, and not every law is enforced.

A policeman walks up behind us so I don't push it and Luke is the only one who tries to get on.

It's a game of teenage boys, same as any group of teenage boys — a little arrogant, a little thrilled with their sudden independence. One kid's T-shirt has a Star of David stitched next to a swastika. Part of me thinks, holy shit. But the other part of me thinks he's just a 14-year-old kid trying to show how cool and defiant he is, not unlike an American teenager who stitches an Anarchy patch on his backpack.

Joining a game is about picking your moment. You don't want to go up to them when they're in the middle of the action. You wait for a window of opportunity — when teams are switching halves or taking a break or when someone's just skyrocketed the ball and is now off to chase it. When Luke sees two kids sit down, jiggling their calves and gulping down water, he takes off, jogging up to the game. He's learned how to say, "Can I play?" in 15 languages but the boys know what he wants before he asks, grabbing his shoulder, introducing themselves, and sticking him on a team, all without a word from Luke.

Ryan films the game, while Ferg films me watching the game. They goof around — not great soccer players, just happy ones. Watching them play, I don't see any staunch adherence to rules; I don't think they'd care if I play.

Luke blasts a shot and the keeper deflects it away, right to the feet of another guy who finishes it soundly into the back of the net. The guy sprints at Luke, jumping onto his back and celebrating wildly, legs wrapped around Luke's waist, arms flying high in the air.

When we are back in the van, Luke sits next to me, loose and relaxed as the smoggy-Tehran air blows in through the windows. Iran, for Luke, is a changed place. When you play, you get to know people in a way that isn't possible from the sideline. His blond hair, damp from effort, sticks straight up and his face is red and sweaty: he's happy. And in this state of happiness, I know he's less convinced the world's going to end if I try to play.

When we arrive at a field on the eastern side of Tehran, close to the neighborhood Saeed grew up in, I stand next to Luke and say, "I could try to play."

He doesn't flinch. "We can ask," he concedes.

We begin to walk up to the gate but I hesitate at the last second and stride as fast as I can back up to Atef, who hasn't gotten out of the van, "Do you think it's OK if I ask if I can play?"

"Why are you asking me?" he says, smiling.

I laugh uncomfortably and stammer, "I mean, will I offend them if I ask to play?"

"Sure you may ask, but I do not know what they will say. Maybe they say no, maybe they say yes," he says shrugging, not getting out, as though staying in the car might ward off implication.

Holding onto my hijab, I run to catch up with Luke, who is standing outside the fence. He looks nervous. It's not easy to approach strangers in a foreign language.

When the ball goes out of play, he speaks his learned sentence: "Can I play?"

The players — a mix of old and young — welcome him to the field, their hands waving him forward. He walks half way out, and says, flustered, in English, as though he's forgotten they speak Farsi, "Can she play too?"

His question is swallowed by a general excitement. Men from both teams are hanging onto Luke's arm and kids along the sideline are yelling what we'll find out later means, "Golden-haired man!"

He tries again, this time pointing at me: "Can she play too?" I shuffle forward.

"Yes, yes," they answer, but I hang back, waiting to make sure they understand.

An old man wearing a nylon warm-up suit jogs up to me and hands me a green bib. (Funny how all over the world, in every country we visit, teams are divided with these same silly bibs, little shrunken basketball jerseys.) I'm nervous putting it on. I pull it over my head, imagining myself accidentally pulling down the headscarf and my hair spilling out. So worried about the head hole, I manage to overlook the armholes. A man strides over to me and lifts the bib so that my left arm goes through the appropriate hole. An Iranian man just helped me get dressed, I think to myself as the game begins.

The players grew up on neighbouring alleys and have played together for 25 years. Everywhere we travel, the field seems to be the place where people are most themselves, and here, on the eastern side of Tehran, this feels especially true. When a man on my team scores a diving header, he sprints around the field, mimicking the celebrations of the professional players, pretending he is going to take off his shirt; of course, he doesn't. He jumps into the arms of a teammate who then falls down. I didn't expect horseplay, I don't know why not.

The Iranians pass the ball to me more than anyone had in any other country. Even when I make no attempt to put myself in any sort of advantageous position, still, they pass it to me. If they are scandalized by my presence, they're careful not to show it. The old man in the nylon jumpsuit who helped me with my pinny appears delighted by me, like I'm the most interesting teammate he's had since the revolution, as if this game and my presence remind him of the past — a freer past perhaps. I imagine him in the park, playing with his daughters. If he lived in the United States, he'd be the kind of dad who did not miss a single game. He'd be in the bleachers, clapping until his hands hurt, walking out of the stadium holding his daughter's shoulder. He cheers whenever I do something good, or even when I try and fail to find him with a pass. He seems to be wanting this for me, happy at the chance to see an exercising of freedom which, in his lifetime, had been taken away.

When the game ends, the players take a picture. They don't ask me to be a part of it. I watch from a few feet away as the Iranians wrap their arms around Luke's neck, joking with him, smiling happily for the camera. They're still kind to me, smiling and nodding in my direction — saying something to me, although Atef doesn't translate. He is rigid along the sideline, arms crossed in front of his chest. It's raining, and he is cold, wet, and distinctly uncomfortable with our cameras and my presence on the field.

Later that night, while I'm lying in bed in the hotel room, I think about a woman in full chador who walked by the field. What did she think, seeing me? She was definitely looking — I thought I saw a smile. But maybe I didn't. Maybe she was thinking, who does that American think she is, coming into her country and brazenly joining in, breaking the laws that prevent her from playing? The chasm between these two possibilities bothers me. It feels wrong to play with men when it's not ok for the Iranian women to do the same; it feels like an unfair privilege. I didn't want to play just because Iranians can't say no.

The next morning we visit the main bazaar in the center of Tehran. Beneath a vaulted stone ceiling, as vendors pedal hand-knotted rugs, designer jeans, spices, electronics, and copper hookahs, we follow behind Atef. There are benefits to a guide: he is able to tell us that the electronic sign flashing Farsi script advertises bridal gowns for sale, and that's the kind of detail we miss while we're roaming other countries on our own. But I don't like being led around. I drift as far as possible away from our guide, out on my own.

In the rug alley, vendors attempt to seduce us into their shops. Not wanting to lead anybody on, I leave and lean over the railing of the balcony, staring down below at the people drifting through the open corridor.

A handsome man with wavy hair, brown eyes, and a stubbled face strolls up to me. In English, he says, "Soccer — it is soccer you want, correct?"

I nod, my hands rapping against the ball I'm holding, worried that this will somehow end with rugs.

He leans down on the rail, pointing across the way. "There — there is a fire station," he says, exhaling cigarette smoke. "In the afternoons, they play until there is a fire." He smiles at me. "Follow me," he says, as Atef comes darting up, panicked.

"You... I always lose you!"

Standing in the opening of the station I'm again a bystander as the firemen talk to Luke. In Italy, this also happened, but while the Italians treated me like the destroyer-of-man-space, the Iranians seem only shy, respectful. They glance briefly at me before their gazes flutter away. Luke and the firemen talk Champions League and handballs and goals-of-the-century, acting it all out in what looks like an enthusiastic game of charades, when Atef, who'd been talking on the cell phone in the corner, comes walking back toward us. I can see from the hang of his face that something in that phone call has made things change.

Before the call, I'd go as far as to say he was buoyant; the mixture of indifference and anxiety that had plagued him since we'd arrived and inquired about soccer had momentarily lifted. Atef didn't like soccer, he told us that the first day when he'd crossed his legs like an academic, pushed his glasses up on his nose, and sneered disdainfully at the game. I'd thought to myself, "Great, we managed to land the one 26 year old in the country who doesn't like football."

But the firehouse was different for him. In Iran, Atef had explained, it is an honour to be a fireman. The majority are former professional athletes who, once past their prime, receive the position as a gift from the government. So there Atef was, hanging out with the gods of his country. Huge men, men out of fables. And you could tell he thought it was cool.

Now Atef is walking toward us incredibly slowly, as though he is making giant decisions over the course of his 25-yard walk, trying to figure out what he will tell us and how much he will tell us. He's got doom on his face.

"You have been reported to the government," he says.

Atef, Saeed and I sit down together on the bench. Atef is clammy, wiped-out. He doesn't know what to do. He doesn't want to ruin this for us. So he just sits with his legs crossed, biting his fingernails as Luke and the firemen begin to play.

Firemen are government officials so there's no chance I could play with them but sitting on a bench outside the station, I don't even feel like trying. Atef's not sure what happened or why we got in trouble. It could be because of our cameras; it could be because I played. I feel naive, like I may have ruined the trip for everyone. We spent US$11,000 we didn't have in order to come here and Atef's face says we aren't taking our footage with us. Maybe he's just letting us film now because he knows we won't get to keep the tapes anyway. Everybody told us not to come and we didn't care. We didn't believe them. But I never really understood that we could end up with nothing.

I sit on the sideline in the courtyard, sipping tea, watching the light bend down the narrow alleyway, breaking against a gold mosque. Three 1940s-style Mercedes fire trucks are parked in a row. A row of lockers line the wall, red helmets and black jackets with iridescent stripes around the sleeves hung onto hooks, boots scattered below. On the other side of the field, men in old-fashioned leather jackets lean against tilted motorcycles, smoking cigarettes, eyes tracking the ball.

They are playing with the *doliar*, the ball Ali told us about in the very beginning, when Iran was still a distant dream. It is purple, tiny, and light, and I only see how difficult it is to control when it is in front of Luke. While his touch is normally perfect, he struggles with the mini-balloon.

When shots fly high, they land on top of the fire trucks. The men heave themselves up the ladder with the speed and familiarity of any fireman, tossing the ball back down to the game.

When Luke has the ball, one guy calls for a pass: "George Bush! George Bush!"

Luke, startled, sends it him, a smiling guy who is big and bulky, brimming with muscles and jokes.

The next time the bulky man has the ball, Luke, with the same casual grace with which he'd serve a through ball, calls out, "Ahmadinejad, Ahmadinejad."

Loud, loud laughter sounds across the field. The bulky guy slaps his hand against his leg, grinning hugely and pointing at Luke as if to say, "Touché."

The station chief watches the action from the doorway of his office, his thumb under his chin, his index finger against his lips. Although he has consented to the game, you can tell he's not a man who lets things slip by.

Luke blasts a shot, which deflects off a defender's leg and rockets into the fire station window, which shatters loudly. We've made it to 23 countries without breaking anything and I regret that this first happens on the property of the Iranian government. I look straight to the chief to gauge his reaction. I don't know what I expected, maybe a frown, a flash of regret for allowing us to play. I didn't expect him to be looking back at me, face full of pleasure as he studies the worry on mine. When our eyes meet, he glances away and walks back into his office with his hands in his pockets, clearly unbothered about the window.

Dusk sneaks in and I know our time is limited. Our cameras can't cope with the dark and Atef can't cope with us being out in the dark. I sit on the bench, itching for interviews, but afraid that this will be too much for Atef.

"Atef," I say, my voice meek. "Do you think we could do just a couple interviews? Just soccer questions?"

While Ferg films the game and Luke plays, Ryan and I nab one of the guys on the bench and take him to a quiet spot behind the fire trucks. We ask him nothing about Iran or the United States, only what soccer means to him. He's an animated guy, open and nostalgic; he grew up playing with his brothers, he wants to play forever. As he speaks, Atef turns to me. "You know, I must tell them that the government will be reviewing your tapes."

I nod, knowing this is the end of it.

Atef walks over to the office. I watch the chief stand up and wave his hands: the international sign to stop. The game ends. The chief whistles over the man we've been talking to. He's silhouetted from the light of the office and I can see his arms flail. He clasps his forehead and talks frantically to Atef. They call Ryan into the office; I follow. "The man wants you to erase the interview tape," Atef explains. "He fears he will lose his job. A fireman is a government official you know. You are American. It is not good."

We erase the tapes, Ryan doing it as quickly as he can, hands fumbling.

On the court, Luke stands in the dark with the other firemen, laughing, clasping each other's arms. None of the Iranians speak English and Luke cannot speak Farsi but you would never know it. This is what the game can do; this is why we're making our movie.

By now it is dark and Atef's distress is at its peak. In the van, he gets phone call after phone call and we lean over the seats and listen. We're so used to listening to languages we can't understand that we've developed a habit of guessing, almost believing we know what's being said from the rush of words and the flinch of the face.

"What's happening?" I ask.

His eyes dart toward mine as he lets out a disbelieving laugh and then sits quietly as though I have not asked him anything.

Finally he says, "We will have to go to the government. They want to see your tapes. I fear they will take them."

The rest of the drive home Atef stares out the window. I feel awful about what we've put him through. At one point, he smiles. "I did not want to be a tour guide forever. It is fine."

Back at the hotel, we are planning to meet Bahram, a friend of Ali. Although meeting him is outside the standard tour group itinerary, it so pales in comparison to our illicit soccer games that Atef seems fine with it, too wasted to protest. He eyes Bahram, as though assessing whether this is someone who might help him control us. As he leans against the reception desk, he seems relieved to have someone to dish us off on.

Bahram looks like a mad scientist — black hair in cottonball-like poofs, wild, enthusiastic hands, round eyeglasses. It is easy to see why Ali and Bahram are friends. Both have a strange mix of rocket scientist intelligence and surfer-cool-lax. Both give off the distinct feel of happiness: they are keen to see, to hear, to taste, to live.

Bahram tells us, "Atef told me not to tell you but you're not going to be allowed to film anymore. And he said I'm not to let you leave the hotel." Bahram just waves his hands, unfazed. I'll learn that Bahram loves Tehran, the hulking puzzle of a city; and that these occasional blockades that pop up are nothing more than small obstacles, annoyances he manages to skirt, almost enjoying the maze as he navigates the ins and outs and shortcuts and ways around.

He sits down on the couch. "I will make you a *doliar*," he says. "It has been a long time. To tell the truth, Ali was always the one who made the ball."

Bahram and Ryan head to a drugstore in search of the twenty-five cent balls and then to Bahram's house to make the ball. I feel envious of Ryan as I imagine him inside Bahram's home, drinking tea with his mother or shaking hands with his father as the rest of us sit inside our sterile hotel rooms. Luke watches an Iranian soccer game on the TV, captivated and impressed. Ferg sorts tapes as she listens to the news. We'd packed double the number of tapes we thought we'd need. For the rest of the trip, Ferg stays up late, making back-up copies in case the government takes the originals.

I lay on the bed, watching the news ticker on the bottom of the screen. Every second piece of news is about the United States. I am fascinated by the presentation, contrasted to the stories American media presents to Americans. In the van, while we drove past murals that said things like "DEATH TO THE USA," we talked to Atef about US/Iran tensions, about all that was at the root of it — the oil, the US embassy, nuclear energy, Israel. He told us about the airplane crash of 1988, when a US missile brought down a plane of 290 Iranian civilians. We'd heard of this, just barely, but we understood it as a terrible

mistake. Atef turned back in the van toward us, "It was not an accident."

When we drove by a mural of the United States flag, the fifty-stars replaced with fifty skulls, we wanted to turn back and drive by it again so that we could film this symbol of the tension between our two countries. Saeed would not turn back. He spoke in fast, emotional Farsi, and Atef translated, "That mural is not how we feel. If you film that, people will think we do not like America. The government paints that, not us. And the men you see who chant 'Death to the US,' they are scooped up from the poor neighbourhoods and paid to chant it — it is not real. It is not how we feel. Please, I beg of you, do not film that sign." We didn't film the sign.

Around 8pm, Bahram and Ryan arrive back at the hotel. Anxious to see beyond the tour-guide-approved Iran, we ask him where we should eat. It is risky to go out, to walk by the man sitting behind the hotel desk, and in retrospect, it seems brash and arrogant to disobey Atef's do-not-go-out mandate. But we do go, Bahram dropping us off at his favourite restaurant before racing off to chemistry cram sessions. "You will like this place," he says, waving his frenetic hands and darting off into the night.

The restaurant is a tiny room lit by candles. The Italian menu is scrawled onto a chalkboard, and the plates of lasagna and bowls of minestrone are passed down a staircase from a woman in a floral smock. There are four or five tables, occupied by groups of friends, men with Latin-lover hair and women with red lipstick whose scarves fall lower and lower as the night goes on. In the two weeks before we left, I read *Persepolis*, *Lipstick Jihad* and *Reading Lolita in Tehran*, books about Iranian lives that unfolded away from the streets, in the privacy of home. Seeing these flashes of hair as the women lean forward across the table — they are little glimpses into the world I know I will not see.

The next morning, we take off for Yazd, two days ahead of our itinerary. Atef is anxious to get us out of Tehran. At the airport, Atef, Luke and Ryan head to men's security, while Ferg and I branch off to the women's. We stick our camera bags and the soccer ball on the conveyer belt, experiencing the familiar airport-security-nerves: will they open our camera bags? Will they see our tapes and if they do, will they care? We've each got several tapes crammed into our pockets as we walk through the screening monitor, hoping we won't beep. A woman in chador summons us through and there is no blaring sound of alert like the one I hear in my imagination. The conveyer belt spits out both our bags and our ball. I pick up our gear and am starting to feel the relief of having once again made it through security when the officer walks up to me and reaches for the ball.

She spins the ball in her hands and I wait to hear what we've done wrong. She walks briskly around the side of the x-ray machine — and then tosses the ball to the other security guard, who attempts to trap it with her chador-engulfed thigh. They giggle together. Here we are in the Tehran airport, and two fifty-year-old

women, government security officials, are juggling the ball and giggling. I feel like I'm in a surreal version of that Nike commercial where the Brazil national team does tricks through the terminal. All over the world, from the ghettos of Argentina to the border control in Togo, the ball has done this. It has the effect of a cute puppy, people stopping to touch it, to play with it, to smile at you like you are lucky.

As we wait at the gate, a very old woman walks toward us, hunched over at the waist, one foot moving at a time. She comes right up to me and her stoop puts her eyes an inch from my own. Breathing heavily, she says, "Where are you from?"

"The United States," I say, my smile unsure.

"Ah!" she says, smiling. Grasping my hands between hers, she says, "Welcome to our country."

Welcome to our country. People keep telling us this and it's no flimsy welcome-to-our-country, no polite offering. They absolutely mean it.

Yazd is in the middle of nowhere. Desert stretches out in all directions. Except for the slow whistle of the wind towers — *badgirs* they are called, and they look like bell towers without a bell; they catch hold of the wind and keep the buildings cool — Yazd is incredibly quiet. A small boy, maybe four years old, kicks a ball against the wall. Two teenagers, barefoot on a motorcycle, draw aimless figure eights in the dust. I call out, "Football" and tap my knuckles against the ball. They slow, standing up on the pegs. The kid in an orange t-shirt and MC Hammer pants dismounts, grabs two bricks from the rubble on a nearby lot and begins to make goals. I lean against the wall and watch Luke and the guys play until dark.

It takes seven hours to cover the 300km back to Tehran. We listen to music, first Atef's ("It is western music — it is forbidden," he boasts), and then ours, because Atef tells us, "I want to hear young American music — my western songs are from my other guests... but they are, well, older." We play our favorite, The National, and all five of us are quiet as we listen to the lyrics and watch the small towns, civilizations from the past, appear on the horizon and then pass.

As we enter the outskirts of the city, all along the grassy banks and sandy medians of the main highway, every 15 yards or so, there are families, eating cheese and sitting on blankets with legs folded beneath them. "On Fridays, we take our picnics," Atef explains. We pass one family after another. The sun is 5pm soft and the city feels calm. I hang onto this calm, even as my mind starts moving toward tomorrow, toward our meeting with the Iranian government.

That night I meet Bahram and his friend in the lobby of our hotel. Ferg has stayed up the past three nights, setting her alarm to go off every hour, dubbing tape after tape — our plan is to leave a copy of the footage here in Iran in case the government takes the originals.

"Hi," I say as I reach for my new friend's hand and then stop, hand freezing mid-air as I remember the no-touching policy in Iran. I sway awkwardly, hand now

embracing my other arm. "Ok, should we go up?" I say, meaning to my room to get the tapes. Bahram and his friends look briefly at each other and start to follow me upstairs until the desk manager surges up from his chair and around the counter, face red, head shaking violently from side to side: "I am sorry. It is impossible. Room, no. I am sorry."

"Sorry," I say. "So sorry." I get up from the couch and run up the stairs, taking them two at a time, face burning as I realize the implications. I am an American hussy who just tried to take two men up to my room.

After retrieving the tapes, I give them over to Bahram, my hands clumsy, guilty. I've never been a troublemaker. I've never flirted with danger. I can still remember the time I let Tiffany Price copy my sixth grade grammar homework: indescribable panic. So now, here, shanghaiing my new Iranian friend, planning subterfuge, I am jumpy. I feel like a drug smuggler. I worry that the man behind the desk will report us. I imagine two men banging at Bahram's front door, raiding his home, tearing at his stacks of chemistry papers, in search of contraband.

Bahram stuffs the tapes into his satchel and we bow awkwardly towards each other, standing on the steps of the entrance. Ferg comes down the stairs as they are about to leave and without thinking, reaches toward Bahram for a hug. He looks miserably uncomfortable with his head smushed against her chest. "Uh, I'm sorry," he says, "but this is illegal in our country." Red patches creep up Ferg's neck.

"Tell Ali I say hello — and to come back to Iran," Bahram calls out as he heads down the street with our dubs.

Bahram gone, the desk manager stops us before we could get upstairs. He says, "There is a field — a few streets away. They play late into the night — 1 or 2am."

I'm moved by this but also confused. Does he know what we are doing? That we are filming soccer? We won't go out and play tonight — there's too much at risk — but his willingness to let us go makes it clear that he has no plans to turn us in. Like everyone else, he just wants to help.

"Thank you," I say.

Later, Luke and I sit in the lobby with the man from behind the desk and the two guys who wait the tables at breakfast, watching Barcelona play Real Madrid.

Packing our tapes the next morning we eat flatbread and prep each other on what to say. "We are twenty-something-year-olds, making a small college documentary; we want to show our pictures of Iran to our friends."

An hour later, we enter the tour agency office. Old posters of China and India are tacked to the walls. "Who is Gwendolyn?" asks a man sitting in the corner desk.

I raise my hand. "So you are the one I have been emailing with," he says. "I am Ahmadreza." Ahmadreza. The head of the tour company that Atef professed no knowledge of.

I look to Atef.

"Ah, Ahmadreza... I knew only his last name."

"How have you liked your time in Iran?" Ahmadreza continues.

Luke, Ryan and Ferg speak up, helping me gush. We talk about the civilizations scattered across the desert, stuff out of the imagination. About the dolmas Atef's mother made for us and the beautiful arches and sideways light of Yazd. Then we are out of chatter and wait to see what's going to happen to us.

"It was a misunderstanding," Ahmadreza says.

He shakes hands and walks out of the office. Soon we are exiting the building, silent and hesitantly excited, walking fast down the tree-lined boulevards until we are far enough away from the office to feel safe enough to ask, "Atef, was that it?"

He smiles his first big smile all week — we can see his gums — and says, "That was it. We shall go for ice cream."

Two days earlier, while we sat in an internet café, I received an email from a friend of a friend of a friend, an Iranian woman named Niloofar who used to play for the national team. I'd emailed her on the off chance she could meet us for a game.

We are licking nutmeg ice cream when I bring it up to Atef, hopeful that because the meeting — the review of tapes, the assessment of the Americans — passed without incident, he will be okay with this idea. But when he nods his head and says, "All right," it is more like we have just broken him down so completely he can no longer muster any resistance.

The field where Niloofar asks us to meet her, the last we'll see in Iran, is an elevated chunk of Tehran with a hazy skyline backdrop. We arrive before Niloofar and climb up on a wall with a vantage point of all of Tehran. Three young guys stand nonchalantly on the overhang, hands in their pockets, backs to the city, ignoring the straight drop behind them.

Ferg spots two women approaching, one carrying a ball in her arms. Across the square, we smile at each other. Niloofar has green eyes, long eyelashes and boyish mannerisms (a wide stance, hand fiddling with her wristwatch). Her friend is stunning: bright purple headscarf, highly arched eyebrows, delicate cheekbones, bright red lipstick, long manicured fingernails. "This is my best friend," Niloofar says of the woman whose features are so striking it's like her face breaks the rules. And it does — the plucked eyebrows, the bronzer, the lipstick, the purple hijab worn far enough back to reveal a few inches of shiny hair — none of it is allowed.

"Will you play?" I ask.

Niloofar laughs and translates, and the woman in purple shakes her finger. "She likes to watch," Niloofar says.

As two other girls approach, Atef stands 15 yards away, his arms around his binder. There are still men playing on the field and I know we won't have much time so I ask to start the interviews right away. It's reverse order — normally we play and then talk, and once we've played, the word "interview" doesn't feel right. You're just talking to another player. But if we wait until after the game,

I worry we won't be able to talk to them at all.

Atef is disapproving and miserable as he translates our questions, saying, "OK, is that all?" after every question. We learn that Niloofar got her moves from watching YouTube videos of Ronaldinho; that her favourite player is David Beckham; that she grew up playing in the streets with her brothers; that all she wants is to play.

When the men finish their game, we take over the field. The guys linger outside the chainlink fence and watch.

"We must wait until they go away," Niloofar says as we make a goal out of shopping bags. No matter how slow we go, the men will not leave, so Niloofar explains that we will pretend to leave. We exit the field as though we have decided not to play after all and wait around the corner until the men disappear. Then we head back onto the field.

The women undo their manteaus but the field owner comes out, shaking his head and finger. They re-button their manteaus reluctantly. I didn't really think they would be good. Two of them played on the Iranian national team but in a country where women's soccer seems barely allowed, I didn't think that would mean much. But, again, I'm wrong. They juggle the ball without spin; they go for the meg; they send through-balls. Every touch is clean. One way or another, they've found a way to not only play but to play well.

When the game ends, it begins to pour, lightning bolts sharp and dramatic across the top of Tehran. We hug goodbye and exchange email addresses. In the van, Atef asks if I had a good time.

"Yes," I answer, grateful. "Thank you so much."

"I would've been too nervous and ruined your fun," he says shrugging, smiling bashfully. "So I waited here."

Our final morning, we pack our belongings, spreading the tapes between us, stuffing them in underwear, side pockets and the insides of running shoes. We drift through security. I am pent-up with nerves as I watch careful inspections of bags, but no one examines the inside of ours. An hour later, we board our

plane and the women begin removing their hijabs as they walk down the aisle, hair spilling out over shoulders.

15 hours later, we pick up our bags and head for United States customs.

Reaching the front of the line, the security guy looks down at our passports and our tickets and makes a choking sound. "Iran?" he says. "Why in hell would you want to go there?"

"Tourism?" Ryan says.

He snorts: "Go to line six."

So we walk to line six to join dark-skinned people with darker beards waiting for American officials to press their fingers against glass.

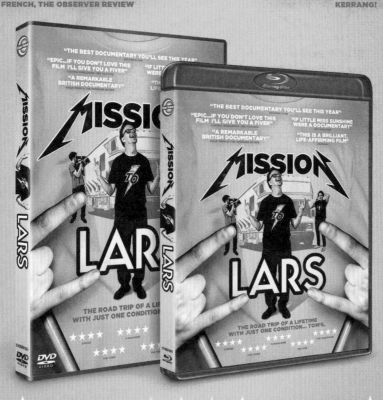

Conflict Management

Dan Gaspar is a key part of Iran's qualifying campaign for Brazil 2014 despite holding a US passport

By Noah Davies

When Dan Gaspar walked out into the massive bowl of Tehran's Azadi Stadium on 16 October 2012, he was greeted by the roar of 100,000 Iranian fans. An athletics track separated the national team's goalkeeping coach from the stands but the eight lanes did nothing to prevent the noise from assaulting his ears. When he stole a glance into the chaotic mass that surrounded him on all sides, he saw tri-coloured flags everywhere. The Iranian men were out in force for the crucial 2014 World Cup qualifier against South Korea. They always came out in force.

In 20 years as a coach, Gaspar had found himself in the middle of passionate fan-bases from South Africa to Portugal. But this was something else entirely. The football field represents one of the few places—perhaps the only space— in which Iranians can express their emotions in public. "It's more than a game for them," he said. "It's an event. It's an opportunity for them to express themselves freely, to sing and chant in unison in a spirited way. I think for them that is extremely important. It's at the football stadium that they are allowed to behave and express themselves in that manner."

But football's significance goes beyond that. "The game is extremely important for the Iranian people, not only here but for the way the rest of the world views them," the 57 year old explained. "Football results are very important for them. The more successful the national team is, the prouder they become." A win over South Korea would have taken Iran level on points with South Korea at the top of their qualifying group at the halfway stage of Asian qualifying, with top two teams advancing to the World Cup, and the third-place finisher meeting the corresponding side from the other group to determine who would make the play-off against a qualifier from South America.

Getting to Brazil 2014 means everything to the Iranian people. Gaspar was in Tehran to help achieve that goal. He joined the Iranian staff when his mentor, Carlos Queiroz, took the job of head coach in April 2011. In some ways, it was just another gig on the endless cycle of international appointments — except that Gaspar was born in South Glastonbury, Connecticut, a little more than 120 miles from New York City. He holds a US passport in addition to his Portuguese one.

But Gaspar is not the only Iranian national team coach in recent history with a strong tie to the United States. His fellow assistant, Omid Namazi, was born in Provo, Utah. Although Namazi's family returned to Tehran soon after his birth, he moved back to the US when he was 18, went to college at West Virginia University, and had a long career with teams around the country between 1988 and 2005. Afshin Ghotbi, the man Queiroz replaced at the head of the Iran team, was born in Tehran but left with his father in 1977 and emigrated to the US. He lived in Los Angeles and attended the University of California, Los Angeles where he played for the Bruins and earned a degree in electrical engineering before embarking on a coaching career that has taken him around the globe.

Despite the tensions between the two countries and sanctions that have been in place since 1979, holding a US passport does not preclude a coach from working for the national team or club teams. That shouldn't be surprising, a spokeswoman at the Iranian consulate in New York explained. No one there would talk specifically about football in Iran, but she was quick to note that the conflict is between the governments, not the people. Iran's general population, especially the younger generation living in Tehran, is more open, liberal, and accepting than the western world realises. So is the city itself.

"It's a strange thing. We live in a country that we know is being suppressed by sanctions, but I don't have that sense of fear. I feel safe. I feel welcomed. I feel respected," Gaspar said. "If I wasn't listening to CNN or BBC, I would have no idea of the perception that Iran has throughout the world. Maybe we are isolated from that as a result of being football professionals, and perhaps we're not exposed to that type of political climate, but I've had no issues being a Portuguese-American."

Namazi, a former defender who was coaching at Semnan's Steel Azin before joining Queiroz's staff, agrees. "Tehran is a metropolitan city with a large population," he said. "Unlike the perception in some of the US, it's safe to live here. I have had no issues whatsoever. I have continued to work during the day and do some site-seeing when I'm not working. It's been fine living here," he said. "People here view the US as a country where people are given an opportunity to grow. It's a positive image."

The tense relations between the two nations do create the occasional logistical difficulty. From 2004 to 2007, Ghotbi served as an assistant coach with South Korea. They had to play an Asian Cup qualifying match in Iran, but the coach could not enter the country because he only had his US passport. The fact that he was born in Iran was not enough to gain him entry.

Having a second, non-US passport seems a requirement for employment as a coach with the national team. As Gaspar shows, it doesn't have to be an Iranian one, but it's highly unlikely that someone like the New Jersey-born and bred Bob Bradley, the former US national team coach who is currently in charge of Egypt, would land a job in Iran. "Being Iranian or Iranian-born made it easier," Ghotbi said, an opinion shared by Gaspar. "My sense is that would be a tremendous challenge for the federation to try to sell."

That said, the US passport in his pocket didn't prevent Ghotbi from landing the job, nor did it stop Gaspar and Namazi from being part of the staff that replaced him. But those ties to the US are probably not part of a larger trend. "I think it's a coincidence," Namazi said. "I don't read too much into it. Obviously, there have been a lot of people who have immigrated to the US at some point in their lives. Maybe that's the reason why there is a higher percentage of Iranian-Americans who have come back and tried to coach. But the next technical staff could be all from Brazil. It just has to be now that there is a staff that has experience coaching in the US."

And he's probably correct. At the end of the day, Namazi and men like him bounce around the globe, looking for jobs. They simply hope to do what they are hired to do: coach. "I have no political agenda," Gaspar explained. "As a result of my profession, I consider myself a global citizen. It's allowed me to open my mind. It's allowed me to experience different cultures. I think that's a valuable, valuable experience. More Americans should do it. It also allows us to appreciate where we come from, but at the same time understand that there are traditions, cultures, and things that you can be enlightened by." There football goes again, perhaps not explaining the world entirely, but certainly helping us understand bits and pieces of this planet a little bit better.

And, at its core, coaching is coaching is coaching, whether it's in the United States, Iran, or elsewhere. The job remains the same all over the planet: get the most out of your players and win. Queiroz, Gaspar, and Namazi have a difficult task since the quality of the Iranian league is not the best in the region, but the national team does have talent, including many players from Persepolis and Esteghlal, the two biggest clubs in the football-mad nation.

Sometimes, however, the country's tinderbox politics intervene. That was the case in 2009 after Ghotbi replaced Ali Daei, the team's all-time leading goalscorer and cap winner who moved into coaching after retiring in 2007. With three matches remaining in the final round of AFC 2010 World Cup qualifying, Iran needed strong results to clinch a berth in South Africa. They had three games in 11 days, away to North Korea and South Korea with a home game against the United Arab Emirates sandwiched in the middle. Ghotbi, who had taken over the team just 30 days before, led the squad to a draw in Pyongyang and a win in Tehran. A victory in Seoul on June 17 would have ensured qualification. The manager needed his troops to focus. But that wasn't possible. On June 12, the Iranian people voted in presidential elections. Mahmoud Ahmadinejad won easily, but irregularities triggered protests in the country and worldwide. It was far from an ideal environment in which to prepare a team for a vital match.

"There were images on BBC and CNN of people being shot, things being burned, and rocks being thrown. It was really a difficult game to get everyone's concentration," Ghotbi said. "Without my knowledge, some players were wearing the green band [of protest] and some players didn't have the green band. That game became a difficult game to win even before it started. We gave up a goal in the 81st minute, and it was a 1-1 draw." Hours later, a draw between North Korea and Saudi Arabia eliminated Iran.

Ghotbi stayed on — "I decided that maybe the only thing that could really keep the peace and at the same time give people hope was football," he said — but resigned after falling in the quarter-finals of the 2011 Asian Cup. It was Queiroz's turn to try to return the national team to the World Cup, a tournament for which it has qualified three times (most recently in 2006, although their most famous result was the 2-1 win over the USA in 1998).

Gaspar and Namazi signed on for the challenge, a journey that started well as the team finished first in the third round and was drawn in the easier quintet for the final stage of qualification, favourites with South Korea to advance from Group A, which also included Qatar, Lebanon, and Uzbekistan. They began the campaign with a 1-0 victory over Uzbekistan and a scoreless draw with Qatar in Tehran. A 1-0 loss to Lebanon, Iran's first ever to the tiny country, was a major set-back. "That was a bitter defeat, one that we weren't expecting," Gaspar said. "Now we'll see what the true football fan of Iran is made of. When you're faced with this type of a result, we're curious to see how the people will respond. Up to this point, it's been a great honeymoon. We haven't lost. We've been through the qualification phases successfully. Now it's a test to see if we can stay united. The press has been very critical."

That was the stage as the coach walked into Azadi Stadium in the middle of October. The crowd passionately and openly demanded a result. A defeat at home to South Korea wouldn't have eliminated Iran from World Cup contention, but it would have been unacceptable in the eyes of the 100,000 strong.

Before kick-off, they chanted, they sang, they screamed. They expressed themselves. They kept up the noise throughout the scoreless first 45 minutes, as the head coach and his assistants searched for a way through South Korea's stout defensive wall. Then, after the break, disaster. The Osasuna midfielder Masoud Soleimani Shojaei, one of the few Iranians playing out of the country, picked up a yellow card in the 48th minute, then a second one eight minutes later. The crowd exploded in protest and despair. Iran, a man down, looked through. But Iran, spurred no doubt by the thousands of supporters, found a goal. Their captain Javad Nekounam, a 32-year-old midfielder for Esteghlal, picked up a deflected free-kick and slotted it home with a quarter of an hour remaining. The fans were still in a state of ecstasy when the final whistle blew on a 1-0 win. The coaches would coach another day. Drama doesn't care about international borders. As Gaspar, Namazi and others around the world are showing, neither, frequently, does football. Ⓑ

Stroke is the third biggest killer and the leading cause of severe adult disability in the UK.

Behind much of the Stroke Association's unique work are people just like you – people who want to do something powerful and lasting through their Will.

To find out more about leaving a gift in your Will please call us on **020 7566 1505** or email **legacy@stroke.org.uk**

stroke.org.uk

Stroke
association

31

Interview

"The church has chosen Rome as
its capital city, and so did Boniek,
because he knew the church
knows what is right."

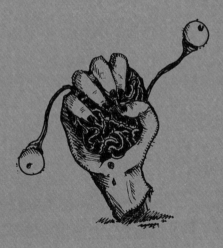

Zbigniew Boniek

The Polish great discusses Juventus, the modern game and his friendship with Michel Platini

By Maciej Iwanski

Zbigniew Boniek is probably the greatest player in the history of Polish football. He scored 24 goals in 80 matches for the national side, was the leader of the team that finished third at the World Cup in 1982 and had a successful career with Widzew Łódź, Juventus, with whom he won the Cup-Winners' Cup in 1984 and the European Cup a year later, and Roma. Elected chairman of the Polish Football Federation (PZPN) last year, he now faces his biggest challenge: despite hosting Euro 2012, Polish football has never been lower.

Fans who loved him and those angered by the on-going problems in the Polish game united to support Boniek in his election campaign, abusing the incumbent president Grzegorz Lato with chants at league games and matches of the national team. Boniek's new era involves creating a new system of coaching from the age of six upwards and modernising the management structure of Polish football. At home, he has been described as the man who ended the era of Communism in Polish football after dismissing a number of officials who had served under the old political system.

Boniek has also worked for many years as a pundit on Italian and Polish television, and has always been a great talker. Sat behind a wooden table in his Warsaw office, he showed just why he is loved by many and hated by some, offering a string of clear opinions and brave ideas.

⊕ *Do you regret the fact that you played in the eighties, without the fame or the money you'd have made today?*

Not at all. Those were good times for football and the quality was high. Of course the intensity of the attention from media and fans is much higher now and the money is better, but I don't like to regret anything in my life. If I was a player now, I wouldn't have lived in those fantastic times...

⊕ *What was so fantastic about living then?*

Everything. Communication between people was much better. Despite not having cell phones, or even telephones at all, and the internet — or maybe because of it. If you wanted to play football as a kid, you'd have to be at a certain place, at a certain time. 3pm at the field and that's it. Everybody came. The way of life was much quieter. I don't intend to sound like an old man — the present is great, too. But those times were very different. If you wanted to date a girl, you had to talk to her, take her for a walk and so on. Now you just send an SMS. The world has changed a lot. But it's OK for me. I like my life and if I were young again it might look totally different. In football and in life now, everything needs to be faster and simpler. Some changes have made the game better — like the goalkeeper being unable to handle a ball passed back to him. Other things are tough — my manager listened to me, not the opposite.

⚽ *You played your best matches in the evening under floodlights. The Juventus president Giovani Agnelli even called you 'Bello di Notte' because you played so well at night. If you played today, you'd play even more games under lights, so would you be rated even more highly?*

It's not like I've played my best games in the night. It's just I never played badly then. I've had good games at different times of the day. If you'd been to my home in Rome, you'd see four statues of *Top Undi* — the prize for best players in Serie A in certain positions. I played six years in Italy and have four statues. Would you like to know what time Serie A matches were played in those days? 3pm. *Bello di notte* came from my perfect performances in Europe. That's not humble, but take a quick look at the facts: with Juve I played in four finals and we won three of them, scoring five goals. Of those five goals, I scored three and a fourth came when I was fouled in the penalty box.

⚽ *Now, you'd have a big marketing machine behind you, adding value to*

your name like Messi and Ronaldo...

Both of them are fine players, out of the top drawer, that's certain. But I tell you something — I haven't seen a single game in which Messi has been marked individually. Somebody comes to him when he gets the ball. It would be the opposite in my time. He would have 50% fewer passes. He wouldn't have the opportunity to play between the lines. [Claudio] Gentile wouldn't even have let him smell the ball.

⚽ *Maradona or Messi?*

You can't compare: the football was too different. But if you were really good in the eighties, life on the pitch was much harder. You were fouled many times and not protected by the referees. A tackle from behind when you were eye-to-eye with the goalkeeper meant... a yellow card. The defenders were brutal. Coming back to this marketing machine, it can produce so-called "great players". Men in green and orange and pink — whatever — shoes. Mine were personalised and always black with a white sole. Some of players are described as giants and they are earning huge money, but they aren't worth it. Why? They didn't win games by themselves, haven't scored goals that gave their club or country the title and yet they are regarded as world-class stars.

⚽ *Such as?*

No names, let's not make a big noise in Europe, especially not when Poland are playing England this year [laughs]. But I tell you something: the players in the dressing-room know who's good and who's not.

🔱 *What was it like in the Juventus dressing-room? Who was the boss — Platini or Boniek?*

It looked very different to how it looks now. We had eleven players, four used regularly as substitutes and the next four were young and talented. Almost every team was like this. It meant that the team was pretty much the same all year. Try to ask Inter, Juve or Roma fans who played for their clubs in the eighties. They will answer easily. And now? It was also much easier to manage for the coach, there were no problems with big names not playing as happens now. Everybody knows the Juve of 1982, and now nobody knows who's in the attack line — Matri and Vučinić, Quagliarella and Vučinić or Giovinco? Different problem: you can see sometimes that the players are fighting for their place in the team so much that there is a lack of power when the game comes! We pushed against our rivals, not ourselves.

And about your question — of course inside the teams there were groups. Some people were friends and some were not, of course. And with Michel, we are still friends now. We have been connected for 28 years. For me, and I'm pretty sure Michel would say the same, we are real friends. Not because he's Uefa President and I'm PZPN president now. We completed each other in the meaning of character, in football, etc. And our wives like each other very much, which helped a lot [laughs]. Seriously one more thing, Juve could buy only two foreigners, so it was natural for us [as the two foreigners] to be close.

🔱 *Juventus from the eighties would today win against...*

Everybody. And that's not just talk. In four years, we only lost to Hamburg, by chance. I see no team capable of beating us in the modern era. If we were at the same physical level, of course.

🔱 *How did it happen that a young player from Poland came to sign for Juventus?*

I knew how to play football. I wasn't just fast, I was also technically advanced and skilful. You can't play for four years for the best team in the world and not be really good. Deyna, Lato, Tomaszewski, Łubanski were allowed to leave Poland at 30 years old for free, as a reward. I started talking about going abroad when I was 22, so by the time I was 26 the Communist authorities knew they had to do something about it and let me go earlier. When I was 23 I had people from great clubs trying to convince me I should go on holiday and never come back, be disqualified and leave Poland illegally... I wanted somebody to pay for me, to make it official. I could have gone earlier to England or Spain. Don't ask the names of these clubs; I won't tell. It doesn't matter now.

🔱 *Swapping Communist Poland for Italy must have been like going to the moon?*

Not at all. I'd played for my country, a couple of times for a World representative team in exhibition matches, European matches with Widzew. That prepared me. I always liked to have a strategy, but I couldn't have thought 10 years ago that I would become PZPN chairman. I matured into this function.

🔱 *Retiring from football was part of the plan?*

When I said *finito* I had 25 clubs at home talking about contracts worth $500,000. But I didn't want to play only for the money. It was better to start a new life. I stayed in Rome. My kids were going to school there and we had a Polish Pope. And thanks to that decision I have Italian citizenship now. I see life this way: try to be comfortable, take care of yourself and your family and make it as easy as possible. The church has chosen Rome as its capital city, and so did Boniek, because he knew the church knows what is right [laughs].

Looking at your life, it's like you had the Midas touch — playing days, business later and now you're head of Polish football. Yet you failed as Poland national team coach...

Everything I did I always tried to do as well as possible. I thought that the coach determines whether the team believes in him. No. The players decide whether the coach is good or not. Players win the matches; the coach can only sometimes lose the match. I did not resign from coaching Poland after five matches for professional reasons. It was 10 years ago. End of story.

Speaking about tough experiences, what should have been your greatest night, the Heysel final, became the worst.

It wasn't only a horrible tragedy for these people [who died] and their families, it was also terrible for us. Yes, we had to go out and play. But the world wants to forget that night. I want to forget it somehow... it was definitely the worst moment of my career. I thought taking the winner's money would be inappropriate, so I donated it all to the

families of the victims. I must tell you one thing. If that game had been played at 20:30 we would have won two- or three-nil, three-one maybe... We won after the penalty, that probably wasn't a penalty because Whelan and I were so fast, the referee couldn't follow us and saw me down in the box. These memories are hard for the players also, the dogs all around, the atmosphere. What happened that night around the pitch was a nightmare. It shouldn't have happened...

An investigation by Europol said over 380 matches might have been fixed in Europe. What do you think of that?

380? Not much.

Really?

I read that article to analyse it. If this were true, these players would have had to sell the match for around €1500. Can anybody believe that? I'm not saying it didn't happen; I'm saying it looks weird. But dishonest people are everywhere and corruption is like doping. You have to fight it, knowing that you won't probably win this fight. The danger is elsewhere. First of all, doping is done by private money and is always a step ahead of anti-doping, financed by public money. The way I see it, the main threat is different. Nobody wants to buy matches now. But you can go on the internet, put some money on a certain result and be dishonest this way. Take four of the team, they bet their money and lose the match... The opponent cannot know about it. The referee can bet also and the effects can be horrible.

You are the face of one of the betting companies in their commercials...

Yes, but they are on the good side. Why? It's easy. It's the betting company can see if too much money is put on a certain match. And they'll inform the police that something seems not to be right because it's them who'll lose their money.

⚽ *Has anybody ever tried to bribe you?*

Speaking about it after 30 years makes no sense for me, but I must tell you something. I never wanted to play unfairly. Once at Juve we played the last match of the season in Cagliari and if they lost they were relegated. We won 2-1. That tells everything. I played football to win.

⚽ *And now you try to change Polish football for the better.*

We've changed a lot. Really a lot and will keep on working so the basics and organisation of Polish football are much better than in the past.

⚽ *Have the problems at the National Stadium in Warsaw been solved, or might it lose the battle with rain again?*

If you lay a carpet on cement and start crying it will also be very wet. Somebody didn't prepare the pitch and that's it.

⚽ *Michel Platini could stand against Sepp Blatter in the elections for Fifa President. Would you vote for him?*

Michel Platini is my friend. No matter what the vote would concern, he always starts with one vote from Boniek.

⚽ *Will he try to be football's most powerful person?*

If I were Uefa president, I'd be totally satisfied with it. Fifa is a different world, different people, different continents... But I think Michel doesn't support my point of view. I don't know what his plans are at the moment but I can assure you that wherever in the world of football Platini comes up for a vote, I'm sure he will get the credit for everything that he has achieved so far. He knows and understands football and that's absolutely what's needed. Ⓑ

37

For the Good of the Game

"Prostitutes outnumbered delegates
while a Filipino rock band filled the
place with ugly noise."

The Only Way is Ethics

Fifa's super-cop Michael J Garcia explains his mission to wash the corruption out of football

By Philippe Auclair

"The FIFA Executive Committee, chaired by President Joseph S Blatter, took another major step in its good governance process today by unanimously appointing Michael J Garcia (USA) and Hans-Joachim Eckert (Germany) as the chairmen of the Ethics Committee during its extraordinary meeting held in Zurich."

This statement, published on Fifa's website on 17 July 2012, was not greeted with wild enthusiasm by what the organisation likes to call 'the family of football'. Reactions ranged from moderate optimism (mostly in Zurich) to scepticism and even derision (almost everywhere else). How could a tainted official body be expected to fear investigations led by people of its own choosing? A number of those members of the Executive Committee who had "unanimously appointed" Garcia and Eckert had good reason to believe they'd be the first targets of a truly independent exploration of Fifa's darker side, of which new recesses seemed to be discovered at every turn. The past two years had been a tumult of scandals. Two ExCo members — Amos Adamu and Reynald Temarii — had already been suspended from all football activities following a sting operation mounted by the *Sunday Times*. The Qatari Mohammed bin Hammam, head of the Asian Football Confederation and would-be opponent of Sepp Blatter in the 2011 Fifa presidential election, chose to retire from football altogether after failing to fight off a series of bribery, fraud and embezzlement allegations. Accusations of vote-rigging, collusion and corruption had preceded and followed the granting of the 2018 and 2022 World Cups to Russia and Qatar in December 2010. The old business of the ISL debacle[1] lagged on, interminably, with no resolution in sight.

---

[1] *The Swiss marketing company International Sport and Leisure — ISL — went bankrupt with debts of £153m in 2001. Court documents released in 2012 showed that the former Fifa president João Havelange and the former president of the Brazilian football federation and Fifa ExCo member Ricardo Teixeira, who now lives in exile in Miami, had received over US$40m in bribes and kickbacks. Swiss law, however, made no provisions for bribes of that kind in its criminal code, which explains why neither was prosecuted in civil courts; they (and others, including the CAF and Conmebol presidents Issa Hayatou and Nicolás Leoz) could, however, still be subjected to investigation and, if found guilty, punishment by Fifa's newly established Ethics Committee.*

This is the landscape which Fifa's 'super-cop' Michael J Garcia discovered in July 2012, an unholy tangle of corporate dysfunctionality and plain human wickedness. He must have known, even then, that very few people expected him to be able or willing to pick up the threads that could lead to the unravelling of a rotten web. His integrity was questioned for no other reason than the belief that, to take on this impossible mission, he had to accept he would not complete it. Eckert was the requisite safe pair of hands, a man with three decades of experience in German tribunals, the current Presiding Judge of the Penal Court, Munich I, to give him his full title. Garcia was a far more controversial figure. He'd made his name as a federal prosecutor with the Office of the US Attorney for the Southern District of New York from 1992 to 2001, taking care of "high-profile cases, involving national security and complex extraterritorial issues, including the 1993 terrorist bombing of the World Trade Center and the 1998 bombing of US embassies in East Africa", to quote from the résumé that is provided by Kirkland, the legal firm of which he is now a partner. He'd also been "Vice-President of the Americas for Interpol and [...] served on Interpol's Executive Committee, the body charged with overseeing the budget and strategic direction of the organisation". The former US General Attorney (2005-2008) had been the architect of the dramatic fall of Eliot Spitzer, who was seen as a genuine contender for the US presidency in Democrat circles and resigned from his post of Governor of New York State in 2008 after a vicious battle conducted in the media as well as in the courts, which hardened the conviction of some in the US that Garcia was in bed with the outgoing Bush administration, a slick politician who'd served the neo-con agenda in order to further his own ambitions.

It should be added that Garcia is one of 18 American citizens who, since April 13 of this year, have been banned from entering the territory of the Russian Federation for alleged (and rather unclear) "human rights violations". This was a direct response from the Russian authorities to the publication of the so-called 'Magnitsky list' in the USA, which named 18 Russian citizens suspected of having played a role in the mysterious death of the lawyer and fraud investigator Sergei Magnitsky in a Moscow prison in 2009. Garcia had been targeted by the Russians for the part he played in the successful prosecution and conviction of the Russian arms dealer Viktor Bout, who is currently serving a 25-year jail term for "conspiring to sell weapons to a US-designated foreign terrorist group" — the Colombian FARC, in this instance.

Not what you'd call a lightweight, then. But could he be trusted to devote the same kind of energy to flush out the slurry from within Fifa, when Fifa itself had cherry-picked him — and was footing his wage-bill?

Setting up this interview, which is published here in full and in the original English for the first time, was a time-consuming or, as Garcia would put it, "time-intensive" task. He is easy enough to get in touch with. His personal email address can be found on the Kirkland website, together with his office's direct line number. Should you wish to share any information about ISL, Russia 2018, Qatar 2022, or any other matter which touches on violations of Fifa's Ethics Code, you know where to go. But, apart from a brief appearance on German television in the summer of 2012, Garcia had politely declined all the media requests that had come his way since his nomination — until he agreed to have lunch with us in a Zurich restaurant. In this case, the game-changer was the publication by *France Football*, on 29 January 2013, of a dossier which dealt in great detail with the particulars of the choice of Qatar as a World Cup host nation for the 2022 tournament. Garcia had the whole dossier translated, found some of it of interest, consented to a meeting on the basis (or so we felt) that we — that is my colleague Eric Champel and myself — would tell him *viva voce* more about the information we'd gathered, and how, and from whom, than we could print; in exchange for which we hoped he'd speak to us on the record. 'Hoped', not 'knew', or 'expected', which might explain why it was with some trepidation that we sat down and waited for our guest. He was flying direct that morning from the USA, which was hit by a bout of cold weather. To our horror, it was so severe that a number of airports and all government offices in Washington DC were shut down; the CNN domestic news bulletins I watched throughout a sleepless night seemed to consist entirely of reports by snow-choked journalists whose overcoats were flapping in a howling wind. Would he turn up? But at 12:30 on the dot, just as the bells of a nearby church rang, Garcia walked in, dressed like an up-dated, upmarket version of Frankie Valli. The handshake was warm, the conversation quickfire yet unhurried. For two and a half hours we listened to him, and this is what we heard.

⊕ *How would you define your role and the exact nature of your mission?*

My role is clearly defined. I've got to investigate the conduct of football people and see if it violates or has violated the [Fifa] governance codes — now or at the time when the violations would have taken place.

⊕ *Where have you got to with your inquiry into the ISL affair?*

If we're talking about ISL, that's slightly different. That's something that landed on my desk the day that I took up my position. I've got to look into the dismissal order of the criminal investigation on Fifa, Teixeira and Havelange and make a report. I've got to take that in it as I'd take in whatever else that might raise the question: "Have there been violations in the conduct of these people?" I have to follow the normal process and report to Judge Eckert, who's the chair of the adjudication chamber; according to the parameters of the code. I'll go to him, he'll read my report and take his decisions. I'll follow the process in this case, while obviously informing the Executive Committee of what I'm doing. I've spent a lot of time lately looking at the facts to see what happened. Who's involved? Have there been violations? There are many other public cases under investigation, like the one on the [vote for the 2018 and 2022] World Cups, which has been referred to me formally.

"Formally", so you're confirming that?

Yes, and it's open. That's the message I'm trying to get across, and I believe that it's very important. This is the time for folks — whoever they are — who have information to come to me. I haven't got any preconceived ideas on what happened or did not happen. Everything is wide open. Sometimes, you hear a lot of talk from people saying they've "got something on this, or they might know that." Well [I'm saying to them], if you truly believe it, the moment has come to show yourself. There are things that we can do under the code that will protect your anonymity. I will work with people on that front.

What I think would be... not helpful is if this review goes forward on that broad area of the bidding [for organising the World Cups of 2018 and 2022], then afterwards, somebody says, "Well, they got the facts wrong," when they knew that before. You know something? Tell me! I'm working, working hard to uncover what's there or isn't there. This is the form, the venue people have got to come forward to if they really think they have something to say. On any side of any issue! On some aspect of some question related to the World Cup. And I believe it's a message that should be out there. People have talked, written articles but what you have now is an official body which is in charge of this case and it's important that people go see me to tell me what they have.

It's a very new role for me. I've been a federal prosecutor, where I had a very wide authority. I could requisition documents or subpoena witnesses before a grand jury, sign search warrants; I had

lots of powers for obtaining information. That's one of the most rewarding things about being a prosecutor in the US, you can use lots of tools to understand what's happened. When I've worked for private companies, generally, I had access to that company's documents, to their employees, to their email systems, etc, all that was at my disposal. It's not the same scope but... it's pretty good.

And in your current role?

Officials in football have an obligation to talk to the adjudication chamber and to establish the facts. They have an obligation to give me records but what I have understood, when it comes to Fifa, as you know well, is that Fifa doesn't function like a big multinational corporation, with one database, one [central] document archive system. It's [an aggregator] of a bunch of confederations and associations, of different personal email systems... It's an honour system almost, when you go outside of Fifa. People who are outside of football, they haven't got any obligation to talk to me. When you go out of Fifa itself and you say, "OK, give me your bank records, give me your personal emails," how do I check if there are other accounts, other email addresses? It's really more difficult. So, when I speak to people and these people are in football, I ask them questions, because there is an obligation [for them] to respond and it would be a breach of the code if they didn't do it. They've got to meet me, speak to me, answer the inquiry commission to establish the facts. And that is good. When it comes to people who aren't in the football world itself, then... I've worked as a prosecutor overseas where I had no authority; we're in the same way of working, we're trying, by various means that you [journalists] all use regularly so that people talk to you [smiles]. We ask questions, it doesn't hurt to ask them, and, sometimes, someone will talk to you.

You've opened a line of communication, open to everyone, which allows people to come to you in complete confidence, knowing that their anonymity will be protected, that sources will not be revealed. Without revealing confidential details, has this initiative been followed by results?

Yes. Yes. Yes, to the extent that people have reached out to me and that some — not all — have been... the best way to describe what I've obtained up to now, it's that I've been sent information of a general character, but also very specific information. And that's really a matter [for me], as for you, to look at your sources and at the 'angles', and I'd tell you there are a lot of angles in this case... After which it's up to you to build something around what people are telling you. This process has started. And there are people [who have come to me] who, I believe, have really wanted to try to be helpful and give me information. We are still at an early stage. To be honest, there has been truly a lot of work for me...

What collaboration have you received from Fifa and...?

[He cuts in] The independent governance commission is also interested in that. In fairness, I would say I've obtained the resources I have asked for and I thought I'd need. I haven't had an issue from that side. Investigating these questions requires an enormous amount of work. It's documents-intensive, travel-intensive, doing lots of interviews. Like when I was a prosecutor, or when I was working for private companies, you have to be very meticulous in the details because that's where you make or break a case. And I've needed assistance for that. I have used people on the inside, I have used external investigators, law firms, in Switzerland and in other countries...

You've used external investigators?

Oh, yes, obviously! I used external investigators, independent lawyers, experts in different legal frameworks, for example, Swiss law. And in all that, there was never an issue when I felt I needed something. There haven't been any disagreements, [comments like], "No, that's expensive." To be thorough, you have to see witnesses, face to face; of course you can speak on the telephone but for real detail, you've got to have them with you, you've got to travel, you've got to review documents [*in situ*]... and you can have people who do that for you. To do it all alone is impossible. It would take too long. It's time-intensive and costly. Myself, I've spent a lot a time on that [laughs]...

More than you expected?

More than I expected! [laughs]. Listen, this is very important, very interesting work. But I've had the support and the resources I've needed.

Have you been supported by Fifa itself? By Blatter in person?

In a general way. I haven't been in personal contact with the Fifa president.

I am in contact with his secretariat, which, by virtue of the code, supports my chamber [of investigation]. When I need to communicate, I generally go through them and, once again, I have never had the slightest issue when I've needed this or that. In fact, they have even been proactive in suggesting, for example, "You need a Swiss lawyer for that," etc. If they had had an issue, it could've been a game-changer. That wouldn't work. I want this to work, and I repeat, "OK, I'm here, perhaps I'll do nothing, but I will certainly listen to whomever who, on whatever subject it might be, says something that is relevant to my jurisdiction." That new whistleblower line is a very good thing. A vast majority of [what we are learning] through that line of access is not relevant to the jurisdiction of the ethics commission, and certain things can be referred to other places, but... it's one more line that people can use to get to my chamber, so we can look into what they have to say — and I look at every single thing. I have a direct access to that system.

⊕ *Some will say, "That's all fine, but it's a way of pretending that something really is being done, and..."*

[He cuts in] One of the keys to that system is that what I've wanted was to have direct access. It's not like I was making a report that I'd deliver to Fifa asking them, "OK, there's what's come across my desk, what do you want to do now?" I am in the system. And every day — every day! — I'm looking into information, I'm asking myself questions, "Do I refer this to the commission, do I need more information?" Every day. At the beginning we were inundated, people who all sent the same things, but

those kinks got worked out over time. It's working well.

⊕ *Let's talk about these investigations. For the ISL one, as Winston Churchill put it, you're "at the end of the beginning..."*

A very good quotation!

⊕ *...but also working in parallel on the investigations into the award of the World Cup [hosting rights]. The one for 2022, have you got the information together, and how much time will that investigation take?*

Very good question. It's a drawn out process, and that depends on what we were talking about before. How much information is still out there? How many people will be proactive and come to me? On the other side, have I got to decide to take the time to travel and convince people they've got to talk? The subject itself is complex. I believe that it's a good opportunity for everyone, everyone will do well out of it. I honestly haven't got any preconceived ideas. As you know when you talk to the people about the [2022] World Cup, they have pretty strong views... or interests. One or the other. Not me. I haven't got a single opinion on subjects such as the date when it has got to take place, etc. But I will listen to everything and I will examine all the information with the same impartiality, whether it comes from the US, from Qatar, from Russia, from Australia. My view remains the same. "What happened? Where were there issues, if there were any? Have they violated the Code?" That is the first of the priorities. And then also to examine certain subjects that you've mentioned in your investigation — were they close [to a breach of the Code]? And is that a problem related to the structure that existed at the time? And has that been considered in the reform efforts? I think that all these questions are very interesting but my top priority is obviously to determine if there have been, or not, breaches of the Ethics Code by football officials.

Who are the people who've helped you in your daily work? Other employees from your law firm Kirkland, for example?

I use some of them. It's fluid. It depends. And there is a subject that I find very interesting, that we haven't spoken about — match-fixing.

Are you taking care of that too?

!t could be a full-time business! In general terms, I'd say that in terms of jurisdiction, it's common ground with the Security Division [of Fifa]. They take care of players, referees; myself, of officials, of the associations... To me it's a fascinating subject in which I would like to involve myself more, and I've started to do that, but I have time imperatives. I need more leverage, I've called on Kirkland people who can serve me as lieutenants. I'm using Chief Justice Robert Torres [a former Guam judge], who is also a member of Fifa's Ethics Commission and who's helped me. He is very good. [I've also called] other lawyers, people who are specialists in technology, people who have the knowhow that I don't have myself. And external investigators, who are very important, because they are doing specific things which, for us others — lawyers, law firms — aren't really our 'thing'. If you have a laptop, and you try

to extract [the data it contains], and there are things that are relevant to a specific expertise, even in a law firm, we contract that out, people on the outside. I do that, and then I use it if I can. You have your investigators who can say, "This is how we have obtained these documents, these came from this server," or who help you know what this witness said or didn't say. You don't want to spread it too widely, since I want to keep control of everything which comes in to us. I try to do as much as I can, but I have to pick my shot.

And then there's the Fifa congress in Mauritius starting on 31 May. Could that be an opportunity of a new 'end of the beginnning' as far as the World Cup investigations are concerned? Or is that too early?

It's too early... Listen, that's a nice marker out there. It would be good if we can make it, but it's too early for me to say that I'm fixing myself a date like that. I hope that significant progress will have been made, one way or another. But I haven't got any idea today where we will be. Or not. But I hope that we will at least have made significant progress on the direction [we're taking], that there will be a crystallisation of specific problems, on which we will be able to concentrate, because we could sit here talking about issues... until the end of the weekend. One part of the work of a good investigative journalist, or of an investigator is, yes, to have all the facts in mind, but also to have in your mind where you would like to go. To know what you've got to do to get there, yes? Whatever the date you want to set or whatever. When I have encountered problems of this kind before, it's because of [the impossibility of] doing that. Because then, you're constantly looking at the whole field without breaking it down and that's terribly ineffective. I hope that with this 'funnel' for [new] information [Garcia is referring to the whistleblower line] we can do this work on the mapping.

◉ *So you haven't got a fixed calendar, no deadline? Your contract is up at the end of May, yes?*

Yes.

◉ *And after?*

[Laughs] That's not up to me, right? That's up to the [Fifa] Congress to decide. Listen, I believe that there is a lot of work to be done, and it'll be a busy time. Where we will be at the end of May... I've never been to a Fifa congress, so...

◉ *Has it been a surprise for you, a lawyer, to come into the football world and see its controversies, its complexities, its universality?*

I understood that football was much more important outside the US than inside. I'd been told that. But there was a big difference between hearing something and seeing it with your own eyes. So, yes, it's been somewhat of a surprise to see the attention that what I am doing brings, or what the Ethics Commission is doing. That's true. But I was at the Ballon d'Or gala and it was so nice to see the beauty of the game, the most beautiful goals, the best players, [I could] feel what people love and admire in this sport, I'm watching football now, my daughter plays... and it's great to see that.

◉ *But have you got the feeling of an adherence to the reform process right at the heart of Fifa?*

Look, I think there's been a lot of good work done in the reform process. I do. I believe it's hard to generalise when we're talking about the position of Fifa because there are different personalities, different approaches at the heart of the organisation. The thing I feel confident talking about is the way in which I've been received and how I've been supported; and the key point for me, is resources [put at my disposal] where it's black and white. Without the resources, you could do all you want, set up all the commissions you want, for nothing. Today I have all the resources I need. I know that there is a whole range of reform propositions but I'm not that knowledgeable on that subject, on who is from what side. What I see is my role in that reform process and to me it's received the support [I wanted].

◉ *There are people who have called into question your independence at Fifa. Are you truly independent?*

Yes, absolutely. And that's very interesting. I hear the criticism: "How can you be independent when you are paid by Fifa?" Well, that's not such an unusual thing in the US. In the US, when a company gets into trouble, we call for an external audit, generally under an agreement passed by the government. This auditor will be completely independent and, generally will report to the government — but he'll be paid by the company. It's certainly not the government who pays for an independent auditor, OK? [Laughs] The key isn't the paystream, it's the audit. Is there a pole that information is made to flow towards, unaudited by the business in question? And, in this case, under the Code, this audit, I've gotten it, just like Hans-Joachim Eckert. It's we who take our decisions together, it's he who gives the ultimate verdict on penalties. My connection with Fifa is the same as an [external] administrator's would be. I use them sometimes to get messages out, or when I can have access to the original [documents] in an investigation, or when I need to reimburse the expenses of an investigator or a lawyer. But there is no supervision of what I do. I am really independent of that organisation. I think that it's not such a strange relationship as all that, seen from an American perspective rather than a European one or the rest of the world, because there are a bunch of cases of this type [in the US].

But where's Sepp Blatter in all this? Does he want to hear what you have to say on Qatar, on Russia?

That's a question... I'll go back to what's my role here: I don't deal with Blatter on that level. I do not report to him. He doesn't talk to me about what I'm doing. I couldn't tell you anything, in one sense or another, on these subjects because we haven't got this kind of interaction. He's kept himself — appropriately — out of my sphere. He is the president of Fifa, he does what he does. I have met him perhaps... once in the first three months of my job.

And if you have concrete information to communicate on the award of the 2006, 2018 and 2022 World Cups to Germany, Russia and Qatar, you will put that on the table?

[Immediately] Absolutely.

Without the slightest hesitation?

Absolutely. Here's the thing: I will put what I have, or what I don't have , on the table, all right? It's not like I've had this idea, "What's in the past is done," and whatever I find, I will put on the table, which will confirm it. I will put on the table what we find and what we haven't found. And I believe that it's in everyone's interest. A fair look. Hard look, but fair look... By listening to everyone, and by making a fair evaluation.

On what basis will you make your recommendations?

I'll send everything to Mr Eckert and there you are. I've got a very good relationship with him. I didn't know him at all before. Obviously, he has a terrific background, he occupies a very prestigious position. He works very hard and he is genuinely interested in the reform process, making this work. We aren't in contact day to day. He isn't directly involved [in my work]; he takes the ultimate decision. If this is proved, what am I going to do? What will be the sanctions? That's his call. It's gone very well. The Code is... very good. In terms of process, it's specific. When I came in, I thought that we would have to set aside time to build a process around the Code, that we would spend a month or two for that to work. And that didn't happen. We were off and running from day one.

Really?

Yes. We got into it from the first day, into precise cases. The structure has really come together to support that code. There will always be someone who will disagree with you, who will think you're crazy because you did this or crazy because you didn't do it. I accept that. I've accepted that throughout my career. What counts is that you have to have faith in the process, whether you will agree with its result or not; that you will be convinced that it's not corrupt or submitted to influence, from one side or another, to pressure to not do something when you have evidence, and that you have relationships in place, or a conflict of interest, or pressure to do something when there is an expectation. "Oh, it's so clearly so, if you didn't do something..." You've got to put these things aside. And you [journalists] are very important in all that. There are so many people who are looking for signs, who read you, and who have got to have confidence in the process even if they think, "This bloke ought to have been charged," etc, but, at least, the process works.

Is it conceivable that with the evidence you have gathered, the 2022 World Cup won't take place in Qatar?

I know everybody is very interested in that. But I think, and I think that Judge Eckert would say as well, that our jurisdiction is limited to people. So... the only thing that we can do is say, "You, football official, violated this provision of the Ethics Code and you, football official, are going to suffer this sanction."[2] But that's only as to people. That what we can do, right? Those decisions, on the venue of the World Cup, you know, that's outside the jurisdiction of the Ethics Commission. That's just a completely different process. Otherwise, it may be a particularly interesting issue, but it's not for me or Judge Eckert, and that's the bottom line of how that process works.

[2] *The Sri Lankan Fifa ExCo member Manilal Fernando, a close ally of the Thai FA president and AFC presidency candidate Warowi Makudi, was suspended on Michael Garcia's recommendation a few days after this interview took place. The precise nature of the charges which led to this ban hasn't been revealed by Fifa.*

THE BLIZZARD BY GOALSOUL
A PARTNERSHIP BORN OF FOOTBALL

BLZZRD03
COMPARING APPLE WITH ORANJE
SIMON KUPER AND DAVID WINNER

BLZZRD08
THE BICYCLE THIEF
LARS SIVERTSEN

The **Blizzard by goalsoul** partnership is a commitment to style and substance in equal measure. Our stunning and original story-inspired, graphic tees look and feel great. Lovingly hand screen-printed on 100% combed-cotton and shrink-resistant fabric – you can be sure of the highest possible quality, durability and wearability.

Available in sizes **S / M / L / XL / XXL** for only **£25** each, plus shipping.

THE BLIZZARD
GOALS ARE OVERRATED
JONATHAN WILSON

BLZZRD03
THE HARMONY OF THE SPHERE
PHILIPPE AUCLAIR

Exclusively available now from **www.theblizzard.co.uk** and **www.goalsoul.net**

Power Play

*The Asian Football Confederation's presidential
elections highlight football's murky governance*

By James Corbett

12pm, 2 May 2013, Kuala Lumpur

**For the small band of sports news
reporters, it was familiar territory:
the anteroom of a five-star hotel
conference room, the expensive
uneaten nibbles, the stale coffee, the
laminates hanging from our necks. For
the uniformity of it all we might have
been in any of sport's staging posts:
London, Zurich, Paris, Doha. But today it
was the turn of Kuala Lumpur.**

Among the delegates who drifted out
of the hall there was a sense of quiet
excitement and relief. A new president of
the Asian Football Confederation had just
been elected. Most people agreed that it
was *politically* the right result, even some
of the defeated candidates. Football was
not mentioned, of course.

One by one the vanquished and the
victors emerged. But, dictaphones
primed, we all only had eyes for one man.

Then there was a charge and there he
was, amid the scrum, the king of world
football himself, Sepp Blatter. He was a
little more stooped and shrunken than
the last time I had seen him, a couple
of years earlier, but still very much
the same; beady-eyed and cunning, a
politician's smile stretching every sinew
of his face.

As 100 or so reporters chased the 77
year old around the hotel, his affable
French press attaché somehow keeping
us all at bay, Blatter said virtually
nothing. Responding to a question
about the tone of the occasionally
bitter election campaign, he smiled and
replied — as only he can — "I have seen
total transparency."

Later that afternoon he put out a
statement praising the AFC for its "unity
as well as solidarity". It might as well have
just said, "Thank you for not choosing my
enemy's friend."

AFC elections have pedigree in
representing some of the very worst of
football. In few other areas of global
sport do national interests, regional
rivalries, corruption and bitterness
mingle into as noxious a mix as they
do in Asian football. At once they have
absolutely nothing and everything to do
with football. They are about power for
the sake of power and are an extreme
example of the way that the game as a
whole is governed worldwide.

The previous presidential elections in
2009 between the incumbent, Mohamed
bin Hammam of Qatar, and Bahrain's
Sheikh Salman bin Ibrahim Al Khalifa,

were a case study in personal abuse, conspiracy theories, alleged vote-buying, corruption and general misbehaviour by men who should have known far better. To many in world football, this was less a leadership election than a referendum on Qatar's role in global sport. At the time the tiny Gulf country was bidding for the 2016 Olympics, the 2022 World Cup and Bin Hammam was said to have an eye on the Fifa presidency. Win the election and Bin Hammam's position as head of Asian football and on the Fifa Executive Committee would have been enshrined, giving him and Qatar huge leverage in contests that lay ahead.

What followed was a concerted effort to stop Bin Hammam. The Korean industrialist and Fifa vice-president, Chung Mong-Joon, aligned with his perennial rival Sepp Blatter to stop Bin Hammam. The Olympic Council of Asia (OCA) headed by the powerful Kuwaiti, Sheikh Ahmad Fahad Al-Sabah, also stepped in on the side of Sheikh Salman. In holding authority over a great swathe of Asian sport and acting as a meeting point between various national political interests and sport, the OCA's importance far transcends sport. "The forces of hell lined up against us," recalled one Bin Hammam associate. "We faced Blatter and Fifa, Chung, the OCA, the East Asian countries… Can you imagine all these individuals and groupings casting aside all their differences just to stop us?"

The volatile atmosphere soon erupted into name-calling, allegation and counter-allegation. Bin Hammam suggested in a TV interview that Chung should be decapitated; his head and arms cut off. "It is a popular, harmless and widely used Arabic metaphor," Bin Hammam later explained, comparing it to the English phrase "Heads will roll", but Chung was unconvinced. "I am afraid that Mr Hammam may be a sick person who needs to be at a hospital rather than at Fifa," he told reporters. "It looks like Mr Hammam is suffering from mental problems. I want to advise him to consider going to hospital." He then went on to allege that Bin Hammam was "acting like a head of a crime organisation" and that Asian football suffered from a serious lack of transparency, democracy and the rule of law.

The allegations also included claims of vote buying. José Mari Martínez, president of the Philippine Football Federation, later alleged that his national association received financial offers as grants from the Philippine National Olympic Council (NOC) in return for voting for Sheikh Salman. The federation declined these offers and supported Bin Hammam (Martínez was accused in a 2012 PWC audit report commissioned by the AFC of receiving $60,000 from an AFC account when Bin Hammam was its president).

In the days leading up to the election, the atmosphere was murky, frenzied and all manner of procedural horseplay went on. It was not clear until the day before the vote whether Kuwait, East Timor, Mongolia, Brunei, Afghanistan and Laos would be allowed to vote. With a constituency of just 46 voters, these are not just the margins by which elections are won and lost, but deciding factors. In the end they were all allowed, and despite facing a grand alliance Bin Hammam won by 23 votes to 21. Two of the ballot papers had been spoiled.

"Unfortunately some bad acts have taken place," Bin Hammam reflected a week later in London. "I hope that we in Asia overcome these bad acts and that we will be able to conduct our [future] elections in a much better way."

For the two years that followed, Bin Hammam kept on winning. It became habitual. Nothing Sepp Blatter, Fifa, the AFC or any of his rivals did could stop him. No matter how big or small the battle, he went on winning. On 2 December 2010, he claimed the biggest prize of them all for Qatar: hosting rights for the 2022 World Cup. It probably represents the most extraordinary — and the most questioned — result in the history of football.

For Blatter, there was one prize that was bigger even than the World Cup: the Fifa presidency. Concession after concession had been put the way of Bin Hammam since he was re-elected AFC president — advisors sacked for upsetting him, political shenanigans overlooked in Asia, muted outrage after the World Cup decision — but when he announced his candidacy for the Fifa presidency in March 2011 he appeared to have crossed the Rubicon.

On 10 May 2011, Bin Hammam appeared at a meeting of the Caribbean Football Union (CFU) to present his election manifesto at the Grand Hyatt in Port of Spain, Trinidad. Because the Fifa Congress adheres to a one-member-one-vote system, in electoral terms Antigua is as important as England; as a voting bloc carrying the CFU, is like carrying half of Europe and twice

as important as the whole of South America. Mindful that this was such a key battleground, at the summit up to 25 CFU officials were each offered envelopes containing US$40,000 in cash to persuade them to vote for Bin Hammam. But the Qatari was betrayed. A file was sent to Fifa, which included sworn affidavits by several CFU members, secret recordings and photographs of the bribes. Bin Hammam was suspended by Fifa two days before the presidential election and subsequently banned from football for life. It meant Blatter was re-elected unopposed. It also meant that the AFC needed a new president.

While Fifa justice dealt with Bin Hammam over the next two years, the AFC was led on an interim basis by China's Zhang Jilong. After the turmoil left in Bin Hammam's wake, it was felt that he represented the steady pair of hands that might bring some unity and redemption to the organisation. As a long-term option, however, some judged him to be overly passive and lacking charisma. Others suggested that the Chinese National Olympic Committee — after coming under pressure from the OAC — told him not to stand for the position permanently. When nominations closed for the AFC presidency in March 2013, Zhang's name was not among the four listed.

The UAE's Yousuf al-Serkal was considered one of the two frontrunners. A vastly experienced sports politician both within the Emirates and Asia, he was a friend of Bin Hammam but without the blemish of corruption allegations throughout his long career.

He was someone to be taken seriously. He employed Vero Communications, the PR agency run by the British spin doctor, Mike Lee, whose campaigning successes included the London and Rio Olympic Games and, of course, Qatar 2022. Unlike the other candidates Al-Serkal actively engaged with the media and published a manifesto that used words like "transparent", "improved governance", and "football". Football, as we will see, was a word often far from the other candidates' lips.

Hafez al-Medlej, a 43-year-old Saudi, who chaired the AFC's marketing committee, was considered a wildcard selection. Although few took his candidature seriously, there was recognition that as the son of a regional superpower anything could happen. "All it takes is two or three calls from the Saudi royal family and the other Arab candidatures are over," claimed one election insider. Al-Medlej would spend most of his campaign waiting for those calls to come.

The inclusion on the slate of Worawi Makudi, a longstanding Fifa Executive committee member, also represented something of a surprise. Makudi had faced a multitude of allegations in his native Thailand concerning ownership of land on which the Thai FA headquarters were built with Fifa grants. Although cleared by Fifa the stink had not quite gone away. Like Al-Serkel he was known for his links to Bin Hammam. Indeed over the subsequent couple of months all three of these candidates would be accused of links to Qatar.

The overwhelming favourite was Sheikh Salman, who, since his narrow defeat

in 2009, had kept his head down, but continued to cultivate support across Asian football — a base that had previously brought him agonisingly close to the confederation's presidency. He was confident of success too. "In 2009 I said that I had a 50-50 chance and I was right," he said in March. "In this election, so far things are moving well. I think now I am 70-80% there."

But amid this support within international football, serious questions were raised about Salman's suitability for high office. In February 2011 the Arab Spring came to his native Bahrain. Pro-democracy protests by the Shia majority challenged the absolute monarchy of its Sunni leaders. The Pearl Roundabout in downtown Manama became a focal point for peaceful protests, which were at one point even encouraged by the royal family. Emboldened, footballers, athletes and other significant figures joined in. It would be the biggest mistake of their lives. As the rule of the Bahraini royal family teetered on the brink of collapse, soldiers augmented by a Gulf Cooperation Council (GCC) force from Saudi Arabia, Qatar, the UAE and beyond swept in to help the Bahrainis ruthlessly put down the protests. Activists claim that four protesters were killed in the operation.

What happened in the wake of the failed protests was perhaps even more shocking. The Bahraini authorities used television and photographic evidence to identify protestors and arrest them. These included doctors and other medical staff who had cared for injured protesters. According to the Associated Press a special sports commission was also established to pick out athletes involved in the protests and as a result

150 sportsmen and women, referees and coaches were arrested. They included the brothers Mohamed and A'ala Hubail, heroes of the national football team, who had brought Bahrain to the verge of qualifying for the 2010 World Cup. "We saw some masked men get out of the car. They said, 'Captain A'ala, get you brother' and we went with them," A'ala later explained in an ESPN documentary. "They put me in the room for the beatings. One of the people who hit me said I'm going to break your legs. They knew who we were... We were forced to endure it. I had to endure it. If I didn't something worse would have happened to me."

Mohamed Hubail was tried in secret and sentenced to two years in jail in April 2011. When Fifa belatedly intervened in June that year he was released on appeal, but with his brother forced to play in exile in Oman. A'ala's case, coming after the Fifa intervention, was thrown out of court. A third national team player, Sayed Mohamed Adnan, left for Australia and played for the Brisbane Roar. None were made available for national team selection again.

Sensitivities ran high in Bahrain about this issue. Peter Taylor, briefly England coach in 2001 and by 2011 in charge of the Bahrain national team, claimed he had never heard of A'ala Hubail. Which was funny, because when I asked him about his non-selection of the Hubail brothers at a post-match press conference in Qatar in November 2011, he erupted into a rage so intense that I feared he was going to jump across the table and assault me. It seemed odd that a player he had never heard about could produce such a volcanic reaction.

But if Taylor was only following orders — which seems the best case scenario for the former Leicester boss — whose were they? This was never clear, but the head of the Bahraini federation was none other than Sheikh Salman. Worse still, the Associated Press alleged that Salman "chaired" the committee that "identified them [the athletes] from photographs of the protests." Salman did not comment on the article at the time, nor has he ever issued an outright denial that he sat on the committee. The furthest that he went was blandly claiming that he has never violated the statutes of either Fifa or the AFC, which seems a strange moral code to invoke when faced with allegations of such magnitude.

It was the day before the election. Kuala Lumpur's Mandarin Oriental Hotel was abuzz with rumour and intrigue. For all its grandeur, the lobby was compact enough for the electoral rivals to have to sit within touching distance of each other through the clouds of cigarette smoke that encircled every delegation. On one side of the room Sheikh Salman's entourage spread out around a coffee table. The president of the Kuwait Football Federation and younger brother of Sheikh Ahmad, Sheikh Talal Fahad Al Sabah, sat wearing a baseball cap, leering at his rivals across the room, a mobile phone permanently attached to his ear.

Opposite him was the sizable Qatari delegation spread out across two tables. An anomaly in the AFC statutes meant that the new president was not automatically assigned a seat on the Fifa Executive committee. The presidential election would be followed immediately by one for the Exco seat, which Hassan al-Thawadi, the charismatic CEO of the Qatar World Cup organising committee, was contesting. El-Medlej and Al-Serkal had decided to step aside for this contest, fanning another series of Qatari conspiracy theories. Behind the Qataris sat the Emiratis, wearing blue-logoed 'Football at Heart' T-shirts. Al-Serkal was omnipresent in the lobby, stalking it, wise-cracking, shaking hands. In a world in which the real business is conducted behind closed doors, this was not a good sign for his campaign.

I watched from the sweeping staircase as the president of the Afghan Football Federation sat with his general secretary. The hotel is a place of opulence and wonder, where rooms start at $300 per night and a coffee and cupcake on the beautiful verandah cost $20 — around a week's average wages in Kabul.

Two years earlier I had embarked on the last leg of an arduous journey that had taken the Afghanistan national team from Kabul to Dubai, then to Delhi, Amman and finally Palestine for a 2014 World Cup qualifier. Criss-crossing Asia rather than flying direct was the cheapest way their impoverished federation could fulfil their fixture obligations. On the bus through the West Bank, the players sat with their legs raised, trying to prevent the swelling and cramps that come from such a lengthy journey. They arrived at their down-at-heel hotel, in which they slept three to a room, 22 hours before the match and went almost immediately to the stadium for a training session. It was a timely reminder that away from the glamour and TV spectacles that we associate with international football in Europe, the reality elsewhere is often

fairly bleak, with players uncosseted and national associations struggling to pay their bills. I'm certain that the modest Afghan players would have been slack-jawed in these surroundings.

The Afghans were joined by the heads of the federations of some of the world's poorer nations: Bhutan, Timor Leste, Burma, Nepal, all at the expense of the Asian Football Confederation. At a time when its annual spending on "football development" is just $12million for the entire continent there seemed something grotesque in so much cash being ploughed into a junket for men in suits. But then football politics exists in a complete vacuum: one delegate was reminded not to feel sorry for the North Korean delegation — all wearing Kim Jong-un haircuts — when one of their number produced from his briefcase the latest and most high-spec MacBook available.

Makudi and Al-Medlej were conspicuous by their absence, but no one considered either a serious candidate by that stage. A colleague had arranged to interview the Saudi a day earlier and was told to meet him in a branch of Starbuck's. "When will I come?" he asked. "I'll be here all day," came the reply, as if he had nothing better to do. El-Medlej had then shown up at the Mandarin early evening and sat in the lobby watching the AFC Champions League on his tablet computer, seemingly oblivious to the frantic handshaking and lobbying going on around him. There was something endearing about the way he approached the inevitability of his defeat and he openly admitted he would be pulling out. At 7pm, a statement from the Saudi FA confirmed the inevitable.

Sheikh Salman, by contrast, appeared here and there, in and out of meetings. He lacked the presence of his rivals and assumed the aspect of a provincial GP; sombre, meticulous, serious. Al-Serkal muttered that he was just a "shadow" of Sheikh Ahmad and one glance would tell you that his perception was accurate. The Kuwaiti towered above everyone and was as loud and charismatic as Salman was demure and unassuming. He was trailed everywhere by a huge bodyguard, who merely had to cast a menacing glare to part the waves of Arab media.

For them this was a circus. I was just one of two journalists to have travelled from Europe, and only one made the journey from Australia. Apart from the newswires, virtually every reporter came from the Gulf. Every night an array of Arab-language networks broadcast live election specials. It was difficult enough to report 500 words of interesting written copy, even harder to fill 30-minute primetime broadcast slots with the day's news. In reality these amounted to extended rants, denunciations and propagation of regional conspiracy theories. Football, as ever, was of secondary interest.

One was often left with the feeling that for them this was 'proper' politics by proxy; that the Gulf Arab candidates, with their vast entourages and huge media interest, would take it less seriously if they had parliamentary democracy in their home countries to fill their time and TV schedules. But under the rule of absolute monarchs — or as parts of the royal families themselves — and in the absence of players and teams that can compete among the global elite, for them football politics fills an important void. To followers of the endless rhetoric, conspiracy theories and, frankly, nonsense in the region's sports newspapers, the AFC election was as close to democracy as they got.

Indeed, there followed a certain logic to their obsession with football politicians. If your country doesn't have a Messi, Rooney or Ronaldo to believe in, why not pin your hopes on a Sheikh Salman or Mohamed bin Hammam? At least Bin Hammam can claim that he helped 'win' his country the World Cup, which is something none of those players can say.

The shadow of Bin Hammam, nevertheless, hung heavily over proceedings. Statements were circulated by the Kuwait Football Association expressing its 'deep concern' about a media report that Bin Hammam had visited various national associations in order to support the candidacies of Al-Serkal, Makudi and al-Thawadi. The fact that he might simultaneously support rival candidacies spoke loudly of the paranoia and complexities of AFC politics.

"Upon my arrival today in Kuala Lumpur I have witnessed that the entire group of the former AFC president was present and speaking to various members of the AFC family," noted Husain Al Musallam, the vice-chairman of the KFA's International Relations and Legal Committee, in a statement. Fifa sent a fax warning that Bin Hammam was not a man people should be talking to. The Kuwaitis obligingly circulated it for them. Earlier that week Fifa's ethics committee had, for reasons unexplained, handed an eight-year ban to Bin Hammam's one-time ally, the Sri Lankan Fifa Exco member Vernon Manilal Fernando. It represented a stark reminder that Fifa justice can be particularly punitive for the Qatari's friends and, perhaps, a warning to those considering a vote for Al-Serkal.

"Where is Bin Hammam? He is not here," said Al-Serkal when we sat down for a chat in the lobby. "Who is here? Sheikh Ahmad is here. The OCA is here. Who is running? I know I am running. Can you tell me is it clear Sheikh Salman is running? Can you picture Sheikh Salman alone? You close your eyes and who do you see? You see someone else. Sheikh Salman is only a shadow."

It was difficult not to like the engaging Al-Serkal, who in manner and demeanour reminded me of Bin Hammam. History has cast the Qatari as one of Fifa's ultimate villains, but I always found him courteous and deeply infatuated with football — attributes that in my experience characterise few in the Fifa family. While he had been accused of many things and wronged many decent people for his own purposes, human rights violations were certainly not among the accusations he has faced.

I asked the Emirati about the allegations made about Sheikh Salman's role in the suppression of athletes involved in pro-democracy protesters. The Bahrain Centre for Human Rights had just written to Blatter calling on him to withdraw Salman, whom they accused of "human rights violations ... against players, administrators, referees and clubs who participated in the democracy protests."

The Gulf's conservative social norms usually make it seem bad form to cast aspersions about neighbouring royals. But Al-Serkal did not hold back. "I, myself

in general think that I am a better choice than Sheikh Salman," he said. "In this case as well, I think I'm fitter. He's not fit. When it comes to politics I'm a sports man. I understand nothing in politics."

Everything suggested Sheikh Salman would win, even if Al-Serkal's worst crime was no more than being friends with the vanquished Bin Hammam. There was no suggestion that he shared any form of culpability in the Qatari's sins. Al-Serkal repeated his concern about the involvement of Sheikh Ahmad and the OCA. The Kuwaiti is a close ally of Blatter and at an earlier election in January 2011 I'd seen how he played a key role in ousting former Fifa vice-president (and one-time presidential hopeful) Chung Mong-Joon. The OCA had proved highly sensitive to these allegations and when a story was published about it booking an entire floor of the Mandarin — the implication being that they were buying favours with their allies — it was promptly cancelled —and then (according to their rivals) switched over to the Ritz Carlton.

Stalking the corridors of the Mandarin, it was obvious that what was going to follow was a carve-up, but it was difficult to see any signs of overt corruption. Even the suspicious Arab media were silent on this issue. There was no sign of the high-end prostitutes for whom five-star hotel lobbies are a magnet throughout Asia.

But if everyone was well-behaved in Kuala Lumpur, elsewhere on the campaign trail things were not as they might have been. Given that most of the candidates came from one of the most socially conservative regions on earth, what they had to overlook or encounter seems surprising.

A key date on the lobby trail, the Asean Football Federation Awards at a resort hotel in Kuantan, Malaysia, in April, was described by one attendee as "seedy and appalling... prostitutes outnumbered delegates while a Filipino rock band filled the place with ugly noise." Who knows what favours were carried out in the name of cleaning up the name of Asian football that night, or on others?

By the morning of the election, a wave of exhaustion seemed to have washed over everyone. On both of the previous nights, many of the election teams had stayed up until the small hours became the wee small hours, watching the Champions League semi-finals unfold six time-zones away.

We journalists waited in the foyer in front of the Congress Hall, trying to read the runes and gain a glimpse of what might unfold inside. One by one they came: Sheikh Ahmad and his man mountain bodyguard, Makudi, Sheikh Salman, Hassan al-Thawadi, Michel Platini, Blatter and finally Al-Serkal. None gave anything away. Only Blatter stopped, exchanging a word with a Japanese photographer who was dressed in a full Brazil kit and wearing fluorescent orange astroboots.

But then, from the corner of my eye, what was this? A senior member of the Qatar delegation embracing Salman? A man they had been at war with for months? This wasn't a subtle act of courtesy, it was carried out in the full glare of the Arab media. Was this Asian football's Judas Iscariot approaching Jesus in Gethsemane? Had a backroom deal carved up the spoils of Asian football,

giving the AFC presidency to Salman with a place on the Fifa Exco for Hassan al-Thawadi? We would soon find out.

Into the hall we trooped and the formalities were under way. A welcome speech by the outgoing president Zhang Jilong. Blatter pleading for unity ("United we stand, divided we fail," he said, misquoting the Aesopian wisdom). A roll call. A vote on whether to afford Brunei voting privileges. And then, finally, the vote. Candidates were called two by two, entering clear glass voting booths to the left and right of the stage. These were apparently introduced after candidates were alleged to have photographed their ballot papers with camera phones in order to prove their loyalty in previous football elections.

A two-thirds majority, or 31 of the 46 available votes, were needed for a first-round victory. Most observers expected Makudi to be eliminated first time round followed by a run-off between Salman and Al-Serkal. But then the Arab media started filling the back of the Congress Hall and it seemed that something was afoot. Camera lights flicked on and a dozen TV reporters readied their microphones for an instant reaction.

Alex Soosay, the AFC general secretary, stood up and told the Congress that all the votes had been counted and they were all valid. The roar of elation from the Kuwaitis and swathes of the media told us that Sheikh Salman was a first-round victor with an astonishing 33 votes. Makudi had seven votes, he said. Al-Serkal had six. There would be no run off. The AFC had a new president.

Twenty minutes later Soosay confirmed that there had been no backroom deal between Salman and Qatar. The Bahraini had prevailed 28-18, although the reality was that there were just five votes in it.

In the darkened hall, my phone glowed with messages and tweets from Bin Hammam's enemies. "Bahrain 2 Qatar 0," one read.

Afterwards, among delegates, exhaustion gave way to relief that the ghost of Bin Hammam had been exorcised. It seemed slightly unfair on Al-Serkal, who had seemingly been made to pay for the sins of his friend. His defeat had been crushing: besides Qatar and his own federation, just four other countries had voted for him. Even the hapless Makudi polled more. "Despite the force of OCA, despite the force of all kinds of countries I accepted to continue with the race and accepted the result whatever it is," he said. Asked for comment, Makudi said simply, "I have no idea."

In the press conference afterwards, there was much talk from Sheikh Salman about "unity", "smooth transitions", "realistic goals". Given the virtual blackout of the western media in the days running up to the vote, it was my first encounter of him at close quarters. There was a civility and seriousness there, but no spark. He seemed a safe pair of hands, probably the right choice after the tumultuous few years that followed Bin Hammam's fall. Even Al-Serkal's friends admitted as much.

The press conference ground on and on, but still the elephant in the room sat there.

I put my hand up.

"Could you just clarify some of the serious allegations that were made against you about sitting on a commission in Bahrain that identified athletes that were involved in the pro-democracy protests, and can you also comment on an accusation made by the Bahrain Centre for Human Rights that you were involved in human rights violations, please?"

Media officer: "I think he has answered it so many times that…"

"Well, can he answer it for me?"

Sheikh Salman: "I have no problem answering it. I have one question: you talk about allegations, but the question is proof. Somebody talks about government, I don't think that this is our business. We are football people. If anybody has proof that the Bahrain Football Association has violated the statutes of Fifa or the AFC let them present it. Otherwise we will move to the other question."

Afterwards, variations of the same answer were given to the BBC and Australia's SBS. In an interview with AFP, Salman went further, suggesting that allegations made against him were the work of an unnamed foreign government determined to smear him. But still there was no denial. The Associated Press stands by its August 2011 report, which alleges his role as chair of the commission.

"Sheikh Salman has talked of the need for reform and accountability at the AFC, but he still has very serious questions to answer about his role in the serious abuses of protestors, including footballers and athletes, in the antigovernment protests of 2011," Human Rights Watch's Nicholas McGeehan told *The Blizzard*. "In replacing Mohamed bin Hammam with Sheikh Salman al Khalifa, the AFC has replaced a man accused of making bribes with a man accused of ordering torture. The ever-increasing involvement of serious human rights violators in the funding and governance of football should be of real concern to anyone who loves the sport."

Article 3 of the Fifa Statutes demands "Non-discrimination and Stance Against Racism". It reads, "Discrimination of any kind against a country, private person or group of people on account of ethnic origin, gender, language, religion, politics or any other reason is strictly prohibited and punishable by suspension or expulsion." Article 14 of the Fifa statutes insist those bound by Fifa rules maintain political neutrality. Article 11, paragraph 1, sub-section R of the AFC statutes demand each member association "manage its affairs independently and with no influence from third party, even if the third-

party influence was not the fault of the Member concerned."

Sheikh Salman may or may not have violated these statutes. He also knows that Gulf monarchies are absolute and that his own country is notoriously intolerant of dissent. The likelihood of a whistleblower going public, or of documents being leaked is so slim as to be virtually non-existent. Equally, the proof he demands may or may not exist: it could be the work of a foreign government, after all.

But what is indisputable is that the careers of the Hubail brothers, Sayed Mohamed Adnan and others now lay in tatters for partaking in peaceful pro-democracy protests at a time when he was president of their federation.

"We are his responsibility and people like him should solve the problem, not ignore it," Mohamed Hubail told the Associated Press on the eve of the election. "I have a lot of anger. I really miss playing for my team and for Bahrain." Ⓑ

Genesis

How a tournament in China in 1988 changed women's football for ever

By Davidde Corran

Heidi Store had never been so completely surrounded, and yet she was struck by how isolated she felt.

Standing in the middle of a packed Tianhe Stadium in Guangzhou, the Norwegian central midfielder looked to her right and saw her childhood friend, right-sided midfielder Liv Straedet.

Hailing from Raade, a tiny town south of Oslo, the two women had known each other since birth. They started playing the game together with the boys who lived on their street and rose up the ranks before entering the national team at the same time.

Straedet had been a reassuring figure for Store throughout her career. There to her right — an outlet ball, a calming face, a friend. At that moment, though, Store could see Straedet's mouth moving, but couldn't hear a word she was saying as 55,000 cheering Chinese fans drowned her out.

It was 12 June 1988 and the 24 year old looked around and took in the scene unfurling around her. Beyond Straedet were her teammates interspersed with players from Norway's fierce rivals Sweden and then, of course, there was the crowd.

Before arriving in China neither team had experienced crowds bigger than around

1,000 people; now they were playing in front of a packed house for the sixth time in twelve days. For many it was the realisation of a dream they'd never fully believed they'd experience — the final of the first official women's international tournament and the pilot event for an eventual World Cup.

A couple of years before that 1988 final, a Women's World Cup was just an idea and ideas can be fragile things — especially when they're being pushed back by years of prejudice and misconceptions. Women's football was a fragmented sport. In Taiwan, players enjoyed almost full-time fully funded careers while in Australia the national team struggled to get anything other than second-hand men's kits to wear during games.

This schism extended into the game's administration. At Fifa, where women's football was finally starting to gain traction, two factions were fighting over the future of the game. The cause for women's football was led by football associations pushing for a World Cup in the belief that only the recognition that would come with an official Fifa tournament could lift the game towards professionalism. The doubters promoted questionable initiatives such as women playing shorter games with a smaller sized ball than the standard size five used by the men.

Watching a presentation from an official Fifa doctor at a seminar in Sweden, Heidi Store experienced that reality first hand. "The first time I heard the discussion about the number four or number five ball I was at a seminar with my head coach Even Pellerud in Sweden," said Store. "There was a doctor saying girls were so small and tiny they couldn't use a number five ball."

Store is tall. She looks like someone built to dominate a football pitch. "Her nickname in our team was 'Lurch', because she was so tall," said the former Australia midfielder Moya Dodd. "Someone's got to get Lurch on the corners! Who's going to get Lurch?"

Pellerud is almost a full head shorter than Store and he wasn't happy at what he'd just heard. "He grabbed my shoulder and he raced me up [to the doctor]," said Store. "Both of us are standing there next to each other and he says, 'Please sir, can you repeat that question?'"

"We thought it was a ridiculous idea," said the former USA international Carin Gabarra of the suggestion women should play shorter games with a smaller ball.

The response from players was almost universal. "I just remember anytime that came up we were so mad," said Joan McEachern, who used to play in midfield for Canada. "It's just so insulting. We would just get mad."

It was in that environment that the notion of a women's World Cup started to form and in which Fifa decided to host a trial event, what the then president João Havelange called a "World Tournament for Women", in China.

One morning the letters arrived. 18 of them dropped into letterboxes across the country. They were addressed to each member of the Australia national women's team and came from the federation's CEO, Heather Reid. "We would always get news by letter," said Dodd. "If you got something in the post from Heather (Reid) you thought, 'Oh, get this one open, something exciting inside.'"

And this letter wouldn't disappoint: an invitation to represent Australia at the first official women's tournament. "We were just completely excited," said Dodd. "The tournaments we went to then were ones where you never quite knew who was going to be there. You'd hear the Italians are coming or the Germans are coming and you'd think let's hope it's the full national team, but sometimes it wasn't. Sometimes it was a state side or a club side and you'd play whoever you could play.

"It had been basically a bunch of friendlies or self-organised tournaments with no official status on the global scale. To move from that to a world where you're having a Fifa world tournament was hugely exciting. We knew that was the turning point, we knew that was the beginning of an era. We knew that was the greatest opportunity probably most of us had ever had in football."

But the opportunity came at a cost: AU$800 (around £350 given exchange rates at the time) per player — a significant sum for an amateur footballer in 1988 to have to find.

In late May, after a five-day training camp in Sydney, the Matildas began their 24-hour journey to China. The importance of the adventure they were embarking upon was reflected in the clothes the players were wearing.

"We got our first travel or formal outfits ever," remembers the midfielder Julie Murray. "It was a skirt and jacket. I'd never had one before. None of them fit. Pretty much up until the morning that we were leaving people were sewing and putting safety pins in our skirts — I had to roll mine over at the top."

According to the team's post-tournament report, the quick adjustments worked. "Also impressive was the travelling uniform, which not only looked good en route, but also made a pleasant change to tracksuits when we attended an official function," it reads. "There were of course some problems with the fit and the shirt was not ideal, but certainly the uniform was well received and supported."

After stopping in Hong Kong, the Australians boarded a state-run Chinese airline plane that "shuddered a lot" for the last leg of their journey. "The seats were quite close together," Dodd said. "There were a couple of larger American tourists who were on the flight as well and they couldn't sit on their seats, they couldn't fit in. I remember they had to kneel on their seats facing the rear with the seatbelts around the back of their

knees for take-off and landing because that was the only way they were going to fit in the seats."

There might have been issues with the travel and uniforms, but the accommodation in Guangzhou was beyond reproach. Sitting on the banks of the Pearl River, the luxurious 28-storey White Swan has seen visitors that include US presidents and Queen Elizabeth II and housed most of the teams at the start of tournament.

Amid the opulence of the White Swan the teams escaped from the city's thick heat and reflected on a growing sense of pressure, not just to perform for themselves and their countries, but for the game in general. "We knew that we were representing our country, but we also thought we were representing women's football," said McEachern. "Because a good showing at that tournament would mean there would be a World Cup. That was our understanding and that's how we viewed it."

As the Canadian team arrived at Tianhe Stadium for the tournament's opening game the first thing they noticed were the bats circling above. With the opening ceremony taking place on the pitch, the Canadians were forced to find a clear patch of ground outside the stadium to warm up. "It was dark because there were no lights and there were bats flying around," McEachern said. "You could actually hear these bats flying over your head and it was kind of hard to concentrate. But then we walked into the stadium.

"I have the picture of the starting XI [before kick-off] and there's one person who's just the smiliest, happiest person, so she was smiling and the rest of us look like we're walking to our execution. We were just terrified. The stadium was full. None of them were cheering for us.

"The Chinese won 2-0 and we were never really in that game and we were nervous. But we knew where the ball was by the noise the crowd made. Every time they made one of these 50-yard long balls in behind our defence the whole crowd would go 'Ohhhhhhh' and we knew to turn and run to our net."

The tournament also offered a fresh challenge for coaching staffs — after years of playing against the same teams from their region over and over again, they now had to prepare to face nations from the other side of the world that they'd never encountered before — something made harder by the fact that it was rare to be able to scout teams using videos.

The Australians had to be resourceful in the lead-up to their first game against one of the tournament favourites, Brazil. "The intelligence we had was based on one of our coaches sneaking off, watching them train and saying they were playing a 4-2-4 formation," says Dodd.

The Australian coaches coupled this information with their belief only the slowest and least talented Brazilians played at the back to formulate their tactical approach. "We had to be able to defend and defend for long periods against four strikers, but [the coaches] felt with a fast transition and a counter attack we would have a chance of scoring," said Dodd.

And so it would prove. During the game Janine Riddington found herself through on goal and scooped the ball over the onrushing Brazilian goalkeeper to put the Australians 1-0 up. "I think scoring actually just floored us," said Murray. "Holy shmoly, we just scored! I would have instantly assumed Brazil were one of the best women's teams in the world. So to score against the best team in the world from what I imagined, I don't think there was any way up from there."

"We had to soak up a lot of pressure," said Dodd. "Back then we were all just playing state club football. So your week in, week out football was at a level of city-based football really. So to go from that to a sweltering stadium in China with 25,000 people in it, playing against Brazil and to be able to lift yourself to the standard, that was what was really heroic about it. I remember coming on as a substitute and we were leading 1-0 and coming on as a left-back. Playing on the left wasn't my usual position and certainly not left-back. So that was a character-building moment to come on when you're leading 1-0 against Brazil and be thinking, 'OK, we need to be still winning this game when I come off,' and thank God we did. I wasn't sure if the bigger emotion was relief or disbelief.

"After we'd beaten Brazil I remember we all wanted somehow contact home and say, 'Guess what? We won, we beat Brazil 1-0.' We weren't sure what reporting had gone home and who knew. So at this hotel you had to book a phone call and they would call you back in your room when the call was on. So they might call you back in an hour or six hours and they might call you back at three in the morning with your phone call back to Australia."

At a time when women's football struggled to get any mention in the Australian papers, it was understandable the odds of people back home finding out about their victory were low. Yet in the days after the match a telegram arrived: a congratulatory message from the minister of sport.

With four Olympic gold medals and two World Cup titles, the USA have dominated women's football over the last 22 years but in 1988, while competitive, the Americans were still trying to bridge the gap between themselves and the Scandinavian nations. A 5-2 win over Japan in their first game was followed by draws against Sweden and Czechoslovakia before Norway sent them home by beating them 1-0 in the quarter-finals.

"Support," said Gabarra when asked what the difference was between this side and the team that just a few years later would start its period of success. "US Soccer supported us, US Soccer enabled us to have more and more training camps together. We didn't have fans [in 1988]. The team was not well known at all because we never played in the US. We always played abroad. So nobody knew we had a team or what we were doing."

With a squad that included the future World Cup winners Mia Hamm, Julie Foudy, Kristine Lilly, Michelle Akers and Brandi Chastain, that would soon change. Brazil and China were the next big nations to fall as they lost their semi-finals, meaning Sweden and Norway, the two teams who made up what was arguably international women's football's first big rivalry, would face off in the final.

They had a huge advantage in terms of financial and professional support. "The players got paid," said Store. "If I had to leave my job for a week or two the federation would pay my salary. They would cover my costs not only for travel and lodging, but for being away from my work. That was a fantastic situation at that time for women's football in Norway. If you needed to practise in the morning you had a discussion with your employer and tried to make a solution where you can go to practice in the morning, go to work after that and then go to practice in the evening again. We practised twice a day with our clubs. It makes it easier, much easier."

Gabarra played against Norway both in the 1988 quarter-final and in the final of the inaugural World Cup three years later, which the Americans won. "You could tell [Norway had more support], because they played together they were fit, they knew how to play soccer, they played like a team," said Gabarra.

So, for the Norwegian players coming into the tournament final, in the most important game they'd ever played, the financial security, the backing of their employers and their federation's support would help make the difference in a 1-0 win. "Norway and Sweden have been fighting and quarrelling for years and at that time Sweden had been a better team than the Norwegian team," said Store. "Norway won over Sweden for the first time in 1987 so this was the second time. That was huge for us as Norwegian players to beat them in what we thought of as the World Cup final at that time."

After they lifted the trophy Store and her teammates went back to their hotel.

There was no partying, no drinking. They went to bed and the next day flew home for another new experience. "We had a reception at the airport when we arrived with media and everything," Store recalled. "That was very unusual for a female football player to have these receptions with media and people from the federation and everything. So then you realise you've been a part of something special."

BC Place lights up the sky on a freezing cold Vancouver night. It's 27 January 2012 and in a couple hours Canada will have walked off the pitch having claimed a 3-1 win over Mexico to qualify for the 2012 London Olympics. On the concourse outside the stadium around a dozen women are gathering. They greet each other like old friends meeting up to reminisce. Someone's brought a Canadian flag along and they all pose for pictures with it.

Around them the crowd continues to build, moving past the group and into the stadium oblivious to the fact they are passing some of the Canada's greatest ever players. Among them is Joan McEachern and after a while she heads up to her seat to watch the game. As she takes in the record-breaking crowd, she can't help but think to herself, "We helped build this".

"The World Cup, the U17s, the Olympics — you don't get that overnight," said McEachern thinking back on that evening in Vancouver. "There's years of struggle and fighting behind the scenes that we can't even imagine. There's players that sacrificed and struggled, coaches who

sacrificed and struggled, administrators. Those accomplishments don't exist if you don't have the years of walking through the desert. So [the tournament in China] was the start of what we're seeing now 25 years later. We wouldn't be here without that. Once we got a World Cup, Fifa's saying it's a valid sport and that just opens doors."

The players who took part in the 1988 tournament were pioneers for their sport. The generation before them had fought hard to raise the profile of women's football in their countries and these players enjoyed the opportunity to take the game onto the global stage. But for many it came at a cost that went beyond the $800 the Australians had to find.

"The truth is all of us suffered career disadvantages from doing it," said Dodd. "For many players they would never ever complain about it, but the fact is most of the playing group have probably suffered some life-long economic disadvantage as a result of their participation on the field because their career advancement has suffered in some way and you never really catch that up.

"But at the same time we've got so much else from the game, no one would complain for a moment about having spent those years representing their country. There's no other feeling like putting on the jersey and going out there thinking I'm representing Australia. There is just nothing like it."

Hesterine de Reus played 44 times for the Netherlands at a time when many nations could go years without a game. She set up PSV Eindhoven's women's team and is now in charge of a talented young Australian outfit with high expectations. But back in 1988 de Reus made a tough decision — she boycotted the women's invitational tournament in protest against some of the decisions being made behind the scenes by the federation.

Since 1988, the Netherlands haven't qualified for a Women's World Cup and, without knowing it, De Reus was giving up what would be her only opportunity to play on the global stage. A sacrifice made all the more significant by the obstacles she had overcome to play football as a child. "I was born in a village and there was not much to do," De Reus explained. "We could swim and play football. Playing football was for the boys and I was not allowed to join the club."

The seven-year-old De Reus, though, refused to give up. Instead she started turning up at the training sessions, tried to act like a boy and quietly watched. "Eventually the coach invited me to play with the boys and that's what I did," she said. "After a while they discovered I was a girl and they felt sorry for me so they didn't want to tell me, 'You're not allowed to come anymore,' and I was allowed to join in the training sessions. But of course every week I would ask, 'Can I play on Saturday?' and every week they had to tell me, 'No you can't.'

"After a year they got sick of me and they decided to let me play again. From that point on I played every week with the boys. It was illegal, because the rules said it wasn't allowed. And so I played from seven to twelve. When I played in the boys competition they knew I was a girl so they weren't friendly to me. So instead of quitting I just thought, 'You wait, you won't touch the ball anymore in the second half.' Sometimes I think how could I be so naïve? I just liked the game and I just wanted to play and I didn't understand that I couldn't because I was a girl. It didn't make sense to me."

But because of her boycott, De Reus stayed at home 25 years ago while 200 women journeyed to China and played 26 games that helped reshape the football landscape. They disproved the prejudiced beliefs many held about women's football and earned much craved recognition for their sport. It led to the 1991 World Cup, the admission of women's football into the Olympics and all the progress that has come since.

All of these players believe women's football still has a way to go, but can take heart from the fact a young girl in the Netherlands no longer needs to pretend to be a boy just to play the game she loves. Ⓑ

69

Theory

"Rinus used to say that if you're
purely a counter-attacking team
you'll win some games but
won't win the title."

The Weight of the Armband

The Argentina coach Alejandro Sabella explains why he made Lionel Messi national captain

By Joel Richards

"There are different types of leaders," explained Alejandro Sabella. **"You have the ones who lead by sheer ability and others who lead because of their personality. In rare cases you have someone who brings together both of those. You could say that is absolute leadership."**

Sabella is wearing his tracksuit at the national team's training facilities in Ezeiza outside Buenos Aires on a rainy midweek afternoon. It is where he sees out the interminable periods of inactivity between matches with his coaching staff, studying his players and future opponents, as well as granting the odd interview with the press. His English is still good from his time at Sheffield United and Leeds, but he prefers to speak in Spanish.

The question of leadership was at the heart of Sabella's appointment as Argentina coach in 2011, though he admits, "I don't know if I did enough to deserve this chance," a short — but successful — stint at Estudiantes having been his only experience as a first-team coach. He inherited a squad of top international talent that was rudderless, and far more damning than the way they scraped through the World Cup qualifiers for South Africa, or that they played with four centre-backs in losing 4-0

to Germany in the quarter-final of that competition, or even that they failed to beat Uruguay despite playing against 10 men for most of the match in the Copa América, was what had happened to the most important player. Leo Messi had not scored in 16 matches.

The introverted and softly-spoken Messi clearly does not tick Sabella's two boxes to qualify as an "absolute" leader, or at least not in public. Yet selecting the Barcelona forward as captain was Sabella's first decision on taking over the national team. Just as the new coach was a departure from previous profiles, so too was the new captain. Diego Maradona's leader was Javier Mascherano. "My team is Mascherano plus 10," he'd say, before that soon evolved, or descended, into "Mascherano, Messi, Jonás (Gutiérrez), plus eight."

Sabella shies away from offering the press catchy headlines in press conferences or interviews. But having been Daniel Passarella's assistant coach for 13 years, and a contemporary of Maradona, he knows Argentina's two World Cup winning captains well. Both Passarealla and Maradona demonstrated "absolute leadership", as Sabella defines it. So why change his captain? "Messi is accepted as the leader," said Sabella, "and Argentinians always need a leader, the father figure who does something for us. Our society is like that. In Leo's case, the captaincy has done him good and he has taken on that responsibility. And what is good for him, is good for the team."

Ever since Messi began to wear the captain's armband, his form for Argentina has flourished. Racking up a goal-per-game strike rate and equalling Gabriel Batistuta's record for goals in a calendar year — 12 — have silenced the complaints that he doesn't sing the national anthem. Yet Messi is necessarily playing a different role for Argentina from the one he does with Barcelona. "We are lacking creative players," said Sabella. "We are lacking those more cerebral players who make things happen, players like Iniesta or Xavi Hernández. Historically we had those players, or at least that style of player. We had Aimar, D'Alessandro, Riquelme, Verón, Gallardo, Ortega... that kind of player with great skill and technique, and who created play, from deep or closer to the area, but who fulfilled that role. We are losing those kind of players."

Messi scores a different type of goals for Argentina. "We can't forget that Messi will play one way with us and one way with Barcelona," Sabella said, pointing to the national team's more direct style. "We have scored a lot of goals on the counter, but most of his goals with Barcelona aren't like that, because they dominate possession and play in the other team's half."

Together with the creative DNA of the players he has at his disposal, continuity from club to country is something that concerns Sabella. "Spain is made up of Barcelona and Real Madrid players, with the odd player from another side. The same [template of a national side largely made up from two clubs is true] for Germany. On top of the quality of those players, you have the understanding among them. Also, Del Bosque continued the work of Aragonés, and Löw continued that of Klinsmann." He did not need to underline how that contrasted from the situation he was in.

Months after he had taken the job, with Argentina comfortably top of the South American World Cup qualifying table, Sabella walked into a packed conference room in the Four Seasons Hotel in Buenos Aires. He was the last speaker at an event that had seen the Argentina volleyball and basketball coaches, Javier Weber and Julio Lamas, explain their vision of what leadership is. Guillermo Vilas spoke of how he and Björn Borg shaped tennis. The event was unusually slick and corporate. "See! Things can be done properly here," said one Argentinian journalist who was still adjusting to life back in Buenos Aires after years in Spain.

Sabella was given an ovation as he walked out. "I recently met with Pochettino," he began, speaking of a recent trip to Spain before the younger of the two had swapped Espanyol for Southampton. "He told me that for him the most stressful part of the job was the team talk. I told him I felt exactly the same. I dread giving that talk."

Despite the nerves, Sabella went on deliver what is his blueprint for leadership. It was as far removed from the old-school superstition or tub-thumping that his predecessors had espoused as is imaginable. "The relationship between the coach and the players is sacred," he said, stressing the importance of brutal honesty. "You have to earn the respect of the players, you can never lie to them." He admitted to having once done so and then feeling so bad that he apologised every week until the player in question asked him to stop. He outlined how he builds that respect with his players, through knowledge, through ability to work and through the personal relationship and bond with the squad.

He recounted stories of how he handled situations before the Estudiantes-Barcelona World Club Championship match, but stressed that the key, no matter the match, is motivating the players. The power point presentation brought up a slide entitled, "The Team Talk and Me" — an eight-point plan of what he drills into his players before a game. It hit on what he expects of his players, from "emotional balance" to

the virtuous circle of "encouragement-support-help" that his players must show — in Spanish it is a more catchy A-A-A (*Aliento, Apoyo, Ayuda*). Forgiving mistakes is key. He paraphrased Kennedy — "ask what you can do for your team," and although he forgot the exact Gandhi quote about humility he was looking for, he had made his point. He said the better person is the better professional, and hammered in the notion of Success Equals Team, and vice versa.

Finally, he brought up what is a constant theme in Sabella's discourse — regardless of where he is speaking — the sense of belonging and the honour of representing the shirt. In his first press conference as Argentina coach, he said they must follow the example and generosity of the Argentinian independence hero Manuel Belgrano, the man who "gave everything for his country" — an absolute leader. Ⓑ

FOOTBALL ART.

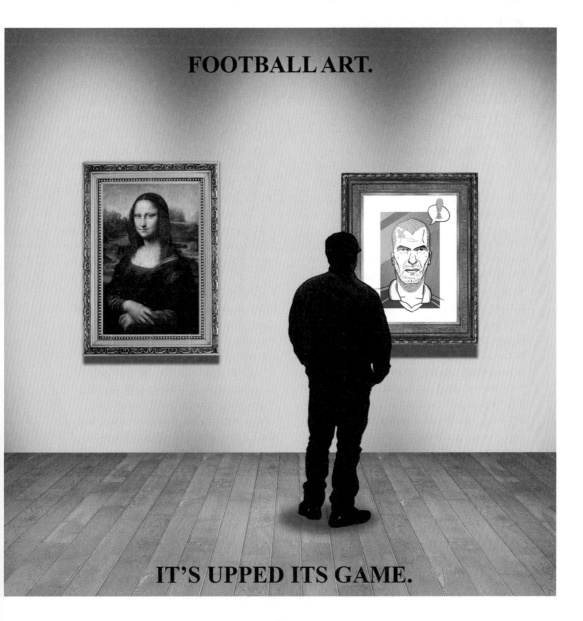

IT'S UPPED ITS GAME.

Pep's Four Golden Rules

How Guardiola made Barcelona the masters of the pressing game

By Simon Kuper

We could all see that Pep Guardiola's Barcelona were brilliant. What's harder is understanding how they did it. That's where my friend Albert Capellas comes in. Whenever he and I run into each other, we talk about Barça. Not many people know the subject better. Capellas is now the assistant manager at Vitesse Arnhem in the Netherlands but before that he was coordinator of Barcelona's great youth academy, La Masia. He helped bring Sergio Busquets from a rough local neighbourhood to Barça. He trained Andrès Iniesta and Victor Valdes in their youth teams. In all, Capellas spent nine years working for his hometown club.

During our last conversation, over espressos in an Arnhem hotel last year, I had several "Aha" moments. I had watched the Barcelona of the Pep Guardiola years umpteen times, but only then did I finally begin to see. Guardiola's Barcelona were great not merely because they had great players. They also had great tactics — different not just from any other team today, but also different from Barcelona teams pre-Guardiola. Barça were so drilled on the field that in some ways they are more like an American football team than a soccer one. Their luscious game wasn't nearly as spontaneous as it looked.

Before getting into the detail of their style, it's crucial to understand just how much of it came from Guardiola. When a Barcelona vice-president mused to me five years ago that she'd like to see the then 37-year-old Pep be made head coach, I never imagined it would happen. Guardiola was practically a novice. The only side he had ever coached was Barça's second team. However, people in the club who had worked with him — men like the club's then president Joan Laporta, and the then director of football Txiki Beguiristain — had already clocked him as special. Not only did Guardiola know Barcelona's house style inside out, he also knew how it could be improved.

Guardiola once compared Barcelona's style to a cathedral. Johan Cruyff, he said, as Barça's supreme player in the 1970s and later as coach, had built the cathedral. The task of those who came afterwards was to renovate and update it. Guardiola was always looking for updates. If a random person in the street says something interesting about the game, Guardiola listens. He thinks about football all the time. He learned from another Dutch Barcelona manager, Louis van Gaal, but also from his years playing for Brescia and Roma in Italy, the country that pretty much invented defending. Yet because Guardiola had little desire to explain his ideas to the media, you end up watching Barça without a codebook.

Cruyff was the single most formative influence on Guardiola. When the Dutchman returned to the Nou Camp as head coach in 1988, he did something that few Barça coaches had ever done before: he went to the pitches where the youth teams played. There he saw a skinny kid in central midfield hitting perfect passes. "Take that boy off at half-time," he told the boy's coach. "Why?" asked the coach. "Because I'm putting him in the first team," said Cruyff. Guardiola went on to spend a decade in the first team.

Cruyff was perhaps the most original thinker in football's history, but most of his thinking was about attack. He liked to say that he didn't mind conceding three goals, as long as Barça scored five. Well, Guardiola also wanted to score five, but he minded conceding even one. If Barcelona is a cathedral, Guardiola added the buttresses. Even in his last, somewhat disappointing, season as coach, they conceded only 29 goals in 38 league games. Sir Alex Ferguson's assistant manager at Manchester United, René Meulensteen, told the Dutch magazine *Voetbal International*, "Pep Guardiola's Barcelona made the biggest change at the top of football, and I'm especially talking about how they played without the ball. They applied very fast and coordinated pressure to win back the ball as quickly as possible." There were four key Guardiola tenets:

Pressure on the ball

Before Barcelona played Manchester United in the Champions League final at Wembley in 2011, Alex Ferguson said that the way Barça pressured their opponents to win the ball back was "breathtaking". That, he added, was Guardiola's innovation. Ferguson admitted that United hadn't known how to cope with it in the Champions League final in Rome in 2009. He thought it would be different at Wembley. It wasn't.

Barcelona start pressing the instant they lose possession. That is the perfect time to press because the opposing player who has just won the ball is vulnerable. He has had to take his eyes off the game to make his tackle or interception and he has expended energy. That means he is unsighted and probably tired. He usually needs two or three seconds to regain his vision of the field. So Barcelona try to dispossess him before he can give the ball to a better-placed teammate.

Furthermore, if the opponent won the ball back in his own defence, and Barcelona can instantly win it back again, then the way to goal is often clear. This is where Messi's genius for tackling comes in. The Argentinian has such quick reflexes that he sometimes wins a tackle a split-second after losing one.

The Barcelona player who lost the ball leads the hunt to regain it. But he never hunts alone. His teammates near the ball join him. If only one or two Barça players are pressing, it's too easy for the opponent to pass around them. Meulensteen said, "You see that few teams have the individual skills to play themselves out from under pressure. Guardiola saw that very well. But Barcelona's is also the playing style with the highest degree of difficulty. You need players with the tactical qualities to shift very quickly from possession to defence, and who are physically capable of doing that constantly. It's a very short moment of hunting the prey."

The "five-second rule"

If Barça haven't won the ball back within five seconds of losing it, they then retreat and build a compact 10-man wall. The distance between the front man in the wall (typically Messi) and their last defender (Javier Mascherano, say) is only 25 to 30 metres. It's hard for any opponent to pass their way through such a small space. The Rome final of 2009 was a perfect demonstration of Barcelona's wall: whenever United won the ball and kept it, they faced 11 precisely positioned opponents, who stood there and said, in effect: "Try to get through this."

It's easy for Barcelona to be compact, both when pressing and when drawing up their wall, because their players spend most of the game very near each other. Xavi and Iniesta in particular seldom stray far from the ball. A packed midfield, with no out-and-out strikers, enhances the compactness. Cruyff has said, "Do you know how Barcelona win the ball back so quickly? It's because they don't have to run back more than 10 metres as they never pass the ball more than 10 metres."

More rules of pressing: once Barcelona have built their compact wall, they wait for the right moment to start pressing again. They don't choose the moment on instinct. Rather, there are very precise prompts that tell them when to press. One is if an opponent miscontrols a ball. If the ball bounces off his foot, he will need to look downwards to locate it and at that moment he loses his overview

of the pitch. That's when the nearest Barcelona players start hounding him.

There's another prompt for Barça to press: when the opposing player on the ball turns back towards his own goal. When he does that, he narrows his options: he can no longer pass forward, unless Barcelona give him time to turn around again. Barcelona don't give him time. Their players instantly hound the man, forcing him to pass back, and so they gain territory.

The "3-1 rule"

If an opposing player gets the ball anywhere near Barcelona's penalty area, then Barça go Italian. They apply what they call the "3-1 rule": one of Barcelona's four defenders will advance to tackle the man with the ball, and the other three defenders will assemble in a ring about two or three metres behind the tackler. That provides a double layer of protection. Guardiola picked this rule up in Italy. It's such a simple yet effective idea that you wonder why all top teams don't use it.

No surprises. When Barcelona win the ball, they do something unusual. Most leading teams treat the moment the ball changes hands — "turnover", as it's called in basketball — as decisive. At that moment, the opponents are usually out of position and so if you can counterattack quickly, you have an excellent chance of scoring. Teams like Manchester United and Arsenal often try to score in the first three seconds after winning possession. So their player who wins the ball often tries to hit an instant splitting pass. Holland — Barcelona's historical role models — do this too.

But when a Barcelona player wins the ball, he doesn't try for a splitting pass. The club's attitude is: he has won the ball, that's a wonderful achievement and he doesn't need to do anything else special. All he is supposed to do is slot the ball simply into the feet of the nearest teammate. Barcelona's logic is that in winning the ball, a player has typically forfeited his vision of the field. So he is the worst-placed player to hit a telling ball. This means that Barcelona don't rely on the element of surprise. They take a few moments to get into formation, and then pretty much tell their opponents, "OK, here we come." The opposition knows exactly what Barça are going to do. The difficulty is stopping it.

The only exception to this rule is if the Barça player wins the ball near the opposition's penalty area. Then he goes straight for goal.

Possession is nine-tenths of the game. Keeping the ball has been Barcelona's key tactic since Cruyff's day. Most teams don't worry about possession. They know you can have oodles of possession and lose. But Barcelona aim to have 65-70% of possession in a game. In the 2011-2012 league season, they averaged more than 72%.

The advantage of possession is twofold. Firstly, while you have the ball, the other team can't score. A team like Barcelona, short on good tacklers, needs to defend by keeping possession. As Guardiola once remarked, they are a "horrible" team without the ball. Secondly, if Barça have the ball, the other team has to chase it, and that is exhausting. When the opponents win it back, they are often so tired that they surrender it again

immediately. Possession gets Barcelona into a virtuous cycle.

Barça are so fanatical about possession that a defender like Gerald Piqué will weave the most intricate passes inside his own penalty area rather than boot the ball away. In almost all other teams, the keeper at least is free to boot. In the England side, for instance, it's typically Joe Hart who gives the ball away with a blind punt. This is a weakness of England's game, but the English attitude seems to be that there is nothing to be done about it: keepers can't pass. Barcelona think differently.

José Mourinho, Barcelona's nemesis, tried to exploit their devotion to passing. In the Bernabéu in December 2011, Real Madrid's forwards chased down Valdes from the game's first kick-off, knowing he wouldn't boot the ball clear. The keeper miscued a pass and Karim Benzema scored after 23 seconds. Yet Valdes kept passing and Barcelona won 3-1. The trademark of Barcelona-raised goalkeepers — one shared only by Ajax-raised goalkeepers, like Edwin van der Sar — is that they can all play football like outfield players. That characteristic will be key in Barça's hunt for Valdes's successor. The club may well choose to sacrifice core keeping skills in favour of ball-playing ability.

The "one-second rule"

No other football team plays the Barcelona way. That's a strength, but it's also a weakness. It makes it very hard for Barça to integrate outsiders into the team, because they struggle to learn the system. Barcelona long had a policy of buying only 'Top 10' players — men who arguably rank among the 10 best footballers on earth — yet many of them have failed in the Nou Camp. Thierry Henry and Zlatan Ibrahimović did, while even David Villa, who knew Barcelona's game from playing it with Spain, has often found himself on the bench.

Joan Oliver, Barcelona's previous chief executive, explained the risk of transfers by what he called the "one-second rule". The success of a move on the pitch is decided in less than a second. If a player needs a few extra fractions of a second to work out where his teammate is going, because he doesn't know his teammate's game well, the move will usually break down. A new player can therefore lose you a match in under a second.

That's particularly true at Barcelona, whose system has such a complex orchestration. Soon after Cesc Fabregàs returned home from Arsenal, he said, "Barça have a very specific system and everyone has to adjust to it. Everything has been studied down to the last millimetre. In my first matches I really had to adjust. I was so used to Arsenal, where I could roam around the whole pitch without worrying about anything.

Here it's really very different. Everyone has his own position and you can never lose it from sight. I had to go back to my youth days at Barça to master the basic principles again."

Barcelona needed Fabregàs precisely because he had once mastered those basic principles. An even better example of this staffing principle is Pedro: not a great footballer, but because he was raised in La Masia he can play Barcelona's game better than stars from outside. The boys in La Masia spend much of their childhood playing passing games, especially Cruyff's favorite, six against three. Football, Cruyff once said, is choreography.

Nobody else thinks like that. That's why most of the Barcelona side is homegrown. It's more a necessity than a choice. Still, most of the time it works pretty well.

No doubt Guardiola will want to transplant most of this system — plus new ideas he has thought up in Manhattan — to Bayern Munich. But in a team that grew up without these principles, such a complex knowledge transfer could easily fail. Ⓑ

Taking the Initiative

Andy Roxburgh, the former Uefa technical director, on how football tactics are changing

By Nick Ames

Andy Roxburgh remembers the day Juninho Pernambucano pitched up in New York. "He'd only just arrived. He went down there, right in the middle, 35 yards out. Looks up here, points to the top right corner. I'm going 'Yeah, yeah, ok'. Steps up, ball hardly spins, whoosh! A little while later, training camp in Florida, he does it again. I got the point! On set pieces, that guy... wow."

Not for the first time in our hour together, he's jumped to his feet, motioning towards the careworn Red Bull Arena pitch below. Wiry and spry, he has been left unscathed by a chilly east-coast winter, even if a crash course in the intricacies of Major League Soccer has had an enervating effect.

You expect he'll cope. His 18 years as Uefa's technical director having begun in an era that saw Europe struggling — in football and wider political terms — to adapt to unprecedented upheaval. He emerged as one of his continent's genuine visionaries, constructing a framework designed to protect a hitherto undefined coaching profession at both ends of the spectrum. A man whose own management career has been understated — seven years in charge of Scotland the only senior experience on his CV — can fairly be credited with a guiding influence on most of Europe's

top coaches, from their education at grass roots to the regular symposia held for Champions League managers by the side of Lake Geneva.

If it was a surprise to see Roxburgh take on a first position in club football in his 70th year, becoming sporting director of New York Red Bulls, questions are allayed by the whippet-like energy he evinces in conversation — fact, opinion and theory bouncing off the walls. IHis contemporary and close confidant Sir Alex Ferguson may finally have retired, but Roxburgh's hunger seems as voracious as ever.

* As well as working with managers at the highest level, you've spent most of your career nurturing prospective coaches. Is it difficult to ask players, or ex-players, to take a more academic view of the game?*

That's a word I really don't like — "academic". I'd just call it "thinking". I don't find that there's anything academic about coaching; it's all extremely practical. Coaching guys for their Pro Licences, the stumbling block is that they're still thinking like players. On the pitch, a player thinks from back to front. That's why, when you've got your tactics board in the dressing-room, you put the goals at the top and the bottom. A coach sees the game from side to side, and it's totally different. As a player, you know what's happening in front and behind; when you're coaching, you're responsible for the whole show. A lot of them just follow the ball around when they start, can't stand back, because it's what they've always done. Sometimes, when you give them a crowded 11-a-side game to work with and say "Stop — what happened there?", they're totally lost. You need to teach them how to isolate a problem within a game and then develop it, and that's an art. You need a trained eye to do it. Some master it straightaway, but others can't take that backwards step and see the big picture.

◆ *In that case, is there a clear advantage in studying for your coaching qualifications while still a player — and recognising both viewpoints at an early stage?*

I came through with Sir Alec [Ferguson] and, as he said to me numerous times when we were players together at Falkirk, he'd decided very early on that his future was going to be in coaching and management — so the quicker he got on with learning about it the better! Like me, he began coaching alongside his playing career and would admit that it completely changed his thinking about the game. I was exactly the same. We applied ourselves in what was an incredibly practical environment. That's why, years later, I used to urge players to enroll on our coaching courses. It'll set you up for your future career and give you a head start, but it will actually help you as a player too. I had them all: Alex McLeish, Gordon Strachan, Willie Miller, Roy Aitken, Tommy Burns. If you're learning about the game like that, it can

really improve you on the pitch. Those guys went on to prove it.

◆ *In an environment where ex-players have often walked straight into jobs with barely as much as an interview, was it initially difficult to assert the value of coaching qualifications?*

Maybe, but we worked hard at it. My 18 and a half years at Uefa can be boiled down to one crusade — a crusade to make coaching a genuine profession in Europe. All 53 countries are now part of Uefa's Coaching Convention and, while it's not complete by any means, the foundation is now in place. Everybody understands what it means and respects its value — the fact that you can't work at the top level without your licence has seen to that. You'll always get a few individuals who are naturally gifted, but relying on that doesn't protect the business at all. To protect football players, at whatever stage in their careers, you need to develop people who know that they're doing — people who know how and when to give input, and who can make you better.

◆ *People who are outstanding teachers...*

Yes — but again, it's much more of a practical business than an academic one. The first thing I'd say about José Mourinho is that he's brilliant at teaching methods. He's wonderfully detailed at organisation, outstanding in terms of knowing how to teach football. You can draw a parallel with Rinus Michels, who was just the same. Pep Guardiola, who's been living here [New York], is another great example: absolutely pragmatic, so clever and shrewd about what he does, always quizzing. I had lunch with him recently — amazing actually, we were in a public restaurant and nobody knew him — and he was asking me what Sir Alec's secret is. You have to know something about working with players to keep going for as long as he has, after all.

◉ *But isn't Guardiola proof that you need much more than the coaching and man-management aspects? By his own admission, he burned himself out while moulding arguably the best club side we've seen. There's so much going on around the role now...*

For a start, your media awareness needs to be far greater than it ever was. Gérard Houllier reckons that the most important 30 seconds of the week for a top coach nowadays is the television soundbite after a match, especially if you've lost. Everybody's listening to it: your players, their wives, the board, the fans. It'll be re-run every hour. During our coaching courses, we started saying that this is the moment you begin preparing for the next game. What you say will already have an impact, and your face is an advert for the health of your team. You've got to become clever at it if you want to be in it for the long-term.

◉ *And isn't that harder than ever?*

No doubt about it. Player power hasn't helped — players are so influential now and club owners take note of it. In the past you'd leave a player out, perhaps he'd tell his father and his father would say, "Aye, that coach is useless." Now he'll just tweet immediately or phone his agent, and the next thing you know there'll be criticism of you all over the media. Agents are another drama, of course. You'll notice that none of this is to do with football. Many colleagues

tell me that the football pitch is the one thing that keeps them sane, because the peripheral stuff around it is so much more intense now.

Training coaches nowadays, you have to make sure they are absolutely ready for everything they're going to face — because if you go into a job and make a mistake, you might never get another crack. I always say that you have to wear three hats: technician, manager and leader. Your technical part might be very good, but if you're not capable of handling the rest you'll have a problem. At the highest level, leadership is the key element — can you persuade people, inspire them, deal with a crisis? How you deal with a defeat will often define your career — the Champions League coaches were all agreed on that when they met last September. If you can't handle defeat well then you'll die a death as a coach.

◉ *In your technical report on the 2011-12 Champions League, you said that the manager's role as "psychologist" to his players is as important as anything else now...*

How a manager behaves will rub off on his players, so the first thing to do is to assess your own behaviour. If you come in on a Monday morning after a defeat and you're wrecked then you have no chance with that team. I believe that talent always rebounds, so if you've any kind of mental strength as a coach — or a player for that matter — you'll bounce back, and that'll filter to your team. That's what all the top guys do, because there are no guarantees about anything.

Last time I saw Carlo Ancelotti he was saying that, for all the power you have, as a head coach, the one thing that you can't control is the result of a football match. You can do all your preparations and make your selections, but it's a world of ambiguity — so you have to stick to a very clear vision of what you want to do and how you're going to handle things. There's so much noise around you, but you have to find a way to be yourself.

With all of these extra strains, can a younger manager really expect to go through his career being more than a coach now?

Again I'll give you Alec as an example — he's more like a CEO than a manager in the conventional sense. He's got all the background, knows all the practical elements, but like the head of any big business he knows how and when to delegate. That in itself is a gift. At big clubs now you have such a massive staff that the key word — and I know it's Alec's favourite — is "control". That's the secret if you're going to stand a chance, whoever you are. You have to be in control of the whole operation, be able to stand back to see everything, hear everything, judge everything. Your staff have to know that you're doing it.

The best way to reach that level and survive is to train your way up, make your first steps as an assistant, perhaps take a job at a lower league club. Make your mistakes there, in an environment where you might have limited resources and are constantly required to deal with tough frontline activity, and build gradually. You see shooting stars who rise quickly and disappear without a trace, but look at the top boys like Alec, Arsène Wenger and Marcello Lippi. They've worked their way up and learned how to keep their eye on

things, while taking that step back when they need to.

In the Euro 2012 Technical Report, you ask whether "overcrowding in the backroom" is becoming an issue. If we accept that the CEO-cum-manager position now exists, is the burgeoning number of specialists beneath him a cause for concern?

I think you can end up with too many. You mustn't just have bodies in there for the sake of it, which is where that "control" word comes in again. It's crucial that there is organisation and structure — sub-leaders for all the groups, be they medical, coaching or anything else. It's an organisational issue and the person at the top needs to be able to oversee the whole show. You can extend it and look at the people players themselves have around them these days. I remember one national coach telling me that his players didn't just bring an entourage with them — they effectively brought a business. He counted out 20 individuals that a particular player had with him: a private physio, trainer, businessman, PR guy, all sorts. The manager needs to be well aware of these "staff" as well as those he is directly responsible for.

Sports scientists, performance analysts and their ilk are presumably included in these swelling backroom numbers. Is their influence becoming such that, at some point, a coach's tactical planning will be overtaken in importance by analytics and statistics?

The bottom line for me is that football is more of an art than a science. Of course sports science has a big influence and it's another element that coaches have had to take onboard, but these analysis programs and tracking systems can be described in one simple word: tools. Most top clubs use them now, but to what extent should you? What many coaches will do is judge with their eyes and use the tool to back up that judgement. If you have the facts at hand, then people will listen to your opinions. If I say to a winger: "You've been lazy in the first half," that's an opinion. If I then hit him with: "You ran 8km on Saturday — you're usually running 10km, is there anything wrong? Should I leave you out?" then I've confirmed it with a fact and he should listen. As tools that support what you are already doing, these facilities are useful — but there is no way they should take over.

⏀ So the relevance of tactics themselves is undimmed?

I prefer to use a word like "principles" — but for me, tactics simply means "how". Does a player know how to recover the ball quickly, how to press in advanced areas? Does he know how to make angles? How will he operate in a certain context or situation? Looking at it that way, it's always going to be critical. Good coaching today is not about drilling or telling — that was the old-fashioned way. One of the gifts of a top modern coach is the ability to ask questions. You're out there creating a practical dialogue: "How would you beat this guy now that he's tuned into you?" or "We're not getting down the line — what would your solution be?" It might seem simple, but you have to know exactly how to get the right response.

⏀ When we last spoke, late in 2007, you referred to a "sense of caution" in

Champions League teams. Elements of the competition seemed stale, predictable. Since then, goals per game have risen by almost 0.3; statistical and visual evidence suggests the trend is reversing. What's changed?

Pep and Alec both said something similar at one of my last Champions League coaches' meetings. They felt that more teams — not everybody, but more — were taking the initiative. If you look down the years, most successful teams at the top level have done that. Rinus used to say that if you're purely a counter-attacking team you'll win some games but won't win the title. That's the Dutch attitude, of course, and it hasn't always been borne out. Chelsea proved last year that a "contain and counter" game could be successful, and José did it with Inter Milan too — he was explicit in saying how comfortable his team was without possession. But I think they've been exceptions; the trend has been that expressive teams like Barcelona and Manchester United will come out on top.

⏀ How do you define 'initiative'?

Look at Borussia Dortmund. They attack with and without the ball, and that's essentially what it means. It's not just about having possession, full-backs and wingers charging up the pitch. Jürgen Klopp is always talking about intense pressing, the 'Barcelona' bit if you like. Barcelona and Spain have set the tone and it's now being shown by a lot of the others. You try to play an aggressive attacking game, but you stay on the offensive as soon as you lose the ball. In the old days, even when I was in charge of Scotland, we would sporadically press if the opportunity was there. Barcelona,

Dortmund and others do it automatically, and it's incredible. You have to be very fit to do it, and also know how to do it properly. And the results justify the style. Xavi said that, five or six years ago, he was about to become extinct — but the bottom line is what Barcelona have achieved by playing the way he and his teammates do.

● *If it's inevitable that trends are followed, does that reduce the scope for new developments?*

Arsène made a good comment that suggests you're right: "We're the generation of coaches that use old shapes; we don't invent any new ones." It's true that results trigger trends. I remember the Spain v France game in Bruges in 2000; they both played 4-2-3-1 and I'd never seen it before. It was unusual, incredibly structured, and a lot of teams obviously went down that road afterwards. The 2002 World Cup final is another example, Brazil playing three at the back with two flying wingers and Germany doing the same. If there's success using a certain shape or approach, people will follow it — and the phase at the moment is about possession play and trying to take the initiative.

● *It's reasonably common to see teams operating without a genuine striker now, though. Did that come out of the blue?*

It's funny actually. In 2002 I sat with Carlos Alberto Parreira and we spoke about shape. He told me that this was the way it was going — we'd soon be at 4-6-0. I thought he was joking, but he was quite serious: "Mario Zagallo told me in 1992 that it'll go that way. I'm sure he is right, but he just didn't

work out how quickly." I asked what he meant — you need depth in your attack, after all — and he explained it would be a back four with an interchanging six, a bit like we used to see from Holland. I still didn't believe him but, sure enough, Barcelona started doing it: Messi up front but not; no real reference points for centre-backs to play against. Spain ended up doing it as well, as we saw last year — Vicente del Bosque says he sweated and sweated about it before thinking "Why not?" And, of course, Spain replicated Barcelona's success.

● *They had the players for it, though...*

The players define the shape. Going back to Barcelona, what they did happened because they had Messi. He was the one that could come out of the middle, with guys like Iniesta and now Fàbregas bombing on past him. So Arsène is actually right, because what they've basically done is to play 4-3-3 without an out-and-out striker. The correct way to put it is that we still don't have any new shapes as such, but variations on existing themes that arise through individual quality.

● *You've travelled the world over the past few decades, primarily to spread the coaching gospel. Are there any areas whose football is evolving at particular speed?*

I've been going to Japan for 15 years or so now, and that's the place that strikes me. The development there is fantastic — the J.League is strong and the national team keeps getting better. It's a similar situation in Korea: there has been a lot of investment and hard work all over the Far East. When the Japanese see a model, they'll develop and adapt it to its absolute fruition, so I have no doubt they will keep getting stronger. Football is flourishing in that part of the world.

⊕ *And are there any more established regions that should be looking over their shoulders?*

South America remains a traditional stronghold, but the only country on that continent that is really starting to embrace coach education now is Brazil. It's a surprise to me, but then you can see that they've based everything on a natural environment that gave them excellent players. That's how it used to be in Europe too, but the environment changed and we had to concentrate on developing footballers — they didn't just come from the streets anymore. It trickles up to how you deal with coaches. At some point they'll be faced with that in South America, too.

⊕ *You're getting a first-hand look at another region of vast potential now. How do you assess the USA's situation?*

Here in America there's vast participation — the biggest of all the sports -- but the problem arises somewhere between the grass roots and the top. I don't really detect a middle. Here's an example: the reserve team here at New York Red Bulls. I expected there to be a small stadium in the area for them to play their games in, capacity of 2,000 perhaps, but there's nothing. You've either a college or university ground, or the huge arena we're sitting in. I came here from Switzerland, where every village had its own stadium — the one at Nyon held 8,000! There's massive interest in MLS now, and then other teams at the

level below, but actual 'local' football doesn't seem to exist. I'm not going to solve it, but the lack of a club structure is certainly an issue for development here.

⊕ *All the same, here you are — in your first club role since you were a player. What took you to New York Red Bulls?*

Somebody asked me to come! I'd already extended my term at Uefa twice and it was an appropriate moment for us both to go in our own directions. It was a very polite parting of the ways, a natural conclusion. I spoke to a number of people after that but Gérard Houllier, whom I've been friends with for 20 years, told me about this project and stressed that it had fantastic potential. It would be a completely different role for me and I'd find it fascinating. So I went to meet the owners twice, and between them and Gérard they really sold it to me. There was a third factor — I came here on holiday last August and went for a walk with Thierry Henry, who tuned me in to everything and added to the impression that this would be a great challenge. Now I'm sitting at this desk, and we're about to open a new training ground that will put us right up there in terms of facilities. I didn't know the finer points of how MLS worked, and I'm getting to grips with them now, but it seemed an intriguing project in an environment that was quickly growing. It just shows you that none of us ever stops learning.

Roxburgh's office is rather sparely decorated, but as we rise to leave he picks up a large, framed photograph from one of the shelves. It's a variation on a famous one: the then-Scotland manager holding aloft a tartan scarf after elimination from Italia 90 at Brazil's hands. "I thought it was the only way I could remind the supporters, everyone back home, that I was one of them — you know?"

I think I do. For all his championing of methodologies, principles and structures, there's something visceral, elemental, that you suspect has sustained him over a lifetime. Half a century in the game has done little to reverse the earthing process he underwent with Sir Alex and their peers back in Glasgow. Tomorrow night, in fact, his old, old friend will be in town: the two will share dinner, doubtless a decent bottle of something, perhaps another chuckle at Guardiola's quest for the elixir of eternal youth. And now, as back then, there's a fair chance that they can do it all as virtual unknowns. Ⓑ

87

The North

"We have to do more than build with lottery money some grand projects, like a football stadium"

City and the City

What does Sheikh Mansour's investment mean for the city of Manchester?

By David Conn

There are very many ways to contemplate the extraordinary story of Manchester City, from the tragic-comic slumped giant slogging round the grounds of the third division as recently as 1998-99, to Premier League victors just 13 years later, thanks to the £38m Sergio Agüero. In that journey the major tributaries of English football's modern transformation can be mapped: the money lapping into the Premier League, the failed stock market floats and cock-ups of English owners looking to cash in for themselves, more recently, of course, the mega-rich buyers from overseas. Through the 1990s, City were cast as the lovable, authentic Manchester alternative to corporate, plc United, who won the treble in the same season City just scrambled up from the third following their play-off final heroics against Gillingham. So even five years after Sheikh Mansour bin Zayed Al Nahyan of Abu Dhabi bought the club, it still feels improbable that he really is here, that he did pick City for his Premier League venture and has poured £1bn in.

The story features home-grown players supplanted by overseas stars — in City's case only Micah Richards, signed from Oldham Athletic aged 14, is clinging on from the club's youth academy (Joe Hart was signed at 19), pushed to the edges by injury and Pablo Zabaleta's professional excellence. The supporters are crucial too, even as Abu Dhabi brands City into a global advertisement and projection of a glamorous image for the dynastic state of which Mansour is one of the inheriting princes. The loyalty the City fans showed down in that third division season, the immovable presence of 30,000 when there was nothing more cheerful to sing than "City Till I Die", was a key component when Mansour decided it was the club for him.

Then there is the new stadium, built for the 2002 Commonwealth Games and converted at the public's expense for City afterwards, the centrepiece of the local council's vision for regenerating post-industrial east Manchester. This was great good fortune for the club and the most concrete reason why City were bought by the sheikh, while Everton, needing a fortune spending on grand, sagging Goodison Park, cannot attract a buyer. The council hit the jackpot with Sheikh Mansour, and now, the stadium renamed Etihad after the national airline of the United Arab Emirates, the club is building a training 'campus' on 80 acres of exhausted land. Jobs are meant to flow in from this, and east Manchester, the former engine room of the industrial revolution, is to be reinvented for the modern era, into a sports and leisure "destination".

I grew up in Manchester and supported City from the age of six; the club, its 1970s cohort of stars, and football itself, bestowed sky blue blessings on my boyhood. As an adult and a journalist, I came to understand the professional game, how it works, the great clubs' volunteer origins and the culture-changing greed and exploitation of the Premier League era partly through investigating the efforts of various new City owners to make money for themselves. This culminated in 2007 with Thaksin Shinawatra, who had just been ousted as prime minister of Thailand in a military coup, arriving to buy out the club.

Thaksin was pursued by Human Rights Watch, which wrote to the Premier League chief executive, Richard Scudamore, to argue that following two murderous episodes in Thailand under Thaksin's rule for which nobody was ever held accountable, Thaksin was "a human rights abuser of the worst kind". He was also formally charged with corruption offences in Thailand before he took over the Manchester "people's club" and the stadium the council built with public money. But none of it was a bar to the owners wholeheartedly recommending that all City shareholder-supporters sell to Thaksin, nor to Scudamore's Premier League approving the man as an owner of one of its major clubs.

Thaksin was in charge of City for just one chaotic year, beginning with the hiring of Sven-Göran Eriksson and the signing of Brazilian midfielder Elano, and ending the following summer with Thaksin on the run and the former chairman, John Wardle, forking out from his own pocket to pay the office staff's wages. That was why Thaksin's

lieutenant was hawking the Manchester club around the Arabian gulf. Mansour, who had been wanting to buy a Premier League club for a while, saw in City the enduring big-club potential, with the loyal cadre of fans, and a new stadium already built. His people told me he paid £150m for the club, which always seemed very much more than he needed to, as Thaksin was a fugitive, his assets frozen in Thailand, and City were sliding towards administration. Thaksin had paid £21.6m to Wardle, David Makin and the other previous owners, and had borrowed £40m. So less that outlay, Thaksin Shinawatra, arguably the least appropriate person ever to be involved in a great English football club, made £90m for himself, from just one year.

In following all of these changes to Manchester City, examining them, visiting Abu Dhabi and talking to Mansour's executives, trying to understand what it all meant to us, one of the most significant documents was research itemising the poverty of the people, in Manchester, living right around the stadium. The official *English Indices of Deprivation*, 2010 ranked every small neighbourhood of 2,000 homes in England, according to accepted measures of social misery. Poverty, worklessness, low life expectancy, "income deprivation affecting children", "health deprivation and disability"; all combined to give a ranking, area by area.

Manchester, despite the two top Premier League football clubs, owned by overseas billionaires, broadcast to 200 countries, its hosting of the Commonwealth Games, the new stadium, velodrome, arena, conference centres, concert hall, metrolink tram system and the makeover of the city centre, was the fourth most poverty stricken local authority area in England. The other three were in London: Newham, Tower Hamlets, and Hackney. Of the northern cities which had grown into metropolises on cotton, coal, steel, docks, shipbuilding, and engineering, Manchester's modern day decline was the worst.

Almost half of Manchester's neighbourhoods, 45.6%, were in the most deprived 10% in England, now suffering another crash, this one of the economy supposed to replace heavy industry: banking, services, consumption. Of those areas, 19 of Manchester's were among the most deprived 1% in the country. The seven worst, the most deprived, for lack of work, desperation, child poverty, physical and mental illness, were in east Manchester, after all those millions spent and made in the regeneration business, greatly to the benefit of the Premier League club, its billionaire owners and millionaire players.

Collyhurst, a football district famous for having incubated United's and England's Nobby Stiles, Brian Kidd and other hardy lads, was second worst in the whole country, for "income deprivation affecting children." Right around the stadium, built almost a decade earlier specifically to revive the fortunes of the area and local population, were still the most deprived Manchester neighbourhoods: Bradford, Miles Platting and Newton Heath, Harpurhey, Gorton South, Charlestown, Ardwick and Gorton North.

I talked before the final, title-winning match of the 2011-12 season to Barbara Taylor, in her neat home on one of the newer estates by the stadium, behind the two pubs City fans were anxiously drinking in. She is a community activist and optimist, who maintains the changes have hugely improved the area and given it a chance of a future, that the Commonwealth Games, stadium and City at least has brought people and some investment to the area, which for 20 years had felt abandoned. But she also said that when she moved here as a girl everybody worked, in the factories or engineering works, leaving home in their overalls — they could go from one job to another the same day. Now, not one person on the estate leaves home in the morning and goes to a regular job, she said.

It is a cliché to compare poverty to footballers' galactic earnings, but the facts are relevant here. Just across the road and over the wall of the stadium bowl, there were Yaya Touré and Carlos Tévez, paid £10m a year.

So with all its dizzying themes, I came to see this modern chapter in the history of Manchester City, in its broadest terms, as a stark, simple, but deeply challenging spectacle. Over the old football club, formed originally in the muck and smog of east Manchester, the poverty and collapse of our industry and economy, is meeting a country that has just found itself one of the richest on earth.

The football clubs used to nestle within the grimy bustle of the cities. They sprang up as outlets in the late 19th century, for lads and men seeking an escape, a breath of air, excitement and sporting benefit, from the toughness of Victorian urban streets and the grind of work. Many of the grounds were thrown up around the scraps of land the players first found to kick a ball on, or later they moved, as City did to the then open space at Moss Side, and built the vast expression of faith in the future of football, Maine Road. The clubs were a part of the great cities, and changed their names from one of the neighbourhoods, Ardwick, or Newton Heath, to represent the name of the city itself. The City badge I fell for as a boy had the Manchester symbols, the red rose and the ship, after the mighty innovation of the canal which made a port of the inland city — but by the time I grew up in the 1970s the shipping was over and the cranes on the docks were rusting relics.

Now the football club, moved to the stadium the council built, a little marooned in acres of car park, prompts a frightening thought. Is this all that remains of real value, that the world actually wants of us?

After Sheikh Mansour first arrived and Manchester had rubbed its eyes and seen the takeover was truly, unbelievably real, a spread appeared in the *Manchester Evening News*, projecting an impression of how Abu Dhabi would transform the area. The artists' impression showed bars, restaurants, hotels, new apartments, the destination east Manchester of the council's dreams. Mansour's men were not slow to make it clear they had no interest in doing any of that. There had been no market or demand for bars and restaurants in an area blighted by economic catastrophe and population-flight for 30 years. They have more money than they know what to do with, literally, with funds devoted to how to spend it, and they have the whole credit-crunched world to invest in. In east Manchester, they were interested in

the football club alone, because Premier League football, with its £3.1bn TV deal, £1.4bn and counting from overseas, is a flourishing industry like the ones used to be which collapsed around the clubs. As Mansour put it in his initial open letter to City fans. "In cold business terms, Premiership football is one of the best entertainment products in the world and we see this as a sound business investment."

In the other sections of the letter, Mansour promised to value the club's history and the loyalty of the fans, its contribution in local community projects. His executives, led by the chairman, Khaldoon Al Mubarak, have been true to that, nurturing the fans' local feeling of belonging in smart ways, while building the club into one capable of winning the Premier League and projecting the glamorous international image they want for Abu Dhabi.

They have been in Manchester five years now and do not appear to have found much else they consider a sound business investment. There is talk of Etihad bringing its European headquarters to Manchester, which would be a coup for the city and the airport, and create jobs, but that does not amount to investing in something Manchester-bred.

When City unveiled plans for the campus, with its 7,000-seat stadium for the reserves — which seems like over-ambition even for Abu Dhabi — the rooms for young recruits from all over the world (ringed by unobtrusive but very reliable security, I was told), it was hailed as a football marvel, and, again, for its regeneration benefits. This is true again;

it is a large development on land which has lain derelict since the last factory, US-owned by then, packed up, and it will add hugely to the rehabilitation of east Manchester. When built it will provide 90 jobs, City said.

Of the 80 acre site, 5.5 acres, around one sixteenth, will be given over to community use, decontaminated at City's expense. The council is hoping it will build a sixth-form college there, because there is no sixth form in the whole of east Manchester. There is also talk of a sports centre and swimming pool being built for community use. While Abu Dhabi plough on with the £140m it will take to build the training campus they hope will rival Barcelona and Manchester United for the best boy footballers, the council must patch together a funding package for the school and sports centre. In an environment in which the council had to cut 2,000 jobs and services, to save £170m over two years cut by the Conservative-Liberal Democrat government, the money for the community benefits will not be easy to find.

What the council has done faced with the apocalypse of industry visited on Manchester from the late 1970s has been admirable, entrepreneurial; the envy of Liverpool, Leeds and other cities. While Liverpool was vainly fighting Margaret Thatcher's Conservative government's assault on local government finances after her re-election in 1987, the former council leader Graham Stringer told me, Manchester made a strategic decision to play as well as they could by her rules. Forced to bid for funding of specific projects competitively with other cities, Manchester became expert at it. They

built their arena, metrolink and G-Mex conference centre while the other cities were still paralysed by their economic disasters. Manchester secured the Commonwealth Games after cheekily bidding twice to bring the Olympics to east Manchester. With public money being squeezed for schools, libraries, social care and parks, that brought the money in: to run the games and build the facilities, including £78m from the lottery to build the stadium which would afterwards re-home a Premier League club. The other £49m the council put in itself, council tax payers' money. Many City fans are under the illusion that after the Games, the club paid to remove the track, lower the pitch and build the new north stand, but that is simply not true. Public money paid for the conversion for football because that was the deal the council agreed with City. In a very Premier League-era arrangement, City had only to pay for the bars, restaurants and corporate facilities they wanted — £20m for that fit-out.

You can argue about the terms City agreed: they had to pay nothing towards the stadium's construction and no rent whatsoever up to the Maine Road 32,500 capacity. Above that, on seats up to the new stadium's 48,000 capacity, City paid a share of income, which the council has said amounts to £2m a year when the stadium is full. I have always taken the view that this was a very generous deal indeed to City, who could never have afforded to build such a stadium themselves, as Everton, a similar club in many ways, cannot. But the council wanted the stadium and games to happen, to be a catalyst for regeneration, and the chief executive, Sir Howard Bernstein, argues it is a good deal, ensuring the stadium was not a white elephant, the rent keeping the other sports facilities around it in good order. The council also controlled any naming rights over the stadium, so when City were concluding their deal with Etihad, the council had to agree. It did so, for a further £2m a year, while Etihad are paying City £35m for the airline's name on the shirt, stadium and campus.

You can argue that the council has been generous, or accept that £2m is decent money for the fourth most deprived local authority in England. Independent auditors have approved both deals. You could argue the council should have squeezed out a little more, or you can applaud it for getting a deal done and securing the campus and its projected economic benefits.

But one central aspect of the stadium deal I could never understand was that it was given to City with no money to return to the council should the club's owners sell at a profit. When the deal was being mooted in the late 1990s, I had travelled my path from wide-eyed sky blue fan to adult understanding that my club was a company. Its shareholders were Wardle, Makin, the kitchen-making Boler family, the former player Francis Lee and even Rupert Murdoch's BSkyB, who had bought a 9.9% share. Lee, Wardle and Makin, with David Bernstein, the future Football Association chairman, an early investor, had wanted to float the club on the stock exchange, which would enable them to make a gain on their shares, if the club was doing well. The council was giving this company, owned by these shareholders, a huge gift of public money, which should have greatly increased the value of their investment. In the event, City overspent during Kevin Keegan's time as manager and arrived at the stadium making losses and in debt. Wardle and Makin, recommending all shareholders sell to Thaksin Shinawatra, wanted out by then, and sold at a loss. Thaksin made his £90m a year later selling the club to Mansour, which would never have been possible without the new stadium built for £127m of lottery and public money, but there was no return for the public.

The Olympic stadium was originally not designed to be converted for football afterwards because the mayor of London's office under Ken Livingstone could not countenance a handover to a Premier League football corporation. When, under Boris Johnson, London changed its mind and decided they would convert the stadium at vast expense for West Ham, they negotiated a claw back of money should the owners of West Ham, David Gold and David Sullivan, sell the club at a profit.

But besides the specifics of the deals they have done, I worry, as a Manchester man, that there is a risk of making too much of the east Manchester regeneration projects. Part of the strategy is to talk up the place and to keep encouraging investment, but I worry that at times the hype can take the place of reality. I found in a regeneration document about east Manchester the following proclamation: "Into the 21st century Manchester has [undergone] and still is undergoing a remarkable economic transformation, moving inexorably towards become the UK's first post-industrial city, where the new economic base will be geared almost exclusively around a service and knowledge-based economy."

That phrase, the "knowledge-based economy", is a difficult one anyway to accept — as if there was no "knowledge" in creating a ship canal and docks, cotton, trains, and engineering. As if all of that was just muscles and brute force. The image of reinvention, conjuring up some kind of Google-land, can also, while understandably wanting to attract businesses, veer into overstating the case. If this had happened so successfully, this "remarkable economic transformation"; including the outlay of public money to create "sport city", then hitting the jackpot with Abu Dhabi, why are the areas right around the stadium still mired in England's worst deprivation?

I worry that some of this, propounding the potential of a football club, its stadium and training ground to revive an economy, can get in the way of a wider proper recognition of where we really are. A more recent study of official statistics by the End Child Poverty campaign found in February 2013 that Manchester is the second worst local authority for child poverty. In Manchester, 38% of children live in households earning less than 60% of median income, the official measure of poverty. Manchester Central ward — right there amid all the costly improvements, a breath away from Deansgate's new, outsized Giorgio Armani store — is the very worst in the whole country. Neighbouring Tévez, Touré, £35m naming rights deals, the football club which beams the international invitation for tourists to visit Abu Dhabi, 47% of Manchester Central's children live in poverty.

Understanding the scale of these social problems which endure in Manchester leads you to the reality of the collapse which caused it, and to question if we have really found a convincing way to economic improvement. Manchester in the 1800s became the world's first industrial city and visitors came from France, Japan and other countries to marvel at its wonders, and grimace at its harshness. Friedrich Engels, Karl Marx's patron, chronicled the city's startling inequality in his classic 1844 work *The Condition of the Working Class in England*. Manchester City football club descends from an initiative by Anna Connell, the vicar's daughter of St Mark's church in west Gorton, in November 1880, forming a football team to promote the benefits of sport, and the church itself, in one of the toughest neighbourhoods.

You can read the 20th century in a city like Manchester as a difficult effort to maintain and modernise the industrial economy in the face of international competition, while the post-1945 welfare state and local authority civilised conditions. The football clubs grew remarkably in popularity from the off, homes of belonging for urban generations, the Football League in effect organising the clubs into an industry themselves, from 1888.

Then, during Thatcher's time, with high interest rates, lack of government intervention, an almost religious belief in the redemptive qualities of "market forces", one factory after another, whole industries, closed down. The records say that 150,000 manufacturing jobs were lost in Manchester between 1979 and 1984, many of them in the districts of the east. Tens of thousands of people left the areas and have never returned. "Firm by firm, there were savage cut backs," wrote Professor Alan Kidd, in his book *Manchester, A History*. "The 1970s and 1980s were decades of national industrial decline in which the Manchester region more than played its part."

Now, the economy which was supposed to replace industry — banking, the stock market, some very vague notions of entrepreneurship and aspiration, "knowledge" — has been exposed as a debt bubble and collapsed. Since then, the crash coinciding with the Manchester City purchase by Abu Dhabi, who have oil, and therefore real, not bubble money, our industrial collapse is slowly being recognised more for the disaster it was. How did we let so many jobs, industries, traditions and skills developed over generations, simply close down? How did we think we could reinvent an economy on "market forces"? What on earth are we going to do about it now? How do we "rebalance" the economy?

These are questions beginning to be asked with more urgency, 30 years on. The answers will surely be that we have to do more than build with lottery money some grand projects, like a football stadium. Even if it enables a club to be bought by a member of the global super rich, who wins the Premier League by paying footballers more than they could earn elsewhere, £10m each, or so. Even if

he then builds a mighty training complex, which will create 90 jobs.

For the 45,000 City fans who danced and wept ecstatically when Agüero scored his 94th-minute title winner last season, the club is the same one they followed to the Gillingham play-off final, only rebuilt. Its remarkable recent history tells us football's story, about how the game has been unleashed by pay TV. And as football always has, the game reflects the world we are living in. Born as a professional sport when workers began to enjoy a half day off on Saturdays, the football clubs in the northern cities are in danger of being a large part of all we have left to celebrate. The meeting of new, rich, lucky Abu Dhabi with post-collapse Manchester speaks of football's irresistible global attraction, the reinvented modern flourish of our traditional clubs. But rather than see in the City story a passport to a better future, the circumstances of its acquisition by Sheikh Mansour should jolt us into facing up, a touch more realistically, to the post-industrial mess we are in.

David Conn's book Richer Than God: Manchester City, Modern Football and Growing Up, *is now out in paperback, priced £8.99*

SPIRIT, STYLE AND QUALITY FROM THE BIRTHPLACE OF THE BEAUTIFUL GAME

AVAILABLE NOW FROM **GOALSOUL ONLINE** OR FROM **CLUB1857**, OUR UNIQUE, FOOTBALL-INSPIRED BOUTIQUE IN SHEFFIELD.

RECENT SIGNINGS

1 **CHILE VS ITALY 1962** THE BATTLE OF SANTIAGO 2 **RUUD GULLIT** THE BLACK TULIP
3 **GABRIEL BATISTUTA** RENAISSANCE SIGHTS 4 **JURGEN KLINSMANN** KLINSMANN'S DIVING ACADEMY
5 **BRUCE GROBBELAAR** A MAN AMONGST MEN 6 **MICHEL PLATINI'S MAGIC SQUARE** CARRE MAGIQUE

 1
 2
 3
 4
 5
 6

CROWD FAVOURITES

1 **MARCO VAN BASTEN** THE SWAN OF UTRECHT 2 **BARESI/MALDINI** THE MILAN WALL
3 **ALEX FERGUSON** HAIRDRYER TREATMENT 4 **ANDONI GOIKOETXEA** THE BUTCHER OF BILBAO
5 **PAUL MCGRATH** NEW YORK GIANT 6 **CLUB ATLETICO BOCA JUNIORS** LA BOCA TANGO

 1
 2
 3
 4
 5
 6

THE SHEFFIELD COLLECTION
CELEBRATING FOOTBALL'S FIRST CITY

1 **SHEFFIELD** FOOTBALL'S FIRST CITY 2 **SHEFFIELD FC** BIRTHPLACE OF THE BEAUTIFUL GAME
3 **SHEFFIELD FC** ORIGINAL RULES AND INNOVATIONS 4 **SHEFFIELD FC/REAL MADRID CF** THE TREE OF MERIT
5 **SHEFFIELD WEDNESDAY** PARLIAMENT OF OWLERTON 6 **SHEFFIELD UNITED** DIAMOND-TIPPED BLADES

 1
 2
 3
 4
 5
 6

KEEPING THE GAME BEAUTIFUL

ONLINE | WWW.GOALSOUL.NET
INSTORE | CLUB 1857, 283 SHARROW VALE ROAD, SHEFFIELD, S11 8ZF, +44 (0)114 266 3374

 goalsoul

Meanwhile Back in Sunderland

How a Tyne Tees documentary on Cup final day 1973 captured the spirit of the town

By Jon Spurling

Ian Porterfield's expression after hooking the decisive goal past the Leeds keeper David Harvey, Jim Montgomery's incredible mid-air twist to deny Peter Lorimer a certain goal, Bob Stokoe's dash across the Wembley turf into the arms of Montgomery, a moment of unbridled joy later captured in bronze outside the Stadium of Light: the victory of second-division Sunderland over Don Revie's mighty Leeds United in the 1973 FA Cup final was replete with iconic images.

It was, in the captain Bobby Kerr's words, "a victory for a one-club city, where literally everyone, from miners to shipbuilders to shop workers drove us onwards." The football club was the face of the whole town. "Even now," the forward Dennis Tueart said, "men and women of a certain age are moved to tears when they talk to you about the game. Our run to the final, and the final itself, created a perfect pitch between the club, its fans and the entire city." In the build-up to the match, documentaries were broadcast by the BBC and Tyne Tees Television that captured perfectly just what was happening in Sunderland and precisely what it meant to everyone connected with the town.

The BBC commissioned Harold Williamson, born in Houghton-le-Spring, to present and narrate a programme called *The Pride and Passion of Sunderland*. Broadcast on the Thursday before the final, when Tueart, Porterfield and the striker Billy Hughes were meeting Suzi Quatro and The Sweet as guests of honour at the *Top of the Pops* studio, the BBC documentary focussed mainly on the impact of the manager — and former Newcastle defender — Bob Stokoe, and how his galvanising presence had lifted the spirit of the town against a backdrop of high inflation, strikes and the impending energy crisis. "Bob was a people person," said Tueart. "One of the first things he did at the club was change the day of midweek home matches so that shipyard workers could attend games. He also changed the kit so we played in black shorts [rather than white, which had been introduced in 1961], which pleased older fans. He understood and connected with supporters in a subtle way."

A young John Motson was dispatched to Wearmouth Colliery, where miners who'd just completed their shift spoke glowingly about Stokoe. "He's saved this town," claimed one. Asked by Motson why he believed Sunderland would defeat Leeds, another miner replied incredulously, "Because we're the better team." Although a brief segment of the Motson interviews survives, *The Pride and Passion of Sunderland* fell victim to the BBC's purging of the archives in the late 1970s. Fortunately Tyne Tees's offering, *Meanwhile Back in Sunderland*, remains fully preserved and is arguably the most treasured social documentary to emerge from the North East.

"I went to see Bob Stokoe and chairman Keith Collings," said the head of features at Tyne Tees, Leslie Barrett. "It soon became fairly clear that we weren't going to get into Wembley, and the BBC and ITV had the team hotel covered to the hilt." So Barrett was forced to think outside the box, and opted to shoot footage in the town from 5am to midnight on Cup Final Day, using four different camera crews. He decided that there wouldn't be a narrator; the people of Sunderland would provide their own narrative to the day. Although the production team was initially disappointed not to be going to Wembley, Barrett tapped into the waves of enthusiasm sweeping through the town and insisted, "If we win, we have got a hell of a programme here."

At daybreak on the morning of the game, the players were sleeping soundly in their Selsdon Park Hotel beds. Some, like Hughes, had supped a couple of cans of lager the night before to ease their nerves; Stokoe, riled by ITV's *Who'll Win The Cup?* late-night show, on which panellists Jack Charlton, Malcolm Allison and Pat Crerand predicted a comfortable Leeds victory, tossed and turned. Leslie Barrett's filming crews, meanwhile, were already hard at work on the streets of Sunderland. By 5.30, groups of supporters, clad in giant red-and-white rosettes, natty red-and-white hats and, for the majority of male supporters,

suits, were making their way to the fleet of Wembley-bound coaches, heading south to the A19, and the station, where specially laid on trains headed to Kings Cross via Newcastle. "About a week before the final," recalled Stokoe, "the town had simply run out of red and white material. You couldn't get a scarf or a rosette anywhere." The documentary explains the shortage: as fans trooped down the streets, virtually every shop window had some kind of candy-striped display; in clothes shops wax dummies were clad in Sunderland garb. Even the undertakers had a discreet rosette tucked to one side.

The FA Cup final was arguably sport's biggest televison event of the year in the seventies, often attracting in excess of 20 million viewers across both BBC and ITV. The BBC commentator Barry Davies argues that the 1973 final was the first time the two broadcasters had really tried to outdo one another with the build-up. ITV were granted a live feed on the Sunderland team bus (Revie refused to allow cameras onto the Leeds bus) and although the technology broke down on more than one occasion, it showed the team in a decidedly relaxed state. They were still grinning about Hughes setting off a "laughing box" during the team's interview with Davies earlier that morning. The players dissolved into fits of giggles on live TV, much to Davies's astonishment. The players' antics contrasted with the far more sombre BBC interview conducted with Revie's squad, who wore pin-striped suits. The Sunderland team watched the Leeds interview on Cup Final Grandstand before leaving for Wembley and Dave Watson recalled the "dread and fear" on the Leeds players' faces. Having watched the tense interview, Tueart became "even more convinced that the day would be ours."

Back home, the locals closed up their shops and descended upon those neighbours who were fortunate enough to own colour televisions. Local boys, accompanied by a dog with a rosette pinned to its collar, had a kickabout in a side street within a few yards of Roker Park and large groups began clustering around Vision Hire on Fawcett Street for an impromptu street party. When the game kicked off at 3.00pm, the town was deserted but for a solitary policeman trudging a lonely beat. Television viewers saw the players emerge from the tunnel on a gloomy London afternoon, with Bobby Kerr, the smallest-ever FA Cup Final captain, surging ahead of his counterpart Billy Bremner. Kerr was yelled at by Jim Montgomery to slow down and his teammates, barely able to control their glee, bounced up and down as they prepared to meet the Duke of Kent.

When Porterfield scored after 31 minutes, the emotion of Sunderland fans at Wembley was mirrored in the houses and streets at home. Plastic hats were thrown into the air, beer was slopped over tables in pubs, working men's clubs and cinemas which broadcasted the game, and teenage girls screamed and wept. The reaction among fans to Montgomery's remarkable double save was one of bafflement initially, because it took so long to understand what had happened. Jimmy Hill, co-commentating, only realised Montgomery had saved Lorimer's shot when he saw a second replay.

As the game reached its climax, the atmosphere was fevered. Many could

barely watch, others chain-smoked; some chain-smoked while not watching. The final whistle was met with a tumult of Klaxons, whistles, and cars tooting their horns. On the streets, groups of women performed renditions of "Ee aye adeo, we won the cup," and men embraced, according to one fan, "in a way Sunderland blokes have never done, except perhaps when we last won the cup in 1937." With the players preparing for their reception at the Savoy, the town partied in inimitable early seventies style. A young woman revealed knickers embellished with Sunderland logos and men with Rod Stewart-style feather cuts got more beers in. Most poignantly of all, a group of senior citizens sang along to a pling-pling version of *You'll Never Walk Alone*, led by a pianist clad in an enormous red-and-white top hat and a drummer with red-and-white twirling drum sticks. "Whenever I see that final clip on the documentary," Tueart said, "I watch it with a lump in my throat, because those older supporters are long since passed away. Many of them had been to the Raich Carter Final of '37, and couldn't believe it when, 36 years later, Sunderland did it again."

Due to Sunderland's backlogged fixture list, they had to travel to Cardiff on Monday (the game ended 1-1) before coming back home on Tuesday, in advance of their final league game of the season against QPR (an understandably exhausted group of Sunderland players were hammered 3-0 by the Second Division runners-up) at Roker Park on Wednesday. "None of us had a clue about what had been going on at home," explained Watson. "We'd been in our Wembley bubble." As the team approached the town, they had a taste of what was to come. "There were supporters hanging over bridges, and cheering from the grass verges. There were cows in fields wearing rosettes and when we got into Sunderland, there were tens of thousands out and Roker Park just buzzed for the trophy parade." Lance Hardy, author of *Stokoe, Sunderland And '73*, estimates that around 750,000 turned out to welcome home the conquering heroes, and thanks to a local amateur film maker, grainy images remain of the Roker Park homecoming, at which around 50,000 crammed in to see the cup paraded. For those who missed it, there was always the QPR game the following night, at which Stan Bowles allegedly knocked the FA Cup off a table by the side of the pitch for a bet, enraging the 43,000 who had squeezed in.

Meanwhile Back in Sunderland was broadcast on the Monday and when the players watched it at a private screening, they were staggered by what they saw. "We'd been out and about in the town during the cup run, meeting and mixing with supporters, so we had a feeling what might have happened, but the documentary reaffirmed exactly how the whole town was involved," said Watson. Only Yorkshire TV and Wales bought the rights to the programme, but it is occasionally repeated in the area now and is accessible on YouTube in all its glory. Several former players still watch

it from time to time, Hughes describing it as "a perfect piece of TV, simple and effective". Stokoe, whose Wembley dash is included at the end of the documentary, is said to have wept when he saw it.

Towards the end of the programme, several supporters insist: "We'll win it next year," and Sunderland were installed as promotion favourites for 1973-74. Things quickly went awry. Tueart and Watson departed to Manchester City and the class of '73 disintegrated amid grumblings about a lack of investment in the team by the board. Stokoe guided the team to Division One three years later but, stricken by ill-health, resigned after a disappointing start. Sunderland, who were losing finalists to Liverpool in 1992, have been unable to match the ecstasy of the '73 final since, but as Tueart notes, "That would be nigh on impossible. You can't recreate what happened back then."

Kerr once described the '73 Cup run as "something that you cannot put into words." Yet, thanks to Leslie Barrett's brilliant improvisation, *Meanwhile Back in Sunderland* does a splendid job of encapsulating the joyous mood of the time and will remain a compelling oral and visual testament to the bewitching power the FA Cup held over Sunderland in 1973. Ⓑ

That Grandish Pile of Swank

Tracing Leeds United's place in the tradition of Northern Realism

By Anthony Clavane

At the beginning of 2013, several announcements were made which caused me to reflect on the connection between football and art. First, Radio 4 announced they would broadcast the complete text of Tony Harrison's poem *V*, which was written in 1985 in the midst of the miners' strike and caused something of a fuss when it was aired, two years later, on Channel 4. Then Leeds Waterstones announced it would commemorate the 50th year of *Billy Liar*'s release at the cinema by holding an event at its bookshop. The government then announced the second phase of the £32bn HS2 high-speed rail network. And, finally, Leeds United announced the sale of their best striker to Norwich City.

At first glance, only the last of these developments relates to a footballing theme. But to those who, like me, are obsessed by such things, they are all part of the contradictory narrative of northern realism.

I should explain. In my book *Promised Land*, I set out to pull together several strands into this one narrative. By "northern realism" I mean the cultural movement characterised by the so-called kitchen sink writers of the 1950s and 1960s. A new kind of man sprang into the public imagination during these

years. A working-class iconoclast and provincial braggart: Northern Man. In novels, the theatre, television and the cinema, he suddenly became the subject of ground-breaking dramas. He found his way into the glare of the spotlight via his writing ability, photography, acting talent, musicianship or football skills. He was an antidote to both the upper-middle class tweediness portrayed by Dirk Bogarde and Kenneth More and the warm-hearted proletarian stereotypes offered up, in a previous era, by Gracie Fields and George Formby.

Before the 1950s, 'the North' had been reconstructed on London film sets; in the classic Fields vehicle *Sing As We Go* (1934), for example, the streets of her home town were rebuilt in the Ealing studios. Filmed on location on the back-streets of Leeds, Bradford, Nottingham and Salford, these social realist films brought a new vitality to British cinema. They were inspired, and very often written by, a post-war generation of edgy, 'tell it how it is' northerners hailing from several cities and towns. A disproportionate number hailed from Leeds and its surrounds. Indeed, West Yorkshire, for a few glorious years in the early 60s, became the unofficial home of an influential movement that drew upon the lives and experiences of the aspirational, newly-socially-mobile working-classes. Keith Waterhouse's *Billy Liar* (1959), for example, told the story of a daydreaming fantasist and his desire to escape the confines of his upbringing. Alan Bennett wrote bittersweet tales of unfulfilled ordinary life. David Storey's *This Sporting Life* (1960) followed the emotional struggles of a bitter young coal miner who was recruited by a rugby team in Wakefield after being spotted fighting outside a nightclub.

Waterhouse, Bennett, Storey, Stan Bartsow, Willis Hall and, a few years later, Tony Harrison, all wrote about working-class anti-heroes — Billy Fisher, Joe Lampton and Frank Machin — who were characteristic of the revivified new north in their energy and belief that the good things of life were within their reach. They were, as Lampton declared in *Room at the Top*, "going to the Top": Leeds "was stirring out of its pre-war, post-Edwardian sleep," recalled Waterhouse. "There was a civic restlessness about, a growing clamour for clearing away the old."

Waterhouse wrote *Billy Liar* in 1958, the year his city's architect insisted the multi-storey block was the only way forward, the first British motorway — the M1 — opened between Leeds and London, and Leeds United signed Don Revie from Sunderland. It was published a year later and, after John Schlesinger's screen version was released in 1963, the name of its eponymous protagonist passed into popular culture. Like Lampton, Machin and Jimmy Porter in *Look Back in Anger*, Billy spoke to a generation of ambitious provincials barging through the privileged ranks of the elite. A working-class anti-hero was something to be.

The rise of this movement was paralleled by the ascent of Don Revie's great, if tarnished, Leeds United team. In my view, this team was the footballing apotheosis of northern realism. The kitchen sink stories could be lifted from any one of their autobiographies. There's Joe 'Dracula' Jordan emerging, like Machin, with his front teeth missing following a clash with a defender. There's Jack Charlton threatening to knock Norman Hunter's block off as a Leeds fan shouts, "Go arn, Norman, 'ave a go at him." There's Big Jack chasing a Valencia defender half-way round the pitch after the Spaniard had punched him. There's Billy Bremner, described by Michael Parkinson as "ten stone of barbed wire", hurling his shirt to the ground after scrapping with Kevin Keegan at Wembley. There's Bite Yer Legs Hunter lamping Frannie Lee after another dive by the Derby striker. There's Gary Sprake decking a lad at the Mecca after being accused of eyeing up the lad's bird. There's a tearful David Harvey telling his unsympathetic team-mates how his pet monkey had switched on the oven and gassed himself. There's Revie giving his players their wages in readies "so you can go straight to the bookies." There's the coach Les Cocker telling his defenders to go in hard with the first tackle, the one the referee never books you for.

Each chapter of *Promised Land*'s section on that team begins with a quote from Waterhouse's classic novel. In the Leeds fanzine *Square Ball*, 'Moscowhite' wrote: "Leeds United — the perennial runners-up, the eternal chokers — are recast as Billy Fisher, the frustrated northern man so convinced of his own potential, if he could only get the breaks, yet who, with everything he ever dreamed of there for the taking, will always leave Liz (Julie Christie! Julie bloody Christie!) alone on the train to London, will always sabotage his own chance of happiness and go back for the milk...

"Leeds United were a team of heroes that existed only through the irresistible force of the will of Don Revie, bearing the indelible hallmark both of his brilliant blueprint for success and of his fatalistic lack of confidence. Chelsea's troupe of flash, brash, nightclub-hopping dandies were an expression of swinging London, but Leeds's greatest side were an expression of the personality of just one man. The sensible haircuts, the carpet bowls, the bingo; the spectacular football, the innovation, the 7-0 wins; the time-wasting, the hard tackles, the win-at-all-costs mentality; the dossiers, the superstitions, the crippling fear of losing; these were all facets of Don Revie, impressed upon a team of players who depended on Revie the way characters in a novel depend upon their author. Revie fused his every character trait — the good and the bad — with the character of his team, until the two were inseparable; like Barbara Hepworth or Henry Moore, he moulded Super Leeds as a monumental reflection of his self, and was every bit as much an artist. 'Revie's Leeds are not often lumped together with Billy Liar, The Beatles, David Hockney, the New Wave writers, the Liverpool poets...' writes Clavane, but he makes a persuasive argument that they, The Beaten Generation, should be. Leeds United as art is not as far-fetched as it may seem: the urban myth still persists that the Smiley badge was designed by Andy Warhol and I could look for hours at a photo of the Super Leeds team, lit like film stars by the tallest floodlights in Europe, waving to the crowd in their matching tracksuits. Don Revie's achievement, and his failure, was to make Leeds United into a full representation of his own personality, its brilliance, its style, and its flaws. It isn't hyperbole to call that a work of art, as well as a work of football management."

I love this idea of Revie's Leeds as a work of art. It certainly runs counter to the popular image of the side, reinforced in David Peace's (2006) seminal novel *The Damned Utd*. How can Dirty Leeds, of all teams, forged in the gritty cynicism of Elland Road brutality, be described in such terms?

Fast forward from the golden age of LUFC to 1987 and we have Channel 4 defying a growing, Mary Whitehouse-led moral panic about "TV obscenity" by broadcasting a film of Harrison performing *V*. After discovering his parents' grave has been vandalised, Harrison composed a narrative that is fiercely confrontational, detailing an imagined exchange between author and perpetrator in a bout of civic-minded mudslinging against the backdrop of Elland Road. Like *The Damned Utd*, it — superficially at least — updates a trope that has been present in popular culture since Charles Dickens described Leeds, in a mid-19th century talk, as a "beastly place": a grim, sullen, down-to-earth, anti-intellectual, proudly independent, no-frills, dark and gritty town. A town — it only achieved city status in 1893 — you would not want to visit, unless looking for material for a dark novel or state-of-the-nation poem; and one which, if born into, you would certainly attempt to escape from at the first available opportunity, preferably on the train to London.

My argument is that Leeds United, as moulded by its 'auteur-manager', embodied the contradictory narrative of northern realism. Revie's team were, in many ways, about escaping a life of provincial confinement, about struggling to become accepted in mainstream society, about grafting for your patch. Like Waterhouse, Harrison, Hall, the Beatles, the Liverpool poets and Hockney, they were part of a cultural insurgency fuelled by full employment and rapidly rising industrial wages. Like their fellow northern iconoclasts, they would not be bought off with a few extra bob — or the odd trophy. They were an angry young northern team who were, by hook or by crook, "going to the Top". Unlike the Lennons, McGoughs and Hockneys, however, they never quite made it. Their biggest fantasies, like winning the European Cup, remained unfulfilled.

Their decline and fall in the late seventies and early eighties was celebrated with a fervour normally reserved for the ceremonial dynamiting of a high-rise. According to their detractors, they had been just another brutalist blot on the post-war landscape. They polluted football in the same way modernist architecture polluted northern cityscapes. Like all those appalling arterial roads, they had ruthlessly sliced their way through cities and communities. Like the out-of-town high-rises, they were an ugly development of a deeply-regretted decade. This is the background to V, which tells of Harrison's visit to his family grave, a traditional family plot in Holbeck Cemetery. The famous poem stands alongside dystopian films like *A Clockwork Orange* — some of whose outdoor scenes were filmed in Leeds

— which lamented the "progress" made in the 60s, particularly the rebuilding of the north. In *Get Carter, Charlie Bubbles, O Lucky Man* and *The Reckoning*, the north's prodigal sons — the *Billy Liar* generation — returned home to discover a concrete wilderness of demolition sites, car parks and crumbling terraces. Their old towns and cities had not only been crippled by the decline of heavy industry but also corrupted by big business and concreted over by urban motorways, flyovers, shopping centres and tower blocks. *Get Carter* begins with our working-class anti-hero catching the train from London to the north, going back to his roots to "sort things out"; a journey into the bowels of New Britain. It ends with him being shot dead.

V was the culmination of a series of broken Britain scenarios documented in the books, plays and films of the 1970s and 80s. It is significant that it was transmitted on Channel 4, a station established with a remit to provide viewing for under-represented groups in society. For, by this time, the northern working-classes briefly feted by The Establishment — and incorporated into an illusory Swinging Sixties meritocracy — had returned to the margins of British culture. When the poem was broadcast, right-wing columnists and Tory MPs declared themselves to be shocked by its "torrents of obscene language" and "streams of four-letter filth". Harrison declared himself to be shocked by both the graffiti Leeds United skinheads had daubed on his father's headstone and his beloved city's descent into the abyss. Written in the aftermath of the miners' strike, and set on a hill-top cemetery in Beeston overlooking Elland Road, the stadium's diamond floodlights the only glints in a decade of decline, the poem used the darkening national mood as a backdrop to Harrison's own internal torment.

At the beginning of the Channel 4 version of *V*, standing — like so many kitchen-sink protagonists had done before him — on top of a hill overlooking his city, Harrison reveals the "panoramic view over the whole of Leeds". He points out the Town Hall, Elland Road, Leeds Grammar School and Leeds University "where I got the education that took me away from this background". There are many conflicts described in *V* — north v south, black v white, Leeds United v everyone else — but it is his own, inner conflict which is the poem's heartbeat; his face-off with a Leeds United hooligan, who has taken the traditional short-cut from the football ground back into town, symbolises his alienation from his "background". In the poem, he tries to erase the drunken fan's graffiti, to scrub away the obscenities. But he couldn't make them, nor indeed his own alienation, go away.

In another poem, *The Queen's English* (1985), Harrison recounts the last time he saw his father — at Leeds Station:

"Last meal together, Leeds, the Queen's Hotel
that grandish pile of swank in City Square
Too posh for me, he said (even though he dressed well)
if you wern't wi' me ah'd nivver dare!
I knew that he'd decided to die
not by the way he lingered at the bar
not by the look he'd give me with one good-eye
nor by the firmer handshake and the gruff ta-ra

But when he browsed the station bookstall sales
he picked up 'Poems from the Yorkshire Dales'
'ere tek this un wi' yer to New York
to remind you of 'ow us gaffers used to talk.
It's up your street in't it? 'ahh buy yer that!
The broken lines go through me speeding South."

Harrison, unlike Billy Fisher, had taken the decision in the sixties not to sabotage his own chance of happiness. The son of a baker, he had escaped his background at the earliest opportunity. At the end of this poem he gets on the train to London, as he has done so many times before, and heads south. But at what cost? A loss of identity? It is almost as if, in catching the train — a metaphor for acting on your fantasies, fulfilling your potential, crossing the threshold — the northern anti-hero becomes estranged from his family, class, community and city.

And as *V* and other fictional and non-fictional works of the period reveal the rebuilt northern city of the sixties, "the Motorway City of the Seventies", the new world of shopping centres and high-rise flats, had turned out to be crass and materialistic. Post-war northern regeneration had been a mirage — as had the fanciful notion that a tired, post-imperial society might reinvent itself as a white-hot technological powerhouse. As the corpses of its dead parent industries slowly rotted, Leeds became a tough and unforgiving place. And Elland Road became the home of a nasty, embittered and racist element. There was a growing aura of menace, a climate of fear and paranoia. A sense of victimhood. The city, like its football club, battened down the hatches and adopted a bunker mentality. It became, once again, identified in the public mind with the darker, more primitive side of life. Property experts advised businesses to move out. The town centre became a night-time haunt of disorderly youths, tramps and alcoholics. The threat of violence was never far away.

As the centrifugal force of seventies Britain quickened the spiral of talent, power and influence down to London, the capital reasserted its authority and Leeds turned in on itself. Manufacturing, the basis of its wealth, collapsed and unemployment soared; in 1976 it reached 5.5% — 15 years later, it had almost doubled. This was an era when many northern towns and cities experienced decline. Between 1979 and 1990, as jobs in the new hi-tech industries were generated in the south, manufacturing employment fell on average 2.8% a year in the region. Leeds, in particular, became a byword for inner-city chaos, violent crime and bigotry. It seemed to be slipping into poverty and isolation and out of the mainstream of British society. The 1984 miners' strike reinforced the view that the Tories were fighting a civil war against the north — and that the police had become a brutal arm of a heartless government. In Leeds, the police's reputation sank to an all-time low. The seventies began with them in the dock, accused of murdering David Oluwale, a homeless black man; it ended with their ham-fisted attempt to catch the Yorkshire Ripper.

According to Peace's bleak *Red Riding* novels, it was during this low, dishonest decade that the West

Riding metamorphosed into a land of endless night, a nightmarish world of foul-mouthed machismo, racism and misogyny. One of his critics has countered that Leeds was, in reality, more like Stodge City than Dodge City. That may be so — measured by national standards, it was not that badly off — but there was a tangible sinking feeling, a perception that, like the country as a whole, it was going to hell in a handcart.

And so to 2013, 50 years after *Billy Liar* first penetrated the national consciousness. "It's easy", Liz/Julie Christie tells the working-class 19 year old living with his parents. "You get on a train and, four hours later, there you are in London." Leeds, Waterhouse's introverted, rather prickly home city has, in a half a century, reinvented itself several times. It has concreted over its dirty past, burst its boundaries to become a metropolitan super-region. It has attempted to become a centre for the global financial services industries, the British city outside London. But its ambition has collapsed in the wake of the worst economic crisis since the war. It has become a two-nation city, polarised between affluence and squalor.

Its football club has spent another decade in the wilderness. Just like in the eighties. It has sold its best players — Jonathan Woodgate, Aaron Lennon, James Milner — to bigger, richer sides. In the last two seasons, no fewer than four of its number have sped south to, of all teams, Norwich City: Johnson, Howson, Snodgrass and, in January 2013, the man who has scored 19 goals to give the club a sniff of a return to the Promised Land, Luciano Becchio. In fact, the majority of clubs in Yorkshire have lurched, like

Leeds United, from well-publicised financial disaster to despair in recent years, tumbling down the divisions and, in several cases, out of the Football League altogether. Only a decade ago, the region boasted thirteen league clubs, seven of which were in the top two divisions. That number has since eroded to 10, with none in the top flight and only four playing as high as the Championship.

And here we have the latest move to revive the north, reinvent Leeds and bridge the north-south divide. A new £32bn rail network which will stop at a new city centre station on the south bank of the River Aire. Speeds of up to 250mph will cut journey times to London from two hours and 12 minutes to 82 minutes. We've had the Motorway City of the Seventies, the Barcelona of the North and now HS2. All part of the dream of a genuinely fluid, open society.

This already feels like a doomed project. Not just because it will take at least 20 years to open. Like the social divisions that torment Harrison, and the protagonists of his fellow northern writers — from the early-sixties fantasists, through the middle-aged prodigal sons to Peace's Yorkshire Noir anti-heroes — the contradictory mindset of Leeds, or more generally West Yorkshire, appears to undermine the city's self-belief that it can, truly, fulfil its potential by crossing the threshold. Why would you want to get to That London in less than an hour and a half anyway? Wouldn't our distinctive Yorkshire identity, our Leedsness, be compromised by becoming, simply, a northern suburb of the Big Smoke?

This mindset has also infected the football club. Leeds United might have been

out of the top flight for 10 years but at least they haven't been tainted by the flashy, glitzy, superficial glamour of the globalised, Fancy Dan Premier League. Back in the day, when pitches were muddy, stadiums were crumbling and foul play was routine, Revie's team earned the right to play by being the toughest club in the land. The Dirty Leeds label did some of the hard work, putting the fear of god into their opponents. The only time George Best ever wore shin pads was at Elland Road. "I hated playing against them," said Best. "They had a hell of a lot of skill, but they were a bloody nightmare." Given their lack of footballing history and culture, they needed an edge. A keep-fighting-till-the-end, don't-let-the-bastards-grind-you-down kind of edge which came from being a bunch of rough-and-ready, provincial outsiders.

When we look back at, say, the Manchester United of Best, Law and Charlton, the Chelsea team of Osgood and Cooke, or the Derby and Nottingham Forest teams of Brian Clough, it is clear that they represent a different mindset. Possibly, a different culture. And Matt Busby, as much as Revie or Clough back then — or, indeed, Alex Ferguson today — was an "auteur-manager", helping to mould, sculpt, create a mindset, a way of playing the game, an attitude not just to football, but to life itself. Interestingly, Peace's latest project — on how Bill Shankly transformed a second division team with a crumbling stadium into a British footballing institution — appears to reinforce the myth of the "auteur-manager", with Shankly, in the author's words, celebrated as a "Red saint".

This positive image of Liverpool and, even more so, of Manchester, provides an interesting contrast to the image of Leeds and Leedsness. These influential north-west cities offer different, more appealing and successful, versions of the north. Versions expressed as much through their great football teams as through their great cultural icons — the Beatles, *Z-Cars*, *Coronation Street*, the Madchester Sound, the Bleasdale-Russell plays, the Hacienda.

A great deal was made of the Y-shaped route envisaged by the HS2 project, with separate railway branches to Manchester and Leeds after Birmingham. It seems to me that the "Y" has replaced the "V" as an apt metaphor for northern realism. Not long after phase two of the project was announced, the *New York Times* included Manchester in its top 50 places to visit in the world. "No surprise to Mancunians," commented the *Guardian*, "who have never been short of pride in a city that is home to two of England's best football clubs, the BBC's MediaCity, the Lowry and Imperial War Museum North."

And no surprise to the inhabitants of Leeds either. From the War of the Roses, through the Industrial Revolution to the Eric Cantona transfer, the Yorkshire-Lancashire rivarly has been played out between Loiners and Mancs. And yet anyone who has any knowledge of the self-appointed capital of Yorkshire will know that the former have made as great a contribution to British culture as the latter.

The dominant view, however, remains that, on reaching Birmingham, and presented with a choice of continuing westwards or eastwards, a journey to the self-confident, swaggering, Manchester would be far more rewarding than a trip to Dickens's beastly city. **Ⓑ**

109

Lev Yashin

"He drank neither wine nor beer —
vodka only. Doctors told him to do
that because of the ulcer."

The Jersey That Wasn't Black

Lev Yashin's widow and Eusébio remember the great Soviet goalkeeper

By Igor Rabiner

Valentina Yashina

Several times during our chat of around four hours, Valentina Timofeevna Yashina asked, "Have I tired you?" or "Maybe you're in a hurry?" My God, how could I have been in a hurry to leave the legendary apartment at Chapaevsky Pereulok, between Sokol and Polezhaevskaya Metro stations, where the Yashins settled in 1964. Just to think that at that kitchen table, Lev Yashin had a meal every day. Franz Beckenbauer, Michel Platini, Gavriil Kachalin, Mikhail Yakushin, all of them ate dinner here. All I wanted to do was ask and ask and ask.

[Yashina indicates an old refrigerator in the corner and starts talking] The fridge has been here since 1971. Lev wasn't able to ask anything for anything for himself. If it was a matter of asking for an apartment or something for somebody else, he did it with great pleasure. But not for himself. He was at a loss: "How will I go about it, what will I say?" These fridges at that time were given for special licences, so he also asked one of his friends to bring him this licence. He was too shy to go and ask for it by himself.

Everywhere we would stand in the queues, as everybody did. Once, after he'd retired, we went to some game at the Luzhniki and met [Nikita] Simonyan there. For whatever reason there were no passes and so these two great former players had to wait at the ordinary ticket office. People were surprised and some of them were outraged: how could Yashin and Simonyan wait for tickets!

◈ *Everybody who remembers Yashin speaks of him as of world champion in kindness. Is it true?*

Yes. His father's second wife told me, that during World War II little Lyova [a diminutive of Lev] kept bringing to their home a boy named Izya, who lived with a large family somewhere nearby, in barracks. Lev told her, "They have nothing to eat," and his father and stepmother always fed Izya. Once he took off sweater and gave it to him, telling his parents, "There are many children in their family and they have nothing to wear." His stepmother was a little bit offended: the sweater was new and Lyova had a younger brother and could have given it to him.

So, this kindness was in him from childhood. On the pitch he would shout loudly at his teammates, but when I asked him about it, Lev replied: "I'm not swearing. I'm giving advice about what to do." And he even gave instructions gently: "Vitek! Tolik!" [which are diminutives of Viktor and Anatoly].

He hated gossips, never blamed anyone or said spiteful things, and he was reticent in general. Sometimes I would say, "Why does this player keep passing to the opponent?" and he would make a helpless gesture. "He's just not able to! He doesn't see the pitch!" It was his favourite saying in general — "He doesn't see the pitch!"— and he transferred it from football to regular life.

The rivalry between different teams never affected off-pitch relations. In the USSR national team he became good friends with Spartak Moscow players. For example, he would call Simonyan and would say things in Armenian [Simonyan's native language] and laugh. He was close friends with him, Isaev, Ilyin and Paramonov and I was with friends their wives. We watched all the national team games together. We still talk on the phone and I'm friends with Khusainova, Paramonova, Ivanova, Ludmila Simonyan...

Once I saw a game between Dinamo and Spartak in which Tolik Isaev ran into Lev with his chest, preventing him from kicking the ball. I asked him after the game at home, "Why did Isaev behave so strangely?" He told me that he had also been surprised and had asked him. Isaev quietly replied, "Sorry, Lev, the coach ordered me to make you anxious." He hung his head, went back to the centre of the pitch and never did it again.

These people had clear consciences; they appreciated each other. They didn't have any choice other than to become friends because they spent all their time together. Imagine: we married just before New Year 1955 and already on January 6 they went to a training camp for two months! And their friendship lasted all their lives.

In all countries, kids would instinctively approach him and that shows his kindness. They would even put him right. In Sweden at the 1958 World Cup, he went across a park, smoked a cigarette and threw the butt to the ground. There was a boy running near him and he ran up, dug a hole and put the butt in. We have dozens of photos of Yashin at his favourite pastime, fishing. There were always kids around him and he would give them interviews.

☙ *Is it true that one of your sons-in-law is a Spartak fan?*

Yes. And I don't see anything terrible in that. When our friends gathered at our home, there were just a few footballers — Shabrov and Tsarev [both teammates of Yashin from Dinamo]. The others were mainly those who had worked with Lev at the aircraft works in Tushino when he was young. One of them became an engineer, another even a director... All them were supporters of different teams and one was a die-hard Spartak fan. They were always chaffing at each other. But even in the national team he almost always played in his club jersey with the letter 'Д' [D]. We have a photo: all the players walking on the pitch with the USSR crest and Lev in a Dinamo shirt. It was allowed at that time.

☙ *I've heard no stories that he had any rivalry with other goalkeepers...*

No! There were none. For many years at Dinamo the reserve goalkeeper was Volodya Belyaev, who maybe surpassed Lev in terms of pure talent. They were even taken to the national team together

— although Belyaev played very rarely. And they were very close in life: we even travelled to his native town of Nalchik [in the Caucasus mountains]. My husband worried about Volodya a lot and blamed himself that Belyaev ended up never leaving Dinamo and never had a chance to be a first-choice keeper at any other team. Lev told him, "Volodya, I'm not eternal. I've played already for many years and I could get hurt at any moment. And then who will go in nets?"

But he ended up playing through three generations of national team players. This way of dealing with his colleagues he adopted from Khomich [Alexei Petrovich Khomich, 'the Tiger', his predecessor in the national team], whose reserve he was at Dinamo. Even when Alexei Petrovich became a photographer, he spent a lot of time behind Yashin's goal taking pictures. There are several photos taken by Khomich of Yashin.

⇨ *I read that at the beginning of his career Lev Ivanovich would not only carry Khomich's goalkeeper's bag but also stayed behind his goal and copied his movements...*

I can confirm that he stayed behind his net. At that time at all Soviet stadiums there were special benches behind goals and the reserve goalkeeper would sit not on the general bench but on this one.

⇨ *Was he friends with other great Soviets, the cosmonaut Yury Gargarin, or the poets who wrote about him, Vladimir Vysotsky, Yevgeny Yevtushenko or Robert Rozhdestvensky?*

No. Lev wasn't a Party man. Only German Titov [the second cosmonaut to orbit the earth] was at our home. When Lev was studying at the Supreme Party School, a replacement for Titov studied with him. He got them together and they met in a restaurant. That's how relations were formed.

⇨ *Why did he go to the Supreme Party School?*

There was a big Dinamo fan teaching political economy there. He asked, "What will Lev Ivanovich do after finishing at the Supreme Coaching School?" Yashin never wanted to be a coach; he didn't think that he had the character for that work. Finally Lev graduated from coaching school but went to the Party school as well. He learned a lot there and even became a good public speaker towards the end of his life — which he wasn't before. I remember how he came home from the school and started to use some unexpected philosophical words. Once he came home out of breath. "There was an exam of political economy," he said. "After 70 years they don't know how to adjust the economy, yet they want me to explain in one hour!" We all laughed.

⇨ *Once I talked with Peter Shilton and he told me that he had admired Yashin's black strip. He thought opposing strikers were demoralised by it...*

Actually it was not black but a very dark blue, a woollen jersey with a number 1 sewn on it. I suppose at his time all keepers played in a dark strip. When, in 2000, I accepted the prize for the best goalkeeper of the century on Lev's behalf, Sepp Maier said, "Formerly all keepers were in black so you couldn't have mixed them up with anyone else.

And now they are red, yellow, blue — like parrots!"

✦ *So it wasn't you who told him to play in dark colours?*

No, he always played in them. For 20 years, he changed jerseys maybe two or three times, when the sleeves on them became worn with holes. But then he took new ones that looked the same.

✦ *You said they were woollen. But in summer, isn't it too hot to play in wool?*

But on the other hand, it's not painful. Also, Lev always wore quilted trunks underneath. He would get angry at colleagues who didn't do that. He said, "I'm telling everybody: you cannot play without them! You could easily hurt your thigh, bruises are guaranteed, your muscles will tear. And you'll start to be afraid of falling down. And how can you play in goal if you are afraid?"

✦ *Have you kept his jerseys?*

No, because you had to return all the kit at that time. Even after Lev had played in his farewell game in 1971, Dinamo sent him an order to return the kit and even the gloves which he personally had sewn up when they were torn. We laughed but he really had to collect everything up and return it. He didn't keep a single Dinamo jersey. It was the same story every year: at the end of the season I washed all his kit to return it looking good.

He kept only one jersey, but it was yellow not dark and had the number 13 on it. It was the jersey in which he kept a clean sheet in London for the Rest of the World team in the famous game that the whole

world saw. Nobody wanted to wear 13, but Lev said, "OK, give it to me. I don't care." After that great game he regarded 13 as a lucky number for him.

Why did goalkeepers of that generation play in dark colours? Because pitches, especially in the spring and autumn, were muddy and on a black kit this dirt was not so noticeable. When he brought home his kit, the whole bath became black and filled with sawdust: goalkeepers' boxes were powdered with it, so goalkeepers didn't sink in the slush.

✦ *One other indispensable accessory of goalkeepers at that time was a cap. Is it true that sometimes, coming for a high cross, Yashin could take off his cap, head the ball clear, and put the cap back on?*

Yes, it happened several times, but only when there were no other players around. At that time penalty boxes were not so crowded as they are now. The first time he headed the ball clear, he came to the dressing-room at half-time and hung his head, thinking that [Dinamo's coach Mikhail] Yakushin would criticise him. The coach could be sly and biting. But he was silent. Lev asked, "Is something wrong?" "No, everything is all right. But you have to take off your cap!" That time he had headed the ball with his cap on. Fans liked it a lot and reacted with a storm of cheers. A few more times he headed it without a cap but later he stopped doing that: the game became faster and tougher.

✦ *Is it true that his cap was stolen when the USSR won the European Nations Cup in 1960?*

Yes. The newspapers later wrote that French police found the cap after the game and gave it back to Lev, but it's a lie. It disappeared forever. At that time, security was not well organised. After the USSR team won the final, thousands of people ran onto the pitch at the Parc des Princes. It was real chaos. Some fan in all this mess took the cap from Lev's head and ran away. The crowd was so huge that it was impossible to find him. Lev said that he looked around but couldn't see anybody with the cap.

⇔ *Is it true that Lev Ivanovich suffered from a gastric ulcer all his life?*

Yes. He had it from childhood as a result of poor food during the war, which started when he was 11. When he was just 16 or 17, he was sent to the south — to have treatment in a health resort. Also hard training sessions made it worse, especially as Lev worked like the damned. Throughout his long career he wasn't late for a single session; he was punctual and demanded the same from others. If I kept him before he left, he would drive me mad.

After every training session, he always remained in the goal and asked other players to take a number of shots at him. Once I saw that, I said that I would never watch it again. He took 30 or 40 of the hardest shots to the stomach — I couldn't watch it. It seemed to me that all his abdominal cavity was punched out. Lev, though, told me that his abdominal muscles were very strong and also that he caught the ball with his hands so it didn't touch his stomach. But I saw that it did.

After some win I met Yakushin at the Savoy restaurant. Mikhail Iosifovich called me over and asked, "Did Lev complain about me?" "No. What happened?" "I

suppose he must have been hurt. He said during pre-game training that he felt stomach pain and he couldn't dive, but I urged him to do it once. He stood back up with difficulty and plodded to the dressing-room at a snail's pace. Naturally, the next day in the game he jumped and dived as usual..."

He had stomach aches permanently and finally he died from stomach cancer. Because of the very high levels of acidity he always had in his pocket some household soda in a small paper bag as well as some water when possible. The heartburn was so bad that if he didn't have water with him, he couldn't wait until he was able to dissolve a teaspoon of soda in a cup of water. Sometimes he poured soda from the paper bag into his palm, put it into his mouth and then desperately searched around for something to take it with.

Once I saw a TV documentary about Lev. Lesha Paramonov said a lot of nice things about Yashin. But I was puzzled about one thing. Talking about his stomach ache and the soda, Paramonov made up the fact that in his other pocket Lev always had a bead of cognac. He said that Lev took soda with cognac and then went to training.

⇔ *Are you sure it's a fiction?*

Absolutely. Not only because it's impossible to take soda with cognac but also because Lev didn't like cognac. He drank it only when there wasn't anything else. Also he drank neither wine nor beer — vodka only. Doctors told him to do that because of the ulcer.

Sometimes you hear such fantastic stories... Once I was travelling on the train from a holiday in the south of Russia and there were two important ladies in the same compartment. One of them was high up, almost on the Central Committee of the Communist Party, and the other was from a trade union. For whatever reason they started to talk about football and the first one said, "I was at a reception at the Kremlin and I saw that all these footballers are alcoholics. Yashin had a big glass of vodka in one hand and a big glass of champagne in the other. He drank the first one and washed it down with the second!"

They didn't know who I was and I kept silent, although I wanted very much to speak. Lev never drank champagne. And he never drank full glasses, just small portions. Yes, he could have been drunk, anything can happen. But he was never an alcoholic or he could have never played 20 years at the top level. But when he was drunk, his conduct was always normal. And he had to take vodka with water, otherwise he started coughing. Even while he was fishing, when he would have to take water from the pond, he had to take water with his vodka.

⇨ *What did Lev Ivanovich like to eat? In the interview in the first ever issue of* Football *[a weekly magazine] in 1960, he replied to a question about his favourite meal saying he liked lobster with mayonnaise, which is best cooked in France...*

It was a joke. Not long before the interview the team travelled to Sweden and one of the guys was unhappy about the quality of the restaurant food. He said, "You should give us lobsters with mayonnaise." Lev was furious with him. After coming home, he said, "You

never ate anything better than carrots at home, but abroad you are starting to show off." Actually, he ate everything. He liked porridge which is not too common among men. And he himself cooked pretty well.

⇨ *Was he a reckless driver of his Volga [a Soviet manufactured car introduced in 1956 that tended to indicate high status]?*

No. He was a very good driver. I felt absolutely safe with him. As a European, he always made way for everybody — both other cars and pedestrians. He stopped at zebra crossings. I never learned if he liked driving fast.

⇨ *Yashin was well-known for his friendships with great footballers. How was that possible when he spoke only Russian?*

I was amazed as well. Even abroad he could stop a pedestrian and find out with a few words and gestures how to go somewhere. Footballers have their own words, terms, gestures, facial expressions... Also, Lev's smile attracted everybody. I remember how in 1971, after his farewell match in Moscow, the Italians also decided to organise a game in Milan. So, he was standing and talking with one group of players, then with another. They were laughing, waving hands — and perfectly understood each other.

Lev, along with some of the other players, was sorry that he didn't learn languages, though. I talked many times to Kachalin and Yakushin, telling them they could organise lessons, given how much time they spent hanging around the training grounds. In the first year of our marriage, I counted how many days

Lev spent at home: just 144 out of 365. But nobody listened to my idea.

⇨ *Sir Bobby Charlton said that Yashin helped to establish good relations between people of different countries and political systems.*

Once he arrived somewhere in South America after a military coup. The situation was rather tense; nobody was leaving their houses or hotels. But it was impossible not to have some sort of reception because of Yashin's visit. So, people from both camps came there, because all of them wanted to see Lev and talk to him.

⇨ *I read that the West German defender Karl-Heinz Schnellinger gave Yashin 15 stylish ties for his Dinamo teammates, which Lev himself wouldn't have been able to afford...*

Yes, it's true. There were a lot of decent people among the foreign stars. For example, Franz Beckenbauer came to Moscow after Lev's death and visited his grave. And when we were flying to Barcelona and I didn't know where to go to change flights in Frankfurt airport, he took me right to the gate.

There was a situation in 1992 when I was invited to a ceremony of announcing the world team of the past half-century and Lev was included in it. Vitechka Gusev [a popular Russian sports broadcaster] called me and said, "Valentina Timofeevna, they are waiting for you here. Please, call the Russian Football Union; the invitation and air tickets were sent there." I called Vladimir Radionov [the general secretary of the RFU at the time], he asked somebody and it was

somewhere in the foreign department: they'd forgotten to tell me about it. But the most important thing was that our comrades bought a return ticket for the following day so I couldn't watch the opening ceremony of Euro 1992. So, what did I travel for — just to pick up the prize and go back?

During this ceremony I met the famous German sportswriter Karl-Heinz Heimann who spoke fluent Russian. He knew Yashin very well. I explained the situation to him and Beckenbauer was walking past us right at that moment. Heimann told me, "Wait just a moment." And Franz in a few seconds settled the problem, and I flew back two days later. I was very grateful to him, because the opening ceremony was beautiful.

⇨ *I talked to Beckenbauer and he told me with great warmness how he had dinner with Yashin at your home. With vodka, of course.*

Yes. But Franz himself was drinking Bavarian beer which we'd found in the Moscow International Trade Centre. Gennady Logofet [a former USSR defender] translated for us. Beckenbauer had a great idea for a book and made it happen. He visited everybody with whom he had played in the Rest of the World team; he went to the home of Pelé, Eusébio, Charlton, Yashin and others, and then he described everything that he saw and sent us the copy of his book.

⇨ *Lev Ivanovich introduced you to Pelé in 1958, right?*

Yes, it was in the hotel where they were all staying. This black boy was running by the stairway and Lev grabbed him by the neck. He told me, "Look at this boy. He'll become the greatest footballer in the world soon." Actually, I doubt that Pelé understood what was going on: there was no translator nearby. Later Lev always regarded Pelé as the best ever.

✦ *Was Pelé ever arrogant?*

No, he always behaved properly. Look at this photo: we are celebrating Oleg Salenko winning the golden boot at the 1994 World Cup with Salenko, Pelé and [the senior Russian football bureaucrat Vyachelsav] Koloskov. The King of Football was there in a bow tie and everything felt at least as good as the Academy Awards. When Pelé visited Moscow, I presented him with a big coloured samovar.

✦ *Is it true that in 1962 Yashin wanted to quit football, when he was blamed for the USSR's early exit from the World Cup?*

Yes, he wanted to quit. When he went onto the pitch in Moscow for first time after Chile, the crowd whistled and shouted many bad things... It happened for two or three games. There was no TV in Russia at that time and everyone only knew about the game against Chile only from a report by the only correspondent of APN [the state news agency], who knew much more about politics than about football. Because of his reports, everybody decided that Yashin lost the World Cup.

✦ *But how can you explain this kind of reaction from fans in Moscow to one failure of a great footballer and person, somebody who achieved so much for his country? Where did this aggression come from?*

It happens not only in football. We are the same with everything... If something bad happens, somebody must be blamed. The big bosses wanted to evade punishment and so shifted the blame onto Yashin. For some time he even didn't train. The [Dinamo] coach Alexander Ponomarev supported Lev and told him everything would be fine. He realised what was going on and let us leave Moscow for a while to go fishing. Much later my husband started to train with the reserve team. His first game back with the first team wasn't until close to the middle of the following season.

✦ *English journalists wrote that at the height of the criticism fans left threatening messages on his car and even broke windows in the apartment. Is it true?*

Yes, our windows were broken twice — but I don't know if there is a connection. There was a street lamp under our window. Maybe hooligans threw stones at it and hit the windows. Regarding writing in the dusty on our car — yes, it happened. Unspeakable words about him. I think, though, that media inflamed it and that influenced people.

✦ *The former Dinamo player Vladimir Kesarev said that Yashin disappeared from Dinamo and you let slip where he was fishing and that it was only then the club sent a delegation to bring him back...*

No, no, we went there together with the children and Ponomarev gave him permission. Lev had a good relationship with all his managers. We had great family relations with the Yakushins, Kachalins, and even went to Karlovy Vary [in the Czech Republic] with Ponomarev and visited [the goalkeeper] František Plánička's home...

Lev didn't come back to the first team in Moscow. It happened in Tbilisi. The atmosphere was more sympathetic there. Somebody shouted with a Georgian accent, "Yashin is in the hole!" and everybody laughed. But it was meant so kindly that even he enjoyed it. You couldn't compare it with what was going on in Moscow.

↪ *Yashin's comeback to the national team was also pretty tough. Right up to his brilliance in the Rest of the World team at Wembley, [the manager] Konstantin Beskov didn't pick him...*

Beskov always called him into the squad when they trained at the base at Ozerki. But every time, not only before the games but also before training sessions, the manager told him, "Lev, you rest, rest!" It went on a pretty long time. Even his teammates lowered their eyes; they felt uncomfortable. He was lonely.

Once I came to their training camp by the suburban train. He told me, "I'll probably go back with you now." "Why?" "Beskov won't let me train. I want to work but he keeps saying, 'Rest, rest.' He doesn't say anything offensive, doesn't drop me from the team, but it's obvious he doesn't trust me." He picked [the Georgian goalkeeper Ramaz] Urushadze that time.

I responded, "He said, 'Rest,' so you should do it. You'll train with your club. But you don't have to leave, because if you do that you'll be quitting both the national team and football." At first he refused and said he'd leave with me. I only just put him off.

In 1963, after his comeback, Lev let in only six goals for Dinamo in 27 games. Urushadze was nonetheless ready to play in the away leg of the European Championship game against Italy, but at that moment Yashin was invited to London and played great there... I watched that game at the radio committee where I worked. I had to pick up our daughters, one from the school, one from kindergarten. I was in a hurry and when the game ended I caught a taxi. The driver said, "Did you hear? We won in London." "We didn't win; we lost 2-1!" "Yashin was in nets in the first half when score was 0-0 and I don't care about anything else!" I wanted so much to tell him that he was my husband... But I was too shy for that.

↪ *What did Yashin think of the fact you worked all your life as a radio journalist?*

We were both from working-class families. In our society it was necessary to work. There wasn't even a question about that.

↪ *Did Beskov change his mind after London?*

No, he still wanted to play Urushadze. Nikolay Ozerov [a famous TV journalist] later told us that there were phone calls from 'upstairs'. Beskov was told, "Nobody will understand it if you don't play Yashin after such a performance in London." That persuaded him and Lev saved a penalty kick from [Sandro] Mazzola to earn a draw that qualified us for Euro 64. Yashin got the Ballon d'Or for that year [1963].

↪ *Where is the Ballon d'Or?*

It's in the Museum of Sport at the Luzhniki. I've been wanting to go there and pick it up for a long time.

✦ *Yashin was one of the great symbols of Soviet sports, but he communicated a lot with foreigners. The KGB didn't have a problem with him doing that?*

It wasn't allowed to walk alone when abroad — to prevent provocations. But I can't remember it being prohibited to communicate in the hotels. But there were some other situations. Once Yashin was invited to Brazil for Santos's anniversary celebration. He was going to perform a kick-off with Pelé. But the functionary who received our invitations was afraid of going to his bosses with them. It was impossible for him to imagine that Yashin should go abroad with his wife but without a 'translator'.

✦ **You mean a KGB officer who would control you?**

Yes, without 'a teacher from the physical training school', as they called them. Lev had already retired by that time and I took time off at my own expense. But then we found out that we were not allowed to go. Next day I went in to my work and one spiteful employee laughed at me. But a couple of days later, Lev met one of federation bosses by chance. That official was surprised by the story and helped to issue all the documents rapidly. The problem was that we arrived in Brazil after all the celebrations were over. The local papers wrote, "The Russians were late as usual."

✦ *Did Lev Ivanovich believe in God?*

No. Neither did his parents.

✦ *They were simple working people, right?*

Yes. His father was a turner or a metalworker. His mother worked at the Krasny Bogatyr rubber factory but died from tuberculosis very young — Lyova was about six years old. His sister was a baby and, when his mother was lying in the hospital, she also fell ill and died. Within a year Lev's father married again — a telegraphist from Central Telegraph. They soon had a son, Boris, who is still alive. When the Great Patriotic War started in 1941, their family moved from Moscow to Ulyanovsk [a city on the Volga river]. An aircraft plant was built there and little Lyova worked as well. After the war, this plant was moved to the Moscow district of Tushino and my husband worked there as a teenager.

✦ *I can't imagine that Yashin had many enemies.*

He had a personality such that you had to do something terrible to become his enemy. Even when he didn't like somebody, he just didn't get close to him but still greeted him warmly.

He had some unpleasant moments after the end of his playing career. One of them was with an important official called Nikolay Rusak, who became chairman of the Soviet Sports Committee. Every spring, Soviet football clubs went to the south of the USSR to prepare for the season. Also there was a conference in which all managers, coaches and referees participated. Lev was a team director of Dinamo. One day the head coach Kachalin and his assistant Tsaryov had some urgent business and they asked Lev to take the training session.

Later he told me that the players had been working and he was sitting on the bench and sometimes telling them something. Every spring he had a worsening of his stomach ulcer, so he sat, holding his body to diminish the pain. At that moment this Rusak came over, sat down near Lev and asked why there were no coaches and how the players could prepare by themselves. My husband replied, "I suppose, I understand something about football. Maybe you want me to explain something to you?" As he was speaking, he held himself even more tightly because of the pain.

The next day that conference happened and Rusak spoke. He said that he visited Dinamo. He said there was no head coach, no assistant, only Yashin sitting drunk on the bench and managing the training session. Oh, how furious Lev was! He stood up, went to the microphone and, in spite of all his gentleness said a lot, how some people who didn't understand anything about football were coming to the sport and wanting to govern it. "What did you say now that was useful?" he asked. "What exactly was wrong with the training? You can't say anything!"

The allegation he was drunk was especially insulting for him. Lev wasn't an ascetic but he never drank in the mornings. And he never drank alone. A bottle of vodka at home could have stayed in the fridge for very long time — until some of his friends came over. And nobody saw him drunk in public...

Also Lev was very offended by and said a lot of bad things about General Bogdanov, the chairman of the Central Soviet of Dinamo sports society. In the seventies there was an extremely talented young striker, Anatoly

Kozhemyakin. Lev even said once that he could become better than Pelé. Once Tolya was in the elevator with his friend and it got stuck between floors. There was a hole to climb out, and his friend did. But as soon as Tolya started to do the same, the elevator started moving and the guy was killed. Lev cried...

But after this episode he as well as Kachalin and Tsaryov were dismissed from working with the Dinamo first team for the bad educational work! For what? What was the connection between Yashin and the accident in an elevator? He was moved to the Central Soviet of Dinamo, to do meaningless paperwork. He was thrown away from the team, from doing live work. Lev felt pretty comfortable as a team director. It was his business — to help players away from the pitch, to make them live better. Also he worked with goalkeepers, even though there was no specific profession of goalkeeping coach that time. And he enjoyed all that.

Paperwork was something very alien to him and he had problems with the chairman Bogdanov. Once Bogdanov said to him, "Your work is bad, you are always travelling." "Where do I travel?" "There are tons of invitations from abroad for you on my desk." Lev was at a loss: "You are keeping them. I don't know anything about them and I'm not travelling." Bogdanov even blamed him for the bad performances of the team, even though Lev was no longer team director.

Lev was very upset about it. At 48, right after that conflict, he had his first heart attack. Not a long time ago I learned from another general that Bogdanov recently told him, "I cannot forgive myself for one thing: that I pressured Yashin and treated him this way. I didn't sort out the real problems. I listened to some functionaries..."

⇨ *One of the popular theories was that smoking damaged his health a lot.*

Doctors said that his heart attack was because of smoking and the leg amputation later was also partly caused by smoking. But I don't think so. I heard from some specialists that if a person is smoking for many years, it's very dangerous to stop at an advanced age. He was smoking even when he was a player and coaches allowed him. Of course, he didn't smoke in the dressing-room in everyone's presence, but Yakushin and Kachalin allowed him to go to some back room and smoke a cigarette. He smoked a pack per day, I suppose.

Once there was a Party meeting in the club. Lev was a member of Communist Party and he was criticised by the Party: everybody discussed Yashin's smoking and even made a resolution to prohibit him from doing that! I think only [the writer] Leonid Soloviev stood up and said, "What are we doing? Yashin doesn't have to run; he is a keeper. We know how well he does it so what are the complaints? Not everybody can stop smoking." Finally, the resolution was rejected.

⇨ *Did he try to stop?*

He didn't smoke for about two months after the heart attack. But later he tried again and felt OK. So he went on. Also for the last couple months of his life, when he felt very bad, he didn't smoke. Coming back to the heart attack, it was caused, most of all, by bad feeling, from the fact that he was turned away from the team and that he didn't deserve the attitude towards him. The second reason was that he stopped playing very suddenly. He didn't play for a veterans team so he didn't have a proper physical load. When he was a team director, he was moving at least, training with the goalkeepers. But when he was pushed to office work, he immediately gained about 10kg. And he had a heart attack. A doctor explained later that Lev as a professional athlete had a very large heart and that's why he had to move a lot to keep blood running. But when he stopped moving and started gaining weight, a lot of cholesterol built up in his vessels. The consequence was not only the heart attack but also the amputation of his right leg later.

⇨ *A few days before his death, Yashin became the first Soviet sportsman to be awarded the star order of the Hero of Socialist Labour medal.*

It happened on 15 March 1990, when Lev was still holding out, although he looked awful. He became extremely ill on the 16th and died on the 20th. The order was given thanks to Nikolay Ozerov. He ran from one office to another to persuade functionaries to give Yashin the star of Hero. Ozerov achieved his goal — it's a pity that it came so late. Lev said, "What is it for? I'll not have time to be proud of it." Ozerov wanted Mikhail Gorbachev to deliver it personally to Yashin but Mikhail Sergeevich didn't have enough time...

⇨ *Was Yashin happy?*

He was happy. I saw that. But he never said this aloud.

◈ *What did you think when Zenit fans at a Zenit v Dinamo game erected a banner saying "Yashin went to hell, Dinamo will do the same"?*

I think it wasn't necessary to make so much noise about that because that's exactly what these people want. I cannot understand why one paper [*Sovetsky Sport*] makes a contest out of banners, provoking such things. There was nothing shown on TV from the game but next day in this paper it was displayed in full.

Soon afterwards, before one home game, there was a meeting at which some officials near Yashin's monument at Dinamo stadium expressed their indignity about the incident. I asked [the sports minister Vitaly] Mutko, "Why did the press make all this noise? If nothing had been published, nobody would know anything about it." At first he agreed but after the meeting he said, "Maybe it was not wrong to make it public. Did you see how the people reacted? They're going to the game and bringing flowers, a mountain of them!" Maybe he is right.

◈ *Do you follow today's football?*

Of course. I support Dinamo as well as people from other clubs who had great relations with Lev. I hardly could have imagined that one day I would pray for Spartak success — but when Volodya Fedotov [the former CSKA striker and Beskov's son-in-law] was in charge of Spartak, it happened. The same with Yury Semin when he worked at Lokomotiv.

Also I support all goalkeepers, even when they play against Dinamo. Because I put them in Lyova's place. When they make a

mistake, I get upset as if it had happened to my husband.

I visit Lev's grave at Vagankovo [the famous cemetery where dozens of footballers are buried] often. At first I was there almost every day, trying to stop some crazy ideas. They wanted to turn the cemetery into a museum — they kept talking such rubbish. In 2010 I was touched when two Dinamo keepers, [Vladimir] Gabulov and [Anton] Shunin on a matchday that coincided with Lev's birthday, brought a very nice wreath. Every year there are a lot of people at his grave, although I don't especially invite anyone. Not only Dinamo veterans come, all the rest as well. Right by the graveside, we take a funeral repast, drinking a little for the peace of Lev's soul.

I personally support [the Zenit goalkeeper] Vyacheslav Malafeev since I went to St Petersburg to give him a prize as the best goalkeeper in the Russian championship that season. I was one of the first people who sent him a telegram with condolences [in March 2011 when Malafeev's wife Marina was killed in a car accident]. I'd like to ask journalists: please, support goalkeepers! I felt terrible for [Alexander] Filimonov when he suffered the same harsh criticism as Lev in 1962 [after a terrible mistake in the final minutes of a decisive qualifying game with Ukraine in autumn 1999, which meant Russia failed to qualify for Euro 2000]. Yes, he let in that goal. But why didn't they score more?

My husband told me about his second game for the Dinamo first team. It was against Dinamo Tbilisi, and a 4-1 lead turned into 4-4 just before half-time. He went in at the break sure he'd be kicked out of the team. But Kostya Beskov approached him, clapped on the shoulder and said, "Lev, don't worry. I'll score now." He scored and Dinamo won 5-4. When keepers make mistakes, it's necessary to rescue them, because on a lot of other occasions they rescue you.

A goalkeeper's work is very hard. I worry about Igor Akinfeev: he's great guy, he's playing well, but he started very early. When goalkeepers get into the starting XI very young, there is a danger that they finish before the right time.

I don't like the brutality towards goalkeepers in today's football. Lev broke his finger, twice he had concussion, he got a big scar on his chin but overall players tried to protect each other. Look at this photo: in the World Cup semi-final of 1966 Uwe Seeler is jumping over Lev! When in 2000 there was a ceremony presenting prizes to the best footballers of the century, Seeler approached me with a translator. "I want to be friends with you. I wanted so much to score against Yashin but I wasn't able to do it even a single time. I hoped to do that at least in the farewell game but no way!" I replied that it was an honour for me to be friends with Seeler. We still send each other cards at Christmas, New Year and other holidays.

⟳ *English players and journalists admired Yashin's fair play when in the World Cup semi-final, in the tensest atmosphere, he ran out of his penalty area to help Seeler who had gone down — even though the game hadn't stopped. The whole stadium stood up and started shouting: "Yashin! Yashin!"*

I was at that game but I don't remember the shouting. But I remember how a few days later, in the game for third place, Eusébio scored a penalty kick against him, then approached Lev and said something. Later I asked my husband, "What did he say?" He answered, "Eusébio clapped me on the shoulder and said, 'Sorry, Lev. I had to do that.'"

Eusébio

I met Eusébio in Lisbon and at first we chatted about recent events: Russia had played against Portugal not long before and Spartak Moscow were playing away to Benfica the following evening. But suddenly Eusébio changed topic and his voice became much louder and more passionate.

"I feel a lot of sympathy for [Russian] football," he said, "and this feeling has a specific cause.

When you write a story about me, please don't forget to mention the level of warmth I feel when I remember my friendship with Lev Yashin. I think about him pretty often, more and more coming to the conclusion that I as a footballer was formed thanks to him. When you're able to score against the greatest goalkeeper in the history of world football, you remember it for your whole life. You realise that you can score against anyone. Every time when I come to Russia, I meet Valentina, Lev's widow. Every time when I come to Russia, I make sure I go to his grave. It's a great honour for me that I knew him in person and was his friend."

I asked how Yashin was able to make friends with so many players when he spoke no language other than Russian. "We spoke the same language," Eusébio said, "the language of football. Here is a ball. [He embraces an imaginary football.] Thanks to it we understood each other to such an extent that we didn't need anything else. I remember how the Soviet and Portuguese national teams played for third place at the World Cup in 1966. We had a penalty kick in our favour. So, Lev asked me with a gesture, 'Where are you going to kick the ball?' And I showed him: in this corner to your right.

"I did that because he was my friend. And it's a double honour to score a penalty having shown the keeper where you will put the ball. It's not cheating. Mário Coluna was the captain of our team that time, and he approached me, 'What are you doing? This is Yashin, he'll save the ball!' I replied, 'No, he'll not get it, although I'll shoot into the corner that I told him.' So, I hit the ball with such power that the ball only touched his gloves.

"I scored and was happy, of course. But my friend was upset, and immediately after the goal I approached him and told him in Portuguese, 'We are friends, but you are a keeper and I am a striker. My job is to score, your job is defend the goal. Lev, I had to do that. I had to.' And I saw that he understood everything.

"I've had a lot of different presents from Russia. But the most valuable of all was a fur jacket Lev Yashin used to wear which his widow once gave me. I still keep it. I've never had a better gift. This jacket touched me in the heart."

I'd read that in 2004, when Portugal beat England on penalties in the European Championship quarter-final, Eusébio had quoted some words of Yashin to the goalkeeper Ricardo, telling him to stay in position to the final second and to stare into the eyes of his opponent. "I really said that to Ricardo," Eusébio confirmed, "and told him that was how Yashin did it. He followed the recommendation and that's how Portugal won.

"Yashin was not only a goalkeeper, he was a master in the goal. And he was also a great gentleman. It was because he was so respectful towards opponents that he had so many friends. His name is written with a golden letters in the history of Fifa, Uefa and football in general, and Yashin will always be the number one goalkeeper in the world." Ⓑ

Yashin in action for Dinamo Moscow

Yashin and Igor Netto (right) return to Moscow after winning the 1960 European Championship

Yashin relaxes on the river

Pictures from the Yashin family archive

Yashin and Pele

Yashin passing on tips to Dmitry Kharin

Pictures from the Yashin family archive

CLASSIC FOOTBALL SHIRTS.CO.UK

THE MOST EXTENSIVE RANGE OF ORIGINAL SHIRTS ONLINE

HUGE CLEARANCE SECTION FULL OF 1000's OF BARGAIN ITEMS

ETAFE	FC YOUNG BOYS	LYON TECHFIT	MARSEILLE TECHFIT	VALENCIA
.11.99	£19.99	£34.99	£22.99	£19.99

CROUCH	NAPOLI CAVANI	NAPOLI HAMSIK	SHORTS, SOCKS, BAGS, JACKETS ETC.
.99	£49.99	£44.99	

130

Polemics

"Football is like strong beer. Some
people just can't take it."

Partisans and Purists

Do fans experience football differently to those who watch without a vested interest?

By Charlie Robinson

After watching a derby between Nottingham Forest and Notts County in 1934, the novelist and playwright JB Priestley observed, among other things and with no little distain, "the monstrous partisanship of the crowds, with their idiotic cries of 'Play the game, ref!' when any decision against their side has been given." To an outside observer, the supposed tribalism of football crowds appears irrational and base. The word tribalism itself carries strong pejorative connotations, a primitive bestiality and a blind obedience to the group. Such partisans are the very antithesis of the purist, an altogether rarer breed. The purist is the embodiment of the rational and unbiased football supporter, a fan of football itself, able to enjoy a heightened aesthetic experience because untainted by the irrational biases of tribal support.

But then that's the average football spectator for you — blind, irrational, partisan. However, despite his disparaging initial remarks, Priestley goes on to say that partisans are "not mere spectators in the sense of being idle and indifferent lookers on; though only vicariously, yet they run and leap and struggle and sweat, are driven into despair, and raised to triumph; and there is thrust into their lives of monotonous tasks and grey streets an epic hour of colour and strife that is no more a mere matter of other men's boots and a leather ball, than a violin concerto is a mere matter of some other man's cat gut and rosin." To enjoy the festival of the crowd, almost a conscious organism in its own right, is part of the aesthetic enjoyment of any sporting event — to lose oneself in the heaving, swaying, singing, braying mass. The psychological benefits of partisanship extend even further, to feelings of identification with the local area, civic pride, and comradeship.

The apparent and supposed superiority of the partisan is emphasised by the philosopher Nicholas Dixon. In a paper entitled "The Ethics of Supporting Sports Teams"[1] he argues that the partisan not only enjoys the psychological benefits associated with offering unconditional support to the local team, but also has an ethical advantage, in that her commitment and passion is more virtuous. He says, for example, that she exhibits "the great virtue of steadfast allegiance to her team even if its fortunes decline." Most 'genuine' football

[1] *Journal of Applied Philosophy, Volume 18 (2001), Issue 2, pages 149–158*

supporters will, of course, display this virtue: if you cut me, I'll bleed black and white; we'll support you ever more.

Dixon thinks the same thing happens when one is in love. At the beginning of a romantic relationship, we come to love our partner's good qualities, but over time we develop something deeper, namely a love of their "unique instantiation of those qualities", their special identity. Furthermore, when some new potential partner comes into our lives, as they often do, we are reluctant simply to 'trade up', even if the new prospective mate scores higher on, or better instantiates, those valuable qualities. Love can also endure change. A partner may lose the qualities to which we were initially attracted, but we stay in love regardless. Despite the changes, there is a constant nucleus that remains the object of our love. In much the same way, I don't change my team with each new defeat — if I did, I'd literally be supporting a new club almost every other week.

Dixon goes even further, suggesting that the partisan displays a side to their character lacking in the purist — the tendency to form bonds with others, especially those with whom we are familiar. Drawing an analogy with the ability to form friendships and lasting romantic attachments, the purist "displays a character flaw that would be condemned from a standpoint of virtue ethics." Quite a claim! But what of the purist? Why is she normally regarded, as Dixon suggests, as lacking commitment, as barely qualifying as a fan at all?

The purist, we might say, is prepared to trade up at any given opportunity. Her support is based purely on their love of the game and is prepared to follow whichever team best exemplifies the virtues and admirable qualities most prized: fairness, excitement, skill and style. In a sense, as Dixon points out, the purist has the moral high ground here, as her choice is based on purely sporting excellence, rather than the arbitrariness of place of birth. If we want to teach our children the value of fairness, at least partly through the games that they play with each other, why should we also give them the strong impression that they should stick with their team even when they cheat and connive, privileging a win-at-all-costs mentality? "Rather than being a genuine fan, the purist approaches each game as a neutral, hoping that his team will continue its excellent play, so that he will be able to continue supporting it."

Of course, the loyal support of the partisan can itself be dangerous, or just plain stupid. Why would I continue to love a partner who continues to abuse and betray me? Asking for me to give them fifty quid every week? Travelling hundreds of miles every other week just to see them for a couple of hours? That really is the limit. Unconditionally to give our love and support to another becomes masochistic if the significant other is genuinely not worthy of it. Perhaps the partisan could do with learning a little from the purist, as some Liverpool and Chelsea fans, in the face of recent controversial incidents, have been unable to do. Therefore, something that could be called 'moderate partisanship' would be the best option: I'll give my whole and undivided support to my team, but there's a limit.

A more robust defence of the purist can be made, however. Stephen Mumford, like Dixon, a philosopher, actively privileges and praises the virtues of the true purist, arguing that the issue turns to a large extent on the respective aesthetic experiences enjoyed by our two different types of supporter. But how and why do different types of supporter have different aesthetic experiences? Obviously, a partisan may enjoy the game less if her team loses, trudging home disconsolately and awaiting the barbs of colleagues on Monday morning, while the purist enjoys the spectacle even if their adopted team loses, shrugs their shoulders and flicks the channel to see if Barcelona are playing. But the differences, according to Mumford, go even deeper than that, as we'll see after a brief journey through Schopenhauer.

Arthur Schopenhauer, the German philosopher, placed an extreme amount of importance on the enjoyment of aesthetic experiences. In *The World as Will and Representation*, he argues that the world is indifferent to human suffering — and suffer we do. Human existence, Schopenhauer says, has no intrinsic meaning or value, and is characterised by suffering, pain, and misery. This is because humans are animals that have will and desire: we have desires (and needs) that we seek to satisfy, and our will drives us on to do so. Unfortunately, as soon as one desire or need is satisfied, another arises, making our lives a continual succession of new desires in need of satisfaction that ends only in death. In fact, happiness may be defined in purely negative terms, as the temporary absence of pain.

Fortunately, we have three choices open to us. Firstly, suicide. Those of us unwilling or unable to end our own lives can consider the second option, that of pursuing an ascetic lifestyle, the denial of the will-to-live, by which we renounce our desires. Sadly, Sky Sports packages are not widely available to the residents of caves half-way up isolated mountains, so the third of Schopenhauer's options might be more viable: we can temporarily remove ourselves from the constant striving and misery of everyday life through art and through the aesthetic experiences that attend our genuine appreciation of it.

Some types of art, however, are superior to others, or at least lend themselves to a superior aesthetic experience. Starting at the bottom of the art form league table, but not yet cut adrift from those above them, is architecture, followed by landscape gardening, sculpture and painting, and poetry. But running away with it at the top of the table is music. The reason for the hierarchical ordering is that Schopenhauer believes that the different types of art allow us better access to the Platonic Forms, or Ideas, the 'in-itself' of the world. The problem with art, excepting music, is that it is still connected to the will and to the striving of everyday life. We cannot experience art (again, excepting music) without understanding it through the prism of our needs and interests, thus distorting it and lending it a subjective bias. But music is different: music releases us from the endless striving and suffering and desiring of life.

Schopenhauer describes it as follows: "When an external cause or inward disposition suddenly raises us out of the endless stream of willing, and snatches knowledge from the thralldom of the will, the attention is now no longer directed to the motives of willing, but comprehends things free from their relation to the will. Thus it considers things without interest, without subjectivity, purely objectively... Then all at once the peace, always sought but always escaping us on that first path of willing, comes to us of its own accord, and all is well with us... For that moment we are delivered from the miserable pressure of the will."

In this sense, the having of a genuine aesthetic experience demands a kind of disinterestedness, a denial of the will and all it strives for. Usually, we see the world around us in the self-interested context of how specific aspects of it might be utilised or manipulated to help us satisfy our desires. But through the aesthetic experience of music, we become detached from ourselves and from the pressures placed on us by our desires and needs, and can enjoy it objectively, for its own sake.

This is beginning to sound rather like our purist, the rational and unprejudiced football fan who supports her team, or teams, for the virtuous qualities it embodies, and Mumford reinforces this impression through his defence of the purist. Just as the quality of our aesthetic experience of art depends on our ability to become detached from our desires, so too does our aesthetic experience of sport. So whereas Dixon sees the purist's flexible and conditional support as a drawback, to the extent that he suggests purists are not genuine supporters, Mumford sees it as a positive benefit, allowing her to enjoy a heightened and authentic aesthetic experience.

The purist, Mumford argues, perceives the game differently to the partisan, the latter having what he refers to as a 'competitive perception'. Reporting on a match he saw between Hearts and Celtic in 1996, Mumford recognises that our desire to see our team win at all costs distorts our perception of the game. Sitting with the Hearts fans, he observes them calling vociferously for corners, free-kicks, and even throw-ins for their team when it was clear that the ball was Celtic's: "In their perception, the ball really did seem to have come off a Celtic player before leaving the field... Were they being disingenuous? Could this really be two different and honest perceptions? I decided it could be."

This leads Mumford to suggest that purists and partisans simply perceive the game differently to each other. Drawing on the thesis of the theory-dependence of observation, he says that "one's beliefs and desires can determine what one sees." Again, this reminds us of Schopenhauer's idea that it's possible to avoid the distorting effects of the will in our aesthetic experience of art. (This is a good reason to demand that referees are neutral.)

But if the purist and the partisan just see the game differently, then on what basis are we allowed to suppose that one interpretation is better than the other? The implication must be that the purist sees the game more objectively, for the simple reason that they lack the unconditional loyalty and passion that might otherwise distort their perception, blinding them to the objective reality of what's in front of them.

This point can be taken even further, for if Dixon supposes that the purist is someone who supports a team for the qualities they embody, then Mumford supposes that the more genuine purist is one who supports no team at all. For the most authentic aesthetic experience, to see the game "for all its beauty and drama", the purist must not have any investment in any one particular team. Thus, they have no interest in where the beauty and the drama come from, only that they can experience it, and without experiencing it through the distorting prism of partisanship. In this way, the true purist doesn't switch allegiance from one game to the next, depending on which team is the fairest or who plays the most attractive and exciting football, for she has no allegiance in the first place (although it might be said that some teams display certain virtues on a more continual basis, allowing Mumford's purist to develop some degree of allegiance).

If this is indeed the case (and I do not think that it is), then the analogy drawn earlier, between supporting a football team and one's love for a partner, is misplaced, or at least the wrong inference is drawn. Mumford agrees, and develops the following analogy: "The purist is more in the position of a parent with a number of children... The parent wants to see all their children do well in life and realise their full potential. They do not choose a favourite among their children and hope for them to do better than their siblings."

In that case, it would be a mistake to think that the partisan is more passionate about the game — it's simply more likely that the passion of the purist is less conspicuous. Invoking John Stuart Mill's distinction between higher and lower pleasures, Mumford says that the purist enjoys the game in a deeper and more satisfying way. They can, for instance, focus more on "the style of play, the tactics, the movement of the ball, rapidity, grace, economy, incisiveness, and so on." To be concerned with the identity of the winner or the final score is "a crude measure of the worth of a game".

A number of objections could be raised at this point. Firstly, why the sharp distinction between partisans and purists? Isn't the dividing line drawn by both Dixon and Mumford artificial and arbitrary? I think so, for the reason that the distinction fails to capture the actual lived experience of many football fans. My evidence here might be considered anecdotal and personal, but I think valid generalisations can be made.

Now, I would count myself as a partisan — I am elated and relieved when my team wins and sometimes depressed when they lose; a grey cloud of misery often hangs over me until the painful memory has faded somewhat. But that does not automatically exclude my having purist, and often sheer puritanical, feelings towards the game itself and even towards my own team. I don't exactly expect my team's players to endorse and then follow a strict moral code derived in the Kantian manner, but I would be ashamed if any of them scored or won a game by cheating. I like to think that I can appreciate the good performances of teams other than my own, even when they beat us. Despite being a partisan, I can also enjoy the finer side of the game, taking an interest in tactics, watching matches from a range of European leagues, and reading the Swiss Ramble blog. And through it all, I remain more than partial to my team, and can't envision a time that I don't support them unconditionally, even though they often depress me and occasionally disgust me.

If this is the case for other football fans, and I think that it is, then the distinction between the purist and the partisan begins to break down. As ever, the truth lies somewhere in between. Making analytical distinctions is a favourite pastime of philosophers, parcelling and packaging the world into discrete and distinct entities that may or may not reflect the lived experiences of those to whom they're relevant. Experience shows us that these distinctions can be broken down, deconstructed, multiplied and subverted and are therefore at best meaningless, and at worst dangerous.

Furthermore, and here's the second objection, the main part of Mumford's argument is based on the theory that the purist actually has a superior or more genuine aesthetic experience, which obviously raises the question: can we enjoy meaningful aesthetic experiences from watching sport at all? Can sport be said to be an art? We can obviously say that sport can be the subject of art, as Lowry's wonderful "Going to the Match" demonstrates on its own. Douglas Gordon and Phillipe Parreno's film/art installation, *Zidane: A 21st Century Portrait*, is also, ostensibly, a work of art, and yet it blurs the line: can Zidane's performance against Villarreal, upon which the film remorselessly focuses, itself be considered art? My temptation is to say yes, as it embodies the grace, elegance, poise, and balance that Mumford thinks are key aesthetic sporting qualities. It also embodies the striving, determination, and occasional brutality of football (Zidane is sent off

for violent conduct towards the end of the match).

Linguistically speaking, at the pragmatic everyday level of language-use, we naturally attribute aesthetic qualities to sport — "that was a beautiful goal", "Xavi's pass was a work of art", etc. Certainly many football players and managers have been obsessed by the supposed superiority of the aesthetic approach, privileging 'attractive' football over the win-at-all-costs mentality, a feature of football brought out nicely by the famous and oft-mentioned enmity between César Luis Menotti and Carlos Bilardo, the aesthete and philosopher versus the arch-pragmatist.

Intuitively, most football supporters understand this, even if they don't necessarily go along with it. We may, for instance, disagree on the exact source of aesthetic enjoyment. After all, we might get just as much enjoyment from watching a valiant backs-against-the-wall 0-0 game, especially if one of the teams is demonstrably inferior to the other, as we do from a 4-3 thriller characterised by awful and comical defending. The increase in the number of Premier League goals per game over the last few years might be cause for celebration for some, but bad news for fans of sophisticated defenders and defending. It depends where we find the beauty of football and that might be at least partly subjective.

But is the aesthetic dimension of football an essential aspect of the game? Again, it depends where you stand. Peter Arnold, among others, makes a distinction between purposive and aesthetic sports. Arnold defines purposive sports, such as football, in the following way: "The aesthetic is not intrinsic to their purpose, which is to win by scoring the most goals, tries, baskets, points or runs." Therefore, there's no requirement, legally or morally, to bring aesthetic qualities to the performance. Aesthetic sports, on the other hand, are obviously based, to a large degree, on the aesthetic aspects of the performance: there is a "concern for the way or manner in which they are performed." The awarding of points in sports such as gymnastics and diving (I'm going to avoid the obvious Luis Suárez/Gareth Bale joke here) qualitatively focuses on relevant aesthetic qualities.

Here's an excerpt from an expert's summary of Ludmilla Tourischeva's gold medal-winning floor exercise at the 1972 Munich Olympics, quoted by Arnold in an article entitled "Sport: The Aesthetic and Art": "Of qualities of form, she displayed poise, controlled balance, cleanness of line, and each in turn — an arched, curled, twisted and extended torso; her long supple limbs described sinuous and circular movements and her shapely flexible fingers made florid gestures in space. Her footwork had a precision at times forceful and firm and yet again dainty with impeccably shaped and patterned placings."

On this theme, Mumford acknowledges the "aesthetic pluralism" of sport, meaning that different aesthetic categories apply to different sports: speed, strength, grace and so on. Furthermore, most sports, and football is a perfect example, provide spectators with a further aesthetic dimension — the unfolding of a drama as the teams battle for a limited resource, namely victory or first place. Some sports,

however, cannot provide such drama — quantitative sports, such as long jump and running, rely on measurements (of time and distance) to determine the winner, while qualitative sports, such as figure skating, rely on the application of aesthetic criteria. According to Mumford, the drama of such sports "tends to be less regular and is not what the nature of these sports is all about." Sports in which teams are in head-to-head competition, on the other hand, optimise the potential for sporting drama.

Nonetheless, the main point is that, despite the enjoyment of observing the unfolding drama of a football match, aesthetic qualities are not necessarily inherent to football, even though they may be highly desirable. Footballers can succeed if they are slow, weak, fat, graceless, and so on, although they're clearly more likely to be more successful if they possess none of those qualities. We can, it seems, say that some players are better than others, depending on the criteria we choose to apply, suggesting that the principle of aesthetic pluralism holds within football as well as without. The question is whether any specific criteria are objectively more significant than others, in this case because they add to the aesthetic experience of spectators — technique, flair, vision, and so on. In other words, and drawing on the insights of lazy football analysts, the kinds of qualities attributable to, say, Barcelona's *tiki-taka* merchants, but not to, say, the Stoke City bruisers. Of course, Barcelona are superior to Stoke because they're simply more successful, but is it possible, or even appropriate, to say that they're superior because they're more aesthetically pleasing?

The extent to which the appreciation of such qualities is objective, or whether they can be applied only subjectively, is moot. Many of the defining philosophers of the Enlightenment, and especially David Hume, argue that there is something more at play than a purely subjective choice when deciding which aesthetic criteria are more significant.

Despite the fact that we all have a feeling or a sentiment towards an object offered up for our aesthetic judgement, there are, Hume argues, "standards of taste". The general appreciation of a work of art over a long period of time is one standard, as evinced by the continued affection of football fans for the Ajax and Netherlands sides of the 1970s, to give but two examples. Another standard is given by paying attention to the opinions of those with refined and delicate sensibilities, such as critics and experts. Of the current crop of the best football teams in the world, which ones will be remembered, and which will be fondly remembered? That's a question perhaps best left open.

Many will resist Hume's conclusion that there are standards of taste that go beyond subjective preferences. We find our enjoyment where we can, and if that means celebrating the ugly goal that wins our team the cup, then so be it. If my team avoids relegation by playing defensive and aggressive football, then what's to be done? There's no point in going down in a blaze of glory after a season chock full of high-scoring defeats. After all, winning friends is easy, winning points less so.

How far are we prepared to push this argument? At some point, aesthetic criteria shade into moral criteria: it's an obvious example, but was Luis Suárez right deliberately to handle the ball and prevent a goal in the World Cup quarter-final against Ghana? Would you praise or blame your player for taking a dive to win a last-minute penalty? Perhaps ambivalence is the most appropriate response to both situations, as it would be if through some unfortunate sequence of events we suddenly found our team gaining promotion under the management of John Beck. I guess I'll just have to put up with the stiff neck, like it or lump it, if that's the price of success. Ⓑ

The Lager of Life

Football is haunted by violence, but can it be blamed for it?

By Tim Vickery

I remain extremely happy to have been born on the same day that Muhammad Ali fought for the first time under the name he chose (the rematch against Sonny Liston which he won with a first-round knockout, if you're interested). But I can't feel the same way about boxing as I once did.

True, the sport has a beautiful purity. In the words of a friend who can still find it in his heart to love the noble art, it is the sport to which all other sports refer. I accept this, but still I shudder. With age comes a greater realisation of human frailty. Those punches dished out by men trained to a peak of destructive perfection — they have consequences.

Of course, we all struggle these days with the basic objective of boxing — to incapacitate the opponent. And we also live in a far softer age than just a few decades ago. This applies to other sports. From a contemporary perspective it is hard to watch the bombardment that Michael Holding gave a 40-plus Brian Close when the West Indies played England in a 1976 Test Match. With precious little protection, Close ended up covered in bruises as he doggedly got behind the line of the ball — more like a missile in the hands of Holding — and attempted to show, with ever decreasing success, that the impact had not hurt him. Every ball could have done him serious harm. How on earth did we ever consider this to be a healthy activity? More than a Test Match, with today's eyes it looks like a test of sanity, which we all were failing.

And yet I watched at the time with barely a qualm. But it was boxing that took me past the tipping point. Little more than 20 years ago I was at White Hart Lane for the second fight between Chris Eubank and Michael Watson, the one which ended Watson's career and came very close to ending his life.

It was a slow burner. Of much of the fight, I can recall little. Eubank had won a controversial points decision in their first meeting. Watson claimed that he had been robbed, but his change of approach in the rematch made it clear that deep down he felt differently. This time he went to work with an added intensity, giving Eubank no breathing space and building up a big lead.

The end is ingrained in my mind, as if it took place in slow motion. Eubank, in the penultimate round, seemed on the verge of defeat when he caught Watson with a devastating uppercut. Watson was out on his feet when the bell rung — he was still out when it sounded again to announce the start of the final round.

From my seat, admittedly some way back, it seemed clear that he should never have been allowed to carry on the fight. His corner, though, were caught up in the emotion of the occasion. Their man was three minutes away from a famous victory. They sent him out. But Watson was already so incapacitated that he appeared unable to carry out the last round ritual of touching gloves with his opponent. The referee, anxious to give him every chance, helped out, grabbing Watson's arm and pulling it towards Eubank's. "Why is this still going on?" I asked myself as Eubank steeled himself for the assault that would cause the referee, surely belatedly, to call a halt. The last image I have in my mind from the ring is that of one of Watson's cornermen, pathetically and absurdly, yelling at the referee in protest at the decision to stop the fight.

Later that night, as I left the ground and wandered up the High Road, I felt confused by my own emotions. There was elation in the mix — I had attended a big sports event, followed all over the nation, which had undoubtedly been dramatic and exciting. But it was already apparent that something was seriously wrong with Michael Watson, and I could not help feeling guilty that his suffering had served as my entertainment. It is a feeling I have never completely shaken off.

What had really disturbed me, though, was the behaviour of the crowd. I am unlikely to forget the piercing noise and the frenetic, excited movement that accompanied the last couple of minutes of Michael Watson's able bodied existence. Ugly, feature-twisting emotion had taken over the collective mind of White Hart Lane, even warping

the judgement of some of those paid to keep a cool head in such circumstances. I remember one figure, an ex-boxer of some renown, slipping away into the night soon after the fight. He had seen enough to know what was at stake up there in the ring. His quiet dignity contrasted with the vein-bulging, adrenalin filled pandemonium that was hissing, squawking and screaming all around — that we have all seen, and maybe been part of, in some football stadium.

"Football," says the Liverpool-based academic Rogan Taylor, "is like strong beer. Some people just can't take it." It is one of the wisest quotes on the game that I know. Our sport, of course, does not have the physical incapacitation of the opponent as an objective — though I have to confess that head injuries are making me increasingly squeamish. But in comparison with boxing it has a greater power of representation — in part because it is a team game, but also as a result of an intense internal contradiction between its simplicity and its complexity. The former means that, with low barriers to entry, almost anyone can join in. The latter means that how you join in says so much about who you are; a player on the ball has so many options available to him that it follows that the choices he makes are in some way culturally formed. Get the ball forward quickly using pace and power, or take the scenic route before suddenly striking, using surprise and deception as a weapon. No other game contains such a variety of movements.

As you live, think and dream, so you express yourself on the football field. And so those who watch feel themselves being expressed, as individuals, and in those moments when a surge of emotion makes a crowd react as one, collectively as well.

Here lies the problem with Rogan Taylor's observation. When a mass of people are overdoing the strong beer all at the same time, their collective intoxication is more like a poisoning of the mind, the hysteria that fascism seeks to generate and feed off. And it can take effect with alarming speed. Some of those at Heysel in 1985 talk of a friendly atmosphere on a lovely spring evening suddenly descending into an inferno. I recall being at a derby in Cali, Colombia, which seemed to be a relatively good-natured affair until one police action turned the stands into a riot zone, with the game halted and disorder reigning for hours afterwards in the streets around the stadium. Or, more than a decade ago, going to the Maracanã by bus to see a Vasco da Gama-Flamengo game, Rio's most potent local rivalry. As we approached the stadium a gun battle was raging — it may have been between rival groups of fans, it might have been the police firing into the air in a bid to control the crowd. No one was keen to put their head up long enough to find out. Everyone was on the floor of the bus, children wailing and old people shaking with fear.

Ah, local derbies. So often the atmosphere they generate is referred to with a blithe smile. To my mind they can often be the most over-rated games in football, almost guaranteed to generate more heat than light, fuelled by demented anger. Being in a big derby crowd can sometimes be like experiencing a 90-minute version of Orwell's Three-Minute Hate. Am I the only one troubled by this? Apparently not. "Stand up if you hate Arsenal," goes the inevitable Tottenham terrace song. Hunter Davies and an elderly fan nearby stayed in their seats. "I'm too old to hate," said Davies. "I'm too old to stand," replied his acquaintance.

Am I too feckless to walk away? I watched the 1985 European Cup Final, stayed with it all the way to the end, perturbed, of course, by the scenes from the stadium, but still curious to see whether Liverpool or Juventus would come out on top. It didn't feel quite right at the time, and it feels worse in hindsight. But I was not the only one. I'm haunted by an image in my mind, a tale recounted on a TV documentary by someone who was on duty at the Heysel stadium that night. He recalls seeing an Italian fan, who had lost his shoes in the deadly crush and whose clothes were covered in dust. But now the match had started this fan was cheering on his side, totally caught up in the emotion of the game. Football is powerful stuff.

For years I carried all of these thoughts in my head, but they were locked away in a guilty little corner, seldom visited. Therapy came from an unlikely source.

Towards the end of last year I had the opportunity to interview Paul Breitner, West Germany's star left-back and midfielder from the 1970s and 80s. His reaction to my opening question did not bode well — I recalled that he had been known for taking political positions as a player, and asked whether he thought this type of stance was missing in today's players. I made no reference to Chairman Mao, but even so he was exasperated at having to fend off an enquiry that touched on the folly of his youthful idealism. Once that was out of the way, though, he was an excellent interviewee, forthright and intelligent. There was one point he was very keen to make: whether it was racism in stadiums or young players unwilling to accept responsibility, his piercing blue eyes flashed and he pointed out that these were not problems of football — they were problems of society that were manifesting themselves in football.

It is a simple observation but a brilliant one. Football matters, and so we tend to load more on the game than it can realistically carry. It had been foolish of me to blame football, even in a little corner of my mind, for the dangerous passions it can unleash. The fault lies not with football. Perhaps, in this case, the idea that society is to blame does not go far enough. It is more fundamental than that. It is a problem of the human being.

Turning against football on these grounds would be like hating democracy because people voted for Thatcher. Give the human being the chance to express himself and the outcome will not always be pleasant. Far better that the ugly side of humanity get an airing at a football match than at a public hanging, or even a boxing bout.

Because football carries within it so much that is positive. One of the driving forces behind boxing success is narcissistic individualism. In football the glory always has to be shared. The far right can make a fetish of competition, but human progress has almost invariably been the result of co-operation. Football teaches us the dynamic between these two forces. The best way to compete is to co-operate — a lesson well worth learning, even if it comes at a price. Ⓑ

143

Past Glories

"Perhaps that's why the myths endure, because the story of the upstart challenging
the grandees and crushed for its temerity
has a universal romantic appeal."

The Nearly Men

Zimbabwe's nostalgia for the Dream Team of Bruce Grobbelaar and the Ndlovu brothers

By Ian Hawkey

In Zimbabwe, a traveller usually knows clearly where she or he is. The pentagon of highways that vein the country is meticulously pegged, kilometre by kilometre. Across Zimbabwe's sparsely populated rural space, a driver appreciates the landmarks.

In the very early hours of 16 December 2012 a BMW X5 was approaching the 471km peg on the Bulawayo to Victoria Falls road when its driver lost control of the vehicle at a curve. A tyre had burst. The vehicle veered off the tarmac, crashed through trees, and shuddered to a standstill leaning on its right side, a mangled wreck. The noise of the collision woke people from the settlement of Lupinyu and drew them to the scene. They found one passenger, Nomqele Tshili, a 24-year-old woman, already dead. The two men in the car were rushed to Victoria Falls hospital in a critical condition. In the dark, and bloodied from head injuries, they had not been recognised as two of Zimbabwe's most celebrated citizens.

The number plate, NUDDY23 GP, told them only that the vehicle was South African. In Coventry or Birmingham or Huddersfield, the personalised 'Nuddy' on the plate might have prompted readier recognition. It is the nickname that Peter Ndlovu, who had been driving, acquired when he moved to England at the beginning of the 1990. It stuck with him through a 13-year career in the Premier League and Championship. At home in Zimbabwe, he was seldom called 'Nuddy'; rather, he was known to team-mates as 'Zonga'.

The other man in the car, Peter's older brother Adam 'Adamski' Ndlovu, died later that Sunday in hospital, aged 42. The Ndlovus had been on their way to Victoria Falls to play in a friendly match for the Highlanders Legends — a gathering of retired players from the principal club of Matabeleland, the region they both come from — against a local XI. It was to have been a day of nostalgia.

In the obituaries for Adam Ndlovu, there would be far more. It is 20 years since Zimbabwe's most famous sporting brothers — a step ahead of the cricketing Flowers, or the tennis-playing Blacks — were spearheading what is now looked on as the nation's finest era in its most popular sport. Mention the 'Dream Team' in Zimbabwe and you shorthand the young Ndlovus up front, a rugged back four and one of football's most charismatic goalkeepers. The Dream Team have an almost folkloric status, although they would fall just short of realising the aspirations they sustained over 15 months, of reaching a World Cup.

The tag Dream Team would first be hung on them during the southern hemisphere winter of 1992, a sobriquet borrowed from the US basketball team at the Barcelona Olympics, an assembly of NBA superstars plunged into a Games that had just discarded the pretence of amateurism. Zimbabwe's football had a sense that it too might draw on an unprecedented expertise from one of the sport's most glamorous professional structures: the English league. From the vantage point of today's Premier League, in which almost every team has at least one African in its line-up, it seems remarkable that in 1992, when the Premier League began, the two established African stars of the top-flight of English football were both Zimbabwean.

Peter Ndlovu, quick, surprisingly sturdy in possession and an awkwardly nimble opponent for many English centre-halves, had been spotted by Coventry City when they toured Zimbabwe as part of pre-season training. Bruce Grobbelaar's route to the dominant English club of that era, Liverpool, from his beginnings at the same Highlanders club as Ndlovu later joined, had been more circuitous, via South Africa and Canada in the late 1970s. His relationship with his national team was complicated, and resolving it would provide an element of suspense in the prelude to the Dream Team's adventure.

In the summer of 1992, Grobbelaar was at a club career crossroads. After a decade of mostly unchallenged ownership of the number one jersey at what had been England's number one club — a period of six league titles, a European Cup and half a dozen winners medals from the major domestic Cups

— Grobbelaar was told his Anfield status was threatened. Liverpool had just expensively recruited David James. And on the very weekend the new Premier League was to kick off, he was offered an alternative to sitting on the bench understudying James. Prem or Zim? For the first time after several years of absence from international football, the maverick Grobbelaar answered a call-up from his national team with an enthusiastic "Yes."

Grobbelaar flew out of Merseyside on the Thursday night, three days ahead of the opening match of the 1994 Africa Cup of Nations qualifiers. He passed through customs at Harare airport using the British passport he had obtained in the early 1980s, by virtue, in common with many of the small but significant minority of white Zimbabweans, of some British ancestry somewhere in the boughs of his family tree. But here was the rub. Grobbelaar had not played for his country for a decade — partly because of a law passed by the government of Robert Mugabe which forbade its citizens from holding both a Zimbabwean passport and a British one. Mugabe's transformation of what had been Rhodesia until the country's first democratic elections of 1980 put his ZANU-PF party in power, is pegged with post-colonial markers like that.

But within ZANU-PF, they were alive to the feelgood power of success on the sports field. "Mugabe was quite clever with the Bruce Grobbelaar situation back then," remembers Pernell McKop, an assistant coach to the Zimbabwe national team in the early 1990s. Grobbelaar wanted in. Zimbabwe's new head coach, a German named Reinhard

Fabisch, made it clear he wanted his best goalkeeper in the team. The people wanted Bruce. The fixture in which he might make his comeback was especially resonant. Zimbabwe were to begin their qualifying campaign for the 1994 Cup of Nations against their neighbours South Africa, who would be competing for the first time ever in Africa as a Fifa-authorised national team after decades of anti-apartheid sanctions. It was a South Africa team endorsed by the president-in-waiting Nelson Mandela, an XI of black, white and mixed-race South Africans, emblematic of their Rainbow Nation. For Zimbabwe, the inclusion of Grobbelaar — a man who once fought as a Rhodesian army conscript in the civil war against Mugabe's freedom fighters — made its own statement about their diversity.

"Even two days ahead of the game, the government were saying Bruce's Zimbabwean passport and his eligibility were down to the Home Office," remembers McKop, "so they used it, to hype up the suspense, kept saying 'it's touch and go' whether he could play." Naturally, he did.

Grobbelaar would also boost the number of Bulawayians in the national team, which was noted. "In some ways Zimbabwean football was quite politicised," says McKop. "The rivalry domestically between Highlanders, from Bulawayo in Matabeleland, and Dynamos from Harare, in Mashonaland, could become very tribalistic." Matabeleland had in the early post-democracy years been subject to brutal oppression by sections of the armed forces. Highlanders versus Dynamos matches bore some of that emotional weight.

McKop remembers Joshua Nkomo, the leader of the ZAPU party whose core constituency was in Matabeleland, giving go-get-'em speeches to Highlanders players. "The composition of the national team," he added, "in terms of numbers of players in it from each part of the country was an issue for the politicians and some in the media." Fabisch, as an outsider, exercised a certain licence to disregard that while some fans from Matabeleland congratulated themselves on the unusually high number of their men in the national team.

Once the Dream Team had momentum, it became harder to interfere in such matters. And on a on a sunny winter day at Harare's National Stadium, the Dream Team gained its traction. Grobbelaar had a sense this might be a watershed match for his country. "When I got the call to come back, to play against South Africa, I was thrilled," he recalls. "I knew they'd be really up for it and it would be a helluva game."

The visitors thought they were the big storyline. Fabisch played up the cowing, underdog status of Zimbabwe — "they are much stronger than us" — though not all his players did. Willard Khumalo, the Zimbabwe midfielder, gave a gem of a quote to those of us covering the game. Asked his opinion of South Africa's insatiably showy trickster of a winger, 'Doctor' Khumalo of Kaizer Chiefs, the Khumalo of Zimbabwe suggested the Khumalo of South Africa risked having to "change his name from 'Doctor' to 'Nurse'."

In front of a crowd of more than 40,000, Zimbabwe demolished South Africa. They went 2-0 up thanks to goals from

Vitalis 'Digital' Takawira and Rahman Gumbo in the opening 20 minutes, and were 4-1 winners. Peter Ndlovu, still a teenager, got the other two goals.

The Dream Team had lift-off. David had whipped one self-styled Goliath of the continent. Over the months that followed they would aim their slingshots at genuine giants of African football as they picked their way through the cluttered calendar. Besides the Cup of Nations qualifiers, there was the qualifying marathon for the USA World Cup, with its two tiers of group phases, with only the top team going through at each stage. In the course of those, Zimbabwe would be required keep their poise on some demanding away trips — notably to Angola, in the first World Cup mini-league, on a baking January day during the Angolan civil war. "Coming into Luanda, we had to circle all the way down into the airport because someone was shooting at planes," recalls Grobbelaar. "In the stadium, they must have had 80,000. It was only supposed to hold about 50,000." A 1-1 draw felt plucky.

Three weeks earlier, Egypt had been beaten in Harare, a peg on the Dream Team's highway as significant as the resonant rout of the South Africans. Peter Ndlovu's slalom and left-foot drive for the first goal in the 2-1 win had been the highlight.

It set up a rousing conclusion to the group, with Zimbabwe needing a point in Cairo to go through to the next phase and eliminate the Pharaohs. By the end of an intense, rowdy night, Fabisch had a cut to his head and Grobbelaar had also been struck by a missile. Egypt had won 2-1. Zimbabwe, armed with television footage, appealed to Fifa. The world governing body's record on righting perceived wrongs caused by lax security, particularly in Africa, is a little haphazard. Yet the Dream Team were awarded a replay of the match, to be played in Lyon, France. Grobbelaar had one of finest nights of his international career in a 0-0 draw that was vividly celebrated 5,000 miles away.

Back home, bad drought was hurting the population and wearing at the country's economy. "Morale was low at that time," says McKop, "and people clung to the idea of the Dream Team and the road to the USA, and to what we felt might be our first time at an Africa Cup of Nations. When we played those qualifiers, started to put together an unbeaten run, those days brought back some of the joy of independence, the feeling of all having a single objective. I think that's partly why the Dream Team label stuck."

Zimbabwe's Cup of Nations qualifying campaign would by the middle of 1993 be overshadowed by a bigger story. When Zambia came to Harare for the final group match, needing a draw to pip the Dream Team for a place at the finals, they had the sympathy and support of the world. Three months earlier the Zambia squad travelling to a match in Senegal had been killed in a plane crash. Against Zimbabwe, a hastily patched-together side fell a goal behind. The Dream Team were on course for their first ever major tournament. Eleven minutes remained when the Zambia captain Kalusha Bwalya directed a header past Grobbelaar.

The road to the USA remained open. To add to the scalp of Egypt, there would be the cutting down to size of Cameroon, Africa's most visible football power thanks to Italia 90, beaten 1-0 in Harare. But Zimbabwe had dropped points with a defeat in Guinea, the also-rans in their mini-league. After the penultimate set of fixtures of the second group phase, Zimbabwe found themselves again one win shy of the target. They had to go to Yaoundé and beat the Indomitable Lions to be one of the trio of African sides at the 1994 World Cup.

For a while, the dream flickered on. When, five minutes into the second half, Adam Ndlovu scored, a hush came over the Ahmadou Ahidjo stadium. A brief respite from a noise Grobbelaar describes as "like a swarm of angry bees, ringing in your ears." But Cameroon were already two goals up by then. Once they added a third, Zimbabwe were broken. On the touchline, Fabisch started throwing US dollar bills around, implying the referee, who had given a contentious early penalty in favour of Cameroon, had been bought. Zim's Dream Team had been 11 minutes from a first ever Cup of Nations. They had been one win from reaching the US. They had neither.

Just over a year after the loss in Yaoundé, Zimbabwe's most famous footballer was on the front page of the *Sun* in Britain. Bruce Grobbelaar would spend the next three years defending himself against allegations of match-fixing during his time at Liverpool. He was cleared of corruption charges. He played for his country for a further four years and later coached the Warriors, but after some vigorous disagreements with officials from the Zimbabwe Football Association, his ties with the country weakened. The dual passport issue resurfaced, too. This time it would not be resolved with a presidential flourish.

Zimbabwe's wait for a first appearance at a Cup of Nations lasted into the 21st century, by which time the country often appeared a ceaseless bad news story: violent general elections, surreal inflation rates, soaring unemployment, desperate emigration. Economic crisis meant Zimbabwe withdrew as designated hosts of the African Cup of Nations in 2000. When, nearly quarter of a century after independence, Zimbabwe finally qualified for a Nations Cup, in 2004, the iconic Ndlovu brothers were still up front for the Warriors. The label Dream Team had not accompanied them. Nor were the Zimbabwe who reached the 2006 tournament in Egypt — where Peter Ndlovu won his 100th cap before another group stage exit — deemed worthy of comparison with the sides of the early 1990s.

Even that peak now seems distant. African football's hierarchy, at least at international level, has become refreshingly fluid in the 21st century. Small nations with little footballing heritage rise suddenly, Togo and Angola have reached World Cup finals, Burkina Faso have finished second at a Cup of Nations. Zimbabwe have not caught that train. They currently live with the ongoing fallout from 'Asiagate', the match-fixing scandal centred on the tour by a sub-standard Zimbabwe team to the Far East in 2009, implicating over a hundred players and officials.

In April 2013, Peter Ndlovu was cleared of culpability in the crash that cost his brother his life and he continues to work as assistant coach to the national team, but it ranks outside Fifa's top 100. Little wonder that a longing, a rose-tinted nostalgia for the so-called Dream Team is easily stirred. Ⓑ

The Grand Griguol

How El Viejo *defied accusations of boringness to inspire the golden age of Ferro Carril Oeste*

By Dan Colasimone

Although largely unloved by the Argentinian press at the time, the Ferro Carril Oeste team that dominated domestic football in the early 1980s is now regarded as defining the era, symbolic of a move back to pragmatic footballing ideologies and proving that, under the right conditions, a 'neighbourhood' club could compete with the giants.

Admired by some for making themselves almost impossible to beat, but denigrated by most for their style of bloody-minded possession football, Ferro were a kind of joyless Barcelona of their time. *El Gráfico* magazine described the team as "a well-oiled machine that reached the summit with simplicity as its emblem… A resounding demonstration of how conviction and total unity can take a group to the very top."

Ferro won championships in 1982 and 1984, and missed out on several more in the early eighties by narrow margins. In terms of consistently challenging for honours, the only side close to them in the first half of the decade was Estudiantes de La Plata. The two teams had a similar outlook, one which contrasted markedly with what had come before.

The Argentinian game has forever swayed between pragmatism and lyricism. During the amateur era and in the early days of professionalism, the overwhelming preference was for highly attacking football. After the *Selección*'s humiliation at the 1958 World Cup, however, defensive tactics became the norm. Osvaldo Zubeldía and Victorio Luis Spinetto[1], both known for producing hard-working, tough-to-beat, defence-minded teams, were the dominant managers of the sixties until the tide turned again at the end of the decade and attacking teams enjoyed another heyday. Then, in the 1980s, the Estudiantes of the Zubeldía disciple Carlos Bilardo and the Ferro of the *spinettista* Carlos Timoteo Griguol ushered in a new era of guarded, tactical football, which culminated in the Bilardo-led *Selección*'s consecutive World Cup final appearances in 1986 and 1990. Estudiantes already had quite a pedigree but the evolution of Ferro from modest suburban team to major player took many by surprise.

Ferro Carril Oeste, founded by rail workers in 1904 (the English translation of the name is 'Western Railway') and based in the leafy Buenos Aires suburb of

[1] *See Jonathan Wilson's piece "The First Bilardista" in Issue One for more on Spinetto.*

Caballito, had, for most of its existence, enjoyed a cosy mediocrity. A mid-ranking side from a very middle-class neighbourhood, it had remained fairly consistently in the top division since first gaining promotion in 1912 without ever threatening to challenge the dominance of the giants. As if to emphasise how middling the club is, its Estadio Arquitecto Ricardo Etcheverri ground is located in almost the exact geographical centre of Buenos Aires. Supporters of the team, whose dark green shirts echo the verdant surroundings, are stoically devoted to the institution, though few are foaming-at-the-mouth fanatics. The sporting club, as is often the case in Argentina, is the focal point of the surrounding community. Caballito residents will stop by the club house for a friendly tennis match or a Sunday dinner, and Ferro's basketball, hockey and volleyball teams are long-established powers in their respective national leagues.

Football remains the club's *raison d'être*, however, and the current plight of the team is a cause of great anguish, not only for Ferro fans, but for many neutral observers who lament the disappearance of such a traditional name from the top division. Ferro nowadays compete in Argentina's second division, Nacional B, occasionally flirting with the possibility of a return to the top flight, but more often than not its supporters are gazing anxiously at the relegation averages. Since a financial meltdown in 2002, blamed on nefarious officials, the club has been in administration; struggling for survival both economically and on the pitch. Such a depressing present reality makes wistfully remembering the glory days of the early eighties the pastime of choice for elderly Ferro fans.

So how did a modest team from a laid-back inner-city neighbourhood help change the course of Argentinian football thinking? Two factors stand out: the decline of the traditional powerhouses and the ingeniously simple coaching philosophies of Griguol.

The political and economic deterioration of Argentina in the late seventies and early eighties under the military dictatorship hit the country's biggest football clubs hard. The nation was in a state of emergency. Turmoil caused by high inflation and the Falklands War led to an increase in violence at football stadiums. General unrest spread to the terraces and as the danger increased, crowd numbers dwindled.

The standard of the league was further reduced when the national coach César Luis Menotti called up his squad for the 1982 World Cup early, in order to give the team an extended preparation for the tournament. Most of the players came from the five *Grandes* (Boca Juniors, River Plate, Independiente, Racing and San Lorenzo), so not only were they stripped of technical ability on the pitch, the general public lost further interest in watching them play, which was another blow for attendance figures. The majority of clubs, already hobbled by poor management, were plunged into financial crisis.

Both Boca and River had overstretched themselves financially by purchasing big-name players they could not afford. In 1982, River had to return the forward Mario Kempes to Valencia when they were unable to complete payments for his transfer. So large had the debt grown that they had to offload the defender Daniel Passarella to Fiorentina as well. Boca were similarly crippled by the purchase of Diego Maradona from Argentinos Juniors in 1981. He was sold on to Barcelona after only a year at the Bombonera. Of the *Grandes*, only Independiente benefited from sensible management, based on a strong social function in the community, and they thus remained comparatively stable financially.

None of the *Grandes* made it to the quarter-finals of the 1982 Nacional tournament, a stage reached by finishing in the top two of one of four groups of eight teams. It was a time for clubs of more modest means to make an impact. Several provincial sides emerged as title contenders but it was Griguol's Ferro, with sacrifice and order as its hallmarks, which was at the vanguard of a new era for Argentinian football.

Two first division championships were played every year in Argentina until 1985: the Torneo Metropolitano, which was a home and away league, and the Campeonato Nacional, which comprised an initial group stage followed by a knock-out tournament. Ferro finished runner-up by a single point to Maradona's Boca in 1981's Metropolitano, then lost the final of the Nacional to Kempes's River. Combining the points gained in both tournaments, Ferro would have finished seven clear of Boca and 11 ahead of River over the entire season. In 1982, Griguol's side won the Nacional without losing a match, while Bilardo's Estudiantes took out the Metropolitano. Estudiantes and Independiente won championships in 1983, with Ferro once again claiming the Nacional in 1984 before finishing second to Argentinos in the Metropolitano. Ferro

remained a force throughout the mid-to-late-eighties but did not win another title. For a side that had never come close to a championship before, two titles and three second-place finishes over four years was an outstanding return.

Argentina's big clubs may have been suffering through a difficult period, but to attribute Ferro's success solely to the misfortune of others would be grossly unfair.

The great Ferro team began to take shape in 1979 under Carmelo Faraone, who brought through many of the players who would reap such success later on. It was with the arrival of Griguol from Kimberley in 1980, however, that the Caballito outfit really began to emerge as a force.

'El Viejo' (The Old Man), as he was known, had spent his 13-year playing career at just two clubs, Atlanta, where he played for three years under Spinetto, and Rosario Central, where he would take up coaching after retiring in 1969. Griguol won his first championship with Central in 1973 with a team dubbed '*Los Picapiedras*' (The Flintstones) because of its rustic style, before a stint in Mexico with América. On returning to Argentina he led Kimberley for only a handful of games before being called on to take charge of Ferro's project. The new coach suited club President Santiago Leyden's austere outlook perfectly. He was already known as a conservative manager and was famous for his habit of slapping players' faces before they ran onto the pitch by way of motivation. "When we first started in Ferro, after the games everybody would ask about the results of the teams who were relegation candidates," Griguol would later tell *El Gráfico*. "It took a year to change that attitude."

Aside from his motivational techniques, Griguol brought with him certain characteristics that would prove invaluable at Ferro. Crucially, he placed great emphasis on youth development when forming his sides. He would staunchly avoid spending money on big names, preferring to promote players from the junior teams. With no superstars in the squad, Griguol demanded hard work on all levels, until it became synonymous with both the way the club was run and the players' attitude on the pitch.

His team played a flexible 4-3-3, with an emphasis on the collective rather than the individual. The basis of the starting XI in 1982 would remain the same for several years. The goalkeeper Carlos Barisio offered a sense of calm security. He still holds the record in Argentina for the longest period without conceding a goal; 1075 minutes in total, beginning in the 1981 Metropolitano. The centre-backs complemented each other with their differing styles: Juan Domingo Rocchia was the dominant leader, the *caudillo* at the back, while Héctor Cúper, who had come through the club's youth system, possessed great technique on the ball and could initiate attacks. Roberto Carlos Mario Gómez, reliable and tactically intelligent, started in the right-back role in 1982, while Oscar Américo Agonil took over as first choice in 1984. Oscar Garré was one of the stars of the team on the left side of defence. Renowned for his attacking tendencies down the flank, he would win the World Cup with Argentina in 1986.

The midfield three were extremely disciplined tactically and could be relied

on to run non-stop. Carlos Arregui on the right and Gerónimo Saccardi in the middle had also emerged from the club's junior ranks. Saccardi's tenacity and technical ability made him a key component of the side. He, like Rocchia, had played under Griguol's mentor Victorio Spinetto in Ferro's 1974 surprise title challenge. The Paraguayan Adolfino Cañete, who was the creative spark in midfield, was usually to be found on the left.

The right-sided forward was Claudio Crocco, a speedy dribbler with an eye for goal. Miguel Ángel Juárez played on the left of the front three. He was initially brought to the club in 1981 as a back-up striker but ended up being top scorer in the championship winning campaign in 1982 with 20 goals. Julio César Jimenez would alternate with Alberto 'Beto' Márcico who went on to become a club legend at both Ferro and Boca, in the centre-forward position. Both would habitually drop back into an attacking midfield role.

The 4-3-3 on paper would adapt easily to whatever circumstances on the pitch required. If, for example, the opposition midfield was proving a handful, Ferro's central midfielder Saccardi would drop back to join the defence, allowing it to fan out wider across the back. Another modification was to form a kind of square formation in the middle of the pitch, with Saccardi and Arregui as its base and Cañete alongside a withdrawn striker, Juárez or Márcico , slightly further forward. At the same time, the full-backs would push forward and convert into dangerous attacking threats.

Griguol also worked closely with the legendary Ferro basketball coach León

Najnudel. He attended training sessions, exchanged ideas and watched videos of the basketball team with the aim of transferring movements and plays to the football pitch. Griguol's system, with its quick interchanging of positions, meant it was very rare for the team to be caught out numerically, especially when players not originally designated as defenders would suddenly appear in a defensive capacity.

When opponents had the ball, Ferro pressed vigorously and constantly in all areas of the field. Once such pressing resulted in a turnover of possession, tight passing triangles were initiated to advance the ball away, regardless of which sector of the pitch they were in. This kind of aggressive defending was likened to that of a Menotti team, supposedly at the opposite end of the footballing spectrum, and could even draw comparisons to modern-day Barcelona's off-the-ball play.

Such movement, both with and without the ball, required superb physical conditioning. Much credit was given to Ferro's trainer, Luis María Bonini, recently seen assisting Marcelo Bielsa at Athletic Bilbao. Bonini had the players working extremely hard in pre-season, and ensured they kept up fitness levels throughout the year.

In an *El Grafico* article in 1984, Natalio Gorin pointed out that in the Griguol era, no Ferro player had forced an opponent to leave the field injured, despite the tenacious defensive tactics. "It is not a team that aims to hurt opponents," he said, "they play hard but fair." Nor did Griguol's teams ever man mark an opponent. They defended zonally, even against the likes of Maradona and

Independiente's brilliant playmaker, Ricardo Bochini.

The same article showed a large diagram of Ferro passing the ball all the way along the back four, then back to the keeper, under the headline, "Are Ferro a Boring Team?". The author concluded that "since football has been football, only teams who play well win."

Sure enough, Ferro were experts at sucking the life out of a game after taking an early lead. "Stingier than Griguol's Ferro," was an expression used at the time to criticise overly defensive sides. The players would famously rotate possession at a leisurely rate, changing shape fluidly, frustratingly, with or without the ball, content to put the onus on opponents to come up with a way of catching them out. Certainly, there were no superstars in the team either. Saccardi, Garré and Márcico may have been adored in Caballito, but they were not players to set pulses racing like Maradona, Kempes or Bochini.

It was a solid, hardworking and tactically impeccable side. Griguol described it thus: "The group was very strong, respectful and had a great deal of heart. For us it was normal to run and keep playing for 90 minutes. For other teams it was a sacrifice to play against Ferro. To that you have to add that if the rest of the teams focused on one wide area, running up and down the wing, we would look to the middle. If you reinforced the flanks, I would play through the centre, and vice versa."

In the 1982 Nacional tournament, which was secured over a two-legged final with a 2-0 aggregate victory against Quilmes, Ferro's record reads: 22 games, 16 wins, six draws and no losses with 50 goals scored and only 13 conceded. The 1983 campaigns were punctuated by the side throwing away numerous 1-0 leads in the final 10 minutes of games while chasing more impressive scorelines — perhaps the criticisms of stodgy play had hit home. The 1984 Nacional triumph, however, was just as impressive as the undefeated 1982 campaign. Griguol's side only lost one game, the away leg to Huracán in the first knock-out stage, on their way to the final against the River Plate of Norberto Alonso and Enzo Francescoli. The first leg was held in River's Monumental and saw perhaps Ferro's finest performance, a 3-0 victory. In the second leg, the Caballito side took an early lead through Cañete, and River fans were so enraged at the humiliation their team was being subjected to that they attempted to burn down the wooden stands of Ferro's stadium. The match was suspended with 20 minutes to go, but the result stood, and Griguol and his team had their second title to cap a golden era.

By this stage, the national sporting press had grudgingly acknowledged Ferro as a team worthy of recognition. The 1982 triumph had been overshadowed in the press by the World Cup in Spain and events off the pitch, most notably the tumultuous economic situation and the Falklands War. Consistently strong showings over following tournaments led to a level of respect, and even some praise amid the barbs about dull play.

There may have been limited admiration for Griguol's Ferro while the side was at its peak, but its place in the history of Argentinian football is indisputable. Griguol showed that a side with a small budget and little brilliance could consistently trump more vaunted opponents through industry and tactical precision. In recent years, as the *Grandes* have once again found themselves in trouble due to poor directorship, 'neighbourhood' clubs like Lanús, Banfield and Arsenal de Sarandí have followed Ferro's lead by winning championships on tiny budgets, while other well-run clubs like Vélez and Estudiantes have thrived as richer, better-supported teams such as River, Independiente and San Lorenzo have floundered.

Many of Griguol's team went on to become coaches themselves. Cúper, Garré, Gomez and Saccardi all became managers, as did others who later played under *El Viejo*. All of them remained faithful to his pragmatic, compact style.

Most importantly, the success of Ferro in the 1980s gave, and continues to give, ammunition to those in Argentina who argue that cautious, defensive football remains the most effective path to silverware. The overriding philosophy at the moment seems once again to favour a demure approach. Boca Juniors pulled themselves out of a three-year lean spell by trusting in the grim but effective playing style of Julio Falcioni, winning the apertura in 2011-12 while the Argentina national team is being led towards the next World Cup finals by the highly pragmatic Alejandro Sabella, a Bilardo disciple. The sands will no doubt shift again and the debate will carry on. The lyricists will forever bring up the likes of Menotti in 1978 and River's La Máquina of the 1940s, while the pragmatists can always point to Zubeldía's Estudiantes, Bilardo's Argentina and Timoteo Griguol's humble Ferro side who carved their own niche in history by turning dreariness into a virtue and simplicity into an art form.

A Dream Denied

But for the politics of Greek football, Ferenc Puskás might have ended up in Athens not Madrid

By Antonis Oikonomidis

Holy Thursday morning. Typically a solemn day for Greeks. This one, in mid-April 1957, was even more solemn than usual. A group of friends left the most fashionable hotel in Athens to travel from the northern suburbs into the centre. They took a taxi, but it broke down. The two passengers laughed, one insisting the breakdown was the result of the other's excessive weight. Neither of them were obese but equally neither was thin, particularly not the shorter one. As they waited by the side of the road for another taxi, passers-by began to recognise them, the shorter one in particular. In a few minutes, word spread. Everybody knew who and where they were: "Puskás and Kocsis are in the Royal Garden." Thousands of people flocked to see the two of the most famous members of Hungary's *Aranycsapat* [Golden Squad], so many that even after the second taxi arrived, what should have been a quick drive lasted for hours.

A few months earlier, in November 1956, Honvéd had been on their way to Bilbao for a European Cup match against Athletic when a revolution against Communist rule broke out in Budapest. Honvéd were one of the greatest club sides of all time and a product of the Communist state, having been taken over by the army when football was nationalised in 1949 and transformed from Kispest, essentially a village club — albeit it one featuring the immense promise of Ferenc Puskás and Jozsef Bozsik —into what was effectively a nursery for the national team: Sándor Kocsis, Zoltán Czibor, László Budai, Gyula Lóránt and Gyula Grosics all played there.

Athletic won that first leg 3-2, after which it was decided, because of the disturbances in Budapest, to play the second leg in Brussels. Honvéd stayed in Antwerp, where Puskás gave an interview, widely quoted in the Greek press, in which he said arrangements had been made for him to come to Athens to play some friendly matches in the spring.

At around the same time, and given far less prominence, the Greek newspapers reported that Ethnikos Piraeus had been in touch with both Honvéd and the Hungarian government to try to secure the registrations of five players who had agreed to move to Athens and play for Ethnikos. The players were not named and the reports stressed that the main sticking point was securing consent from their families.

The move was typical of the power and ambition of Ethnikos at the time. Ethnikos had been established in 1923 and remained always in the shade of the great club of Piraeus, Olympiakos. The key person in their development was Dimitris Karellas. Born into a family of noted businessmen, he was the owner of Aegeon, the biggest textile manufacturer in Europe with infrastructure and facilities unique in post-war Greece. He was powerful and rich and, having been invited onto Ethnikos's board in the early fifties, aimed to make the club a competitor to the traditional big three of Greek football — Olympiakos, Panathinaikos and AEK.

His investment soon paid off and, in 1956, Ethnikos finished second, a point behind Olympiakos, their best ever finish. Karellas thrust himself to the forefront, keen to exhibit his power, not merely in terms of finance, but also in the courts, the mass media and public opinion. He was also adept at playing political games behind the scenes, something that has always been of great importance in Greek football. For the Greek football establishment, used to the same three teams dominating, he became a tremendous irritation.

Honvéd drew the second leg against Athletic 3-3 and so were eliminated. The Hungarian authorities ordered them to return, but the players had no desire to return to a war zone and began using the contacts they had made in their years as superstars to try to smuggle their families out.

The team manager, Emil Östreicher, arranged a tour to Latin America, which drew the wrath of the Hungarian football federation. In early January 1957 it banned the team from using the name or colours of Honvéd. They adopted the name Hungaria (and were sometimes

known as Free Hungary, while the press at the time dubbed them 'Puskás & Co'), wore a kit in the colours of the Hungarian flag and, undaunted, set off for Rio de Janerio. Fifa threatened sanctions, both for Hungaria and any team who played them, which led to Santos and Vasco da Gama cancelling matches, but they nonetheless managed seven exhibition games in Brazil, Venezuela and Mexico, raising significant revenue.

The players returned to Europe in February, where they discovered the football federation had taken the decision to dissolve the club. They were warned to return home by March 31 and that if they didn't, they would face serious penalties. Even those who did return found themselves facing bans of several months. Puskás, Kocsis, Zoltán Czibor and Gyula Grosics, though, all issued statements saying they were unwilling to go home.

Ethnikos, meanwhile, were living up to expectations. They qualified with some difficulty from their regional division to reach the 10-team final stage of the national championship, but then beat each of the traditional powers in the first round of games. Karellas, meanwhile, was throwing his weight around off the pitch as well. Since the war, the big three had played a moneyspinning Easter tournament, inviting an overseas guest — and, on occasions, more than one. In 1957, the team they invited was Progresul from Romania.

Karellas decided to shake up the comfy arrangement. After months of contact with the representatives of Honvéd/Hungaria, he sent the infamous fixer Sotiris Volonakis to Vienna, where the majority of the exiled members of the team were staying and reached an agreement for them to come to Athens to play a friendly — at precisely the time of the Easter tournament.

Although the Hungarians were still to be declared political refugees, and their ban was still to be ratified by Fifa, Ethnikos sought authorisation —which was granted —from the Greek government for the games. And so, on Holy Wednesday, thousands of fans descended on the airport to greet the Honvéd players, something unprecedented in Greece at the time. At around the same time, as the ultimatum for returning home expired, the Hungarian federation issued its penalties: a one-year bans for Puskás and Czibor (who had gone to Italy expecting to sign a contract with Roma), six-month bans for Grosics, Kocsis and István Szolnok, and four-month bans for Gyula Szabó and Ágoston Garamvölgyi.

The friendly against Ethnikos was scheduled for the Monday after Easter Sunday. In the four days they were in Athens, every public appearance by Honvéd's players prompted a frenzy. The newspapers charted their every step, from that morning out in the centre of Athens to their visit to the Acropolis, to their first training session at the Karaiskakis Stadium, the shared home of Olympiakos and Ethnikos, to the way they celebrated Easter Sunday in the traditional Greek style. Karellas — along with Volonakis and the Hungarian coach of Apollon Athens, János Zsolnay — followed them, making the most of the opportunity for publicity. He went with Puskás to watch Panathinaikos play Progresul on Holy Saturday. The crowd was small, and Puskás's thoughts on the

game generated more publicity than the match itself. The establishment's irritation grew, and all the more so as rumours emerged that Ethnikos intended to sign the cream of the Hungarian squad.

That wasn't apparent at the friendly against Hungaria. With 30,000 fans squeezing in, they thrashed Ethnikos 7-0. But that wasn't the worst thing for Ethnikos and their leader's ambitions; that was the gravel pitch. Kocsis said it was like playing in Sudan. Grosics, for the first and only time in his career, wore knee-pads. Puskás said it was "a road made for bicycles and cars".

The next day it was announced that a second game against the national team of the armed forces would be played two days later. It was then that Ethnikos confirmed the rumours, announcing that the team had agreed terms with five Hungarian players: Szabó, Cholnok, Zsámboki, Garamvölgyi and Sági, all of whom had signed the relevant registration forms. All that remained to finalise the deal was to get the consent of their families, with the players available after their bans from the Hungarian federation had expired at the beginning of the following season.

Hungaria were defeated 2-1 in their final friendly by the Greece national team, the last game of the renamed club's brief existence. The squad stayed on in Athens for a few more days, Karellas continuing to make the most of their presence. He went with Puskás to watch Olympiakos play Panathinaikos in the Easter Tournament. Midway through the first half, Panathinaikos's players, aggrieved by the refereeing, walked off the pitch. They agreed to carry on only an hour later, and then only with reserve players. The referee would not consent to that, though, and refused to continue the game. Puskás left his seat and, encouraged by fans, trotted onto the pitch, taking the whistle and offering to referee the match himself. In the end a compromise was reached and the original referee carried on the game, but Puskás's actions, with Karellas always in the background, again took all the publicity.

Ethnikos were the big winners. They won new fans, recognition and publicity. They won in terms of revenue and strengthening their squad, and looked set to dominate Greek football. A few days after Hungary's departure Karellas brought Internazonale to Athens for a friendly. These were big events for Greek football and an unambiguous threat to the established order. Karellas pushed harder. He arranged a tour of Egypt and sought permission from the Hungarian federation to use Garamvölgyi and Szabó as well as three Under-23 internationals, Tamás Fridwalszky, József Kuzman and István Sztancsik, on that trip.

Finally the grandees of the Greek game acted. The Greek federation decided the contracts with the Hungarians breached its rules on amateurism, refused to acknowledge the licence granted by the Greek government for Ethnikos to play the friendly against Hungary and imposed a huge fine and a two-month ban from sporting activity.

The penalty was transparently unjustified as there was no evidence the players were anything other than amateurs. The Hungarian federation might have

renounced its players but it would never have declared them professional because to do so would have meant giving up the gold medal Hungary's footballers had won at the 1952 Olympic Games.

So the Greek federation took further action, accusing Ethnikos of bribery and match-fixing — the second such allegation made that season, which perhaps says something about the work Karellas did in the background. This time, though, the charge didn't stand up. For one thing it related to a game Ethnikos had lost against Proodeftiki and, for another, the player who lodged the complaint soon withdrew it. The damage, though, was done. The accusation was enough to remove the suspended nature of the two-month ban and the tour of Egypt had to be cancelled.

Karellas took on his enemies in the civil courts, demanding compensation for the cancellation of the tour. Ethnikos were not allowed to play their final four games of the season; they had been two points behind the eventual champions Olympiakos, whom they would have played in their next game.

That same week, in June 1957, Fifa at last acted on the issue of the Hungarian players, confirming the penalties imposed by the Hungarian federation. The agreements with Ethnikos were terminated and so was the ambition of Karellas to change the established order in Greek football. That summer, the Greek federations, responding to an appeal by Fifa, reduced Ethnikos's penalty, allowing them to compete in the championship the following season[1]. But it never won anything again.

---

[1] *The Brazilian federation similarly reduced a penalty imposed on Botafogo for playing against Hungary.*

Yet it had come close. It remains one of the enduring myths of Greek football that Karellas had reached agreement with Puskás, Grosics and Kocsis to continue their careers at Ethnikos. Certainly Karellas wanted them to and he had the financial capacity to persuade them. If things had gone differently, he may well have achieved it. But the stories that claim Hungaria's stars played friendly games in Ethnikos shirts simply aren't true — they simply trained with Ethnikos a couple of days before the first match.

The penalties imposed on Ethnikos are still considered one of the greatest scandals of Greek football and clearly had less to do with Hungaria's arrival than with the establishment's desire to run down Ethnikos. Perhaps that's why the myths endure, because the story of the upstart challenging the grandees and crushed for its temerity has a universal romantic appeal.

Emil Östreicher, the general manager of Hungaria, was eventually taken on by Real Madrid and ended up taking Puskás there in 1958. He failed in an effort to land Koscis, who joined Czibor at Barcelona. Karellas remained active at Ethnikos and was the team's only sponsor until the late eighties. So dedicated was he that he sold personal property to keep funding the side. He ended up broke and emigrated to England, where he died in the early 1990s. His beloved team limped on another two decades before being overwhelmed by debt and shut down in 2011.

He did at least see a dream fulfilled as Puskás came to Athens, being appointed manager of Panathinaikos in May 1970, 13 years to the day after the first penalty was imposed on Ethnikos. A year later, Karellas was at Wembley to see Panathinaikos lose to Ajax in the European Cup final, still a fan of the man he had pursued to the point of destroying his club. Ⓑ

161

Fiction

"Off he went, speaking ostensibly of football
yet invoking only patterns, shapes, affinities,
compensations, illustrating the rat-a-tat
theorems with baroque diagrams"

In Search of Punditaria

*An anthropologist heads into the jungle to discover a
society founded by stranded football journalists*

By Scott Oliver

Emerging from a fever that might have
lasted several minutes or months,
Wim Dahlmann blinked intently into a
violent tropical light, rubbed his eyes
vigorously, then peered through the
scintillating air at his doctor's beatific,
lunar face, before promptly falling into
a more restful sleep. Upon awakening,
he spent a week convalescing under
the benign shade of the jacarandas that
guarded the old mission hospital of
Itaituba from the chaos of the jungle
beyond, eating with ever less obligation
and slowly restoring his body to its
former convictions. He then set his
mind to the puzzle that had brought
him this far.

Pacing down the wide, cool corridor
one final time, only the humming fans
perturbing the drab reassurance of its
viscous air, he poked his head in on
Carlos, his neighbour. Intoning solemnly
that all Men of Knowledge would find
something within, he handed Wim a
book — a Portuguese translation, the
spine of which had long abandoned its
rectilinear form ("verticality", the Peruvian
called it) and with that the requirement
of holding things together, its title
embossed in black on the rough orange
canvas: *Os Ensinamentos de Dom João*.
Dahlmann spent his last 10 minutes on
the makeshift pontoon flicking back and
forth through the parched leaves (noting

that page 14 was missing altogether)
while the boat that would take him
upriver docked in an elegant half-turn of
controlled deceleration in the manner he
had seen Bergkamp perform hundreds
of times before: receiving the ball back
to goal, he would, with eerie Newtonian
intuition, bring his overeager marker to a
momentary standstill (like some Regency
grandfather clock pivoted precipitously
to the top of a flight of stairs), then,
gravity ceding to celerity, swivel away
and fire off his unerringly accurate darts
(unerring as his memory was erratic).

That apparition, and the purpose
of his journey, reminded him of the
uncomplicated and vast joy that
football had once provided him, a
joy later asphyxiated by pragmatism
and the iron imperatives of money.
(Even winning would eventually lose
out to money.) Dahlmann had been a
midfield anchorman onto whom were
projected various Calvinist virtues, but
whose uncanny positioning was as
much compelled by his own morbid
fear of shooting as any big-picture
acumen ("less Blind than blind" he
would joke, many years later). There
came a time, a few months before his
teenage retirement, when he could do
nothing in possession save pass square
or backwards. *De Krab*, they called him.
But that ordeal belonged to a previous

life, for he was now an anthropologist of renown, with tenure at the LSE and a string of well-regarded publications to his name.

It was recollecting the impact of Dahlmann's earliest papers on football hooliganism and the magic of their conversations on the Ajax terraces that an old postgraduate friend, sympathetic to the vectors of academic eccentricity and now editor of *De Telegraaf*, had commissioned him to cover the 2014 World Cup, writing colour pieces, reportage, following his nose like some old New World creator. His brief was to seek out the sacred in football just as, during two decades' research in ethnobotany, he had sought it in nature's primordial bounty. "Where better than Brazil?"

Mindful of the paradox that as scientific understanding of the world — and he included football in that — increases, so, all too often, pleasure diminishes, he nonetheless hoped profoundly to see a carnivalesque tournament unravel and, in unravelling it, that he might rediscover the raptures of his youth. Yet barely four days into his assignment — 540 minutes — Wim had wearied of the Machiavellian football and its insincere, technocratic exigencies and concluded that there was no rainbow to unweave. Sat cross-legged and despondent on the floor of his Cuiabá hotel room — the centre of the continent — like some penalty-shanker or scuffer inconsolable in the centre circle, contemplating football's growing monoculture with resignation, it occurred to him (with a little help from Caetano Veloso) that the stultifying football was far less interesting than the myriad professional watchers and

gabblers and silk-purse makers following this tournament like pilot fish round a great shark. So, the next morning, with editorial blessing, Dahlmann booked himself on a flight to Salvador where, a day later, England, the game's senescent dreamers (in the sense of fantasists; fantasists in the pathological sense, rather than footballing *fantasistas*), would face Côte d'Ivoire in a ticklish must-not-lose game.

No sooner had he crabbed along to his window seat than he became involved in one of those conversations so engaging and pregnant that its early niceties were leapfrogged for some future encounter. Dahlmann gave a moderate though unambiguous account of the angst, the ennui that had recently overtaken him, his futile search for an irruption of creativity in the timorous systematicity, sparking a gunpowder trail to his neighbour's synapses. Off he went, speaking ostensibly of football yet invoking only patterns, shapes, affinities, compensations, illustrating the rat-a-tat theorems with baroque diagrams. The Dutchman moaned that no-one seems to want to beat their man any more, to take the initiative, to dance, that it was all speed and counter-attack; his companion started to chide him using Viktor Maslov's observations about planes and streamlining when, 35,000 feet above the Mato Grosso, the Tu-154 suddenly began to shake and tremble in what they assumed was a heavy thunderstorm (all resistance in the electric skies) forcing the flight to reroute through Brasilia. After an hour or so on the tarmac — an hour to contemplate the rickety old Russian plane allocated to this C-route skyway — they soared up again above Lúcio Costa's plane-shaped city, over the shimmering menorah of Lake Paranoá (enough time for a spectral Bergkamp to ask his countryman whether an 'I' was missing), then on to Salvador. He separated from his nameless companion, caught a cab to his pastel-hued Pelourinho pousada, then set off uphill toward the Fonte Nova, shimmying through the throngs of inky, pink men tipping schooners of *cerveja* down necks like blancmange.

The game, predictably, was dismal. Roy Hodgson deployed his team in a Scanglonavian 4-4-2 as rigid as English sex and Swedish furniture, while Côte d'Ivoire looked haunted and indeed played as though their pallid opponent were ghosts, succumbing 1-0. (To another ghost in the *Sun*, Jimmy Rodnipp frothed: "Côte d'Ivoire — it's like Spain calling itself Bullfighting".) But the truth is that the game itself and the engorged punditariat milling about it — the tippy-tappy-typists; the pitchside mic paparazzo, arms frozen like some bronze Stalinist homage to ale-quaffers; the studio opinioneers, legs asplay and knees bumping in the budget airline overintimacy of the seats — were of less concern than the accumulating omens: Maslov, the aerial view of Brasilia, Bergkamp. So, rather than head to Manaus for the Group C decider, Dahlmann ensconced in Salvador a few days, a decision that would prove to be his saviour.

He had read somewhere that reality favours symmetries and slight anachronisms, and it was there, listening to Caetano Veloso in the window seat of an omnibus — around the time charter flight VAR4231, carrying the bulk of English football punditry, plunged into the bowels of the Amazonian rainforest before the 2014 World Cup had produced enough goals for even a mediocre Goal of the Tournament — that Dahlmann met Oswald de Andrade, a man who knew much about the soul of Brazil and, *ipso facto*, its football. Dahlmann told his new friend about his task and his quest — the search for *jogo bonito*, for *brazilliance*, for knowledge — while Oswald (whose burnished face was, Wim noted, the precise shape of his name's initial letter) explained how the Europeanisation of Brazilian football was "both neo-colonialism and sell-out". They graduated to caipirinhas, following the England squad inadvertently into The Cockpit, a bar whose staff wore the (decidedly skimpy) cabin crew uniform of some erotic airline, where Oswald discoursed hither and thither about how, though "puritans" traduced Brazilian football as individualist circus, its flicks and feints and swerves and dribbles were not cosmetic showboating but a *molecular* dismantling of the opposition. Wim wasn't sure he knew exactly what his Socratic interlocutor meant (he would) but, upon the resumption of his gonzo "metajournalism", invited his new friend to accompany him along his nomadic interary, after which — partly in the name of research, partly to relive prodigious Amsterdam coffee-shop summers — he headed out with Oswald beyond the hackneyed corruptions of the city to spend a week with Carlos, a shaman, imbibing the sacred *ayahuasca*, or *yagé* (the basis of "Tropic and Psychotropic", the paper he delivered when he returned to the LSE).

He and Oswald maintained a vigorous correspondence — about Brazil's syncretic football, about transcendence and Spinoza's immanent God (Oswald had never sailed entirely from the harbour of his mother's Catholicism), all the unholy mixtures that once appalled Dahlmann's taxonomic temperament — until, some eighteen months after Rio's absurd final, Oswald mentioned in passing that a drawing of a cross had been found washed ashore in Itaituba. The Brazilian had interpreted that symbol as a sign of anthropophagy: "the indigenous peoples of the Amazon disgorging the cross as they had once rejected the Roman church and the Creoles' attempts to civilise them." However, contrary to both poetic and reasoned judgement, Dahlmann knew (or felt) instantly that the English pundits had somehow survived; that the sketch was a football formation, a 4-1-1-3-1 not a crucifix, and that the man he had met on the plane — who spoke of "balance", the need for "an attacking defensive midfielder" and "a defensive defensive midfielder" — was responsible. He asked Oswald what was on the back. "It says 'Maslow', alongside a V and A, upper case, with a picture of a triangle and 'self-actualisation' written above." Dahlmann flew out to Rio the next day, eventually rendezvousing with Oswald, there on the banks of the Tapajós while skim-reading *Os Ensinamentos*.

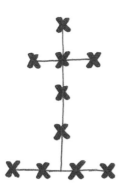

Spurred on by that solitary clue, anthropological curiosity and a simple sense of adventure, the two men rode the steamboat 70km south, disembarking at Jacareacanga where, under a brilliant orange sky, they made camp alongside the mercury river, then at sunrise headed into the oblivious forest, following its scent of autochthonous rumour. For five long days they pushed on beneath the unyielding canopy, pursued by a flotilla of flesh-nibbling flies, by bugs eavesdropping on lengthy disquisitions on Dutch and Brazilian football, the chafing of old dichotomies. Dahlmann's grandfather was a German soldier who had helped the Dutch Resistance before settling beside the shattered frontier of Baarle-Nassau; his grandson had entered the world in that same town on 30 July 1966 — while his father (paradoxically) organised a Provo happening — and had always considered himself profoundly Dutch. Yet now he told Oswald he wished he were more Brazilian; the Brazilian affirmed that he wished to escape the question itself since "the nation is an invention, a convention", then asked, gnomically, "Do we create the nation or does the nation create us?"

Wim, in that old habit of his, shadowed his slippery, probing companion and was about to assert that the latter was true, that without system there was chaos, when the *malandro* told the anthropologist (who was now unsure whether they were talking about football or society): "When you are one-on-one with an assailant, Wim, no knowledge of the law is going to help you. More to the point, the Law won't help you; not in that moment. You have to think and act there, on the spot. *Jeitinho*. Brasilia doesn't run this forest, the insects do…"

"See, system. There must be some order".

"Order, yes," he told the anarchist's son, yawning now, "but no boss. Wim, you must learn from the forest," prompting Dahlmann to ponder the seasonal expansion and abscission of the foliage, its balance of photosynthesis and respiration, which of course evoked in him the pulsating choreography — the ecology of *totaalvoetbal*.

At dawn on the sixth day, with supplies approaching half-time turnaround, they reached a high ridge and surveyed the ungodly wilderness, impervious even to Google's godlike gaze. Oswald chose a moment — or perhaps simply ran out of them — to inform his companion that, being *mestiço*, he could scarcely guarantee his own safety with the occasionally flesh-eating Tupi tribes of the region, let alone his. The thought didn't seem to concern Dahlmann as much as intruding unwittingly into some checkpointless animal territory there in the heaving acreage, and it was while distractedly and unhelpfully contemplating ants that could strip a body in hours, snakes the size of a goal frame, that they stumbled across the head of the former Magpies marksman Alain Chirà (despite the Gallic name, as English, as north-eastern, as Hetton-le-Hole) impaled on a spear. Whether this was the work of Tupi or the pundits was uncertain, but with the receding shock both agreed it was a sign of life beyond.

They found a stream and followed it to a clearing where sunlight attained the penumbral floor in exhausted shafts; there they discovered strange markings which, to their astonishment, revealed themselves as a compact football pitch:

the centre circle, the box, penalty spots... They sat in silence — mournful silence — a few minutes there on the geoglyph of (they felt sure) a lost civilisation, before noticing technical areas, then a dugout in which two rows of six seats salvaged from the rent fuselage had been installed. They saw a mixed zone, and above, remarkably, the "Heath Robinson Press Box" with guarana, breadfruit, pineapple and peanuts laid out alongside a complaints box ("bit exposed"). Out back was a twine ladder which Dahlmann climbed in awed silence up to a high-angled platform — a TV gantry, perhaps — beyond which extended a system of runways providing a bird's-eye-view of the game: the interaction of heads not faces.

Suddenly, there was a rustle in the leaves, startling the men as might a crypt opening in a chapel. "Welcome to Estadio El Dorado," boomed a dishevelled figure with the disconcerting and unseemly pride of a despot showing dignitaries around an arena that only yesterday had hosted a public stoning. Wary, the explorers — the *scientists* — kept their distance. "How many are you?" "A somewhat bloated squad of 81," joked Henry Summer, salaciously, "trimmed down to 47."

Faces appeared, additions to the already mindboggling biodiversity: TV pundits, gnarled reporters of tabloid and broadsheet, columnists, generalists, scoop-hunters, quote-harvesters, angle-finders, insight-mongers, tittle-tattlers, pluck-filled platitude merchants and a clutch of Europeans bringing *je ne sais quoi* that trumped the Anglos' x-factor. They had survived, Dahlmann learned, through rudimentary silviculture, fishing (Dean Dublin assiduously working the channel that flanked the stadium), and foraging and hunting excursions overseen by the Napoleonic Garton Strychnine: "when our lead man stops to explore, the man behind bombs on, right, so no mobile food source escapes."

It turned out that their fatal confrontation with the cannibals had been deferred indefinitely by a simple homeostatic mechanism: Tupi mythology spoke of the arrival of "a roaring white bird that speaks in flames", creating a perhaps undue wariness for the largely harmless hacks (here, the sword was mightier than the pen); conversely, the embryonic lore of the pundits' proto-society had not yet codified its Götterdämmerung, though news of Chirà's skewered head was incontrovertible evidence of their encirclement by hostile forces and served to cauterise professional rivalries, all bound by the hope of their deliverance.

Once the basic exigencies of staying alive had been tended, other urges clamoured. Yet while the insistences of sexual reproduction — the siring of *punditos* — were still a distant throb ("We don't know how long we're going to be here," joked or hoped Libby Grogan. "Amazonia might be ravaged before we are.") the currency of *social* reproduction, storytelling, was ubiquitous. Night after night they gathered to relive great games they had played in, seen, read about — presenting a whole new anxiety for some among these folk paid to talk about football. Here, a prosaic footballer and his pedestrian yarns turned him into a potential meal. Yet it wasn't this orality that convinced Dahlmann the pundits had regressed to a sort of primitivism so much as the fact that the spotlight was circulated, as though to ward off the

consolidation of prestige. "Acephalous society," he underlined, a curious tribesman peering over his shoulder. "It means 'headless'," he told Bobby Savage, scribbling on: "The paradox of Cruyff, the great leader whose power, on the cusp of being instituted and made absolute, was snuffed out by an act of regicide/group suicide."

But this was no anarchist arcadia. Sharing what was likely to be the sole plane crash of their lives had not been sufficient to engender conviviality. Displaying that inexhaustible human capacity for division, even from the most seemingly homogenous of materials (far easier to love a person who hates football than one who likes it in the wrong way), this group of globetrotting fitbaphiles soon fissured along lines dictated not by clubs, nor even their publications' market or ideology (not consciously, anyway), but simple taste, positional proclivities — those who regarded the heartbeat of the team to be the mystical 10, the *enganche*, and others favouring deep-lying playmakers (the *regististas*). Factions were formed, idols carved; blood was shed over whether the channel should be named Danube or River Plate.

As the alluvium of their early socialisation — the jockeying and harrying, striving and suppressing — slowly sedimented, a hierarchy — albeit a hierarchy with latitude for social mobility — began to form. Decisions needed to be taken — on hunting, sacrifice, the ever-present question of attacking the Tupi — and so initiation rites were established. To acquire a vote, one had to name the England World Cup-winning XI; to enter the Supreme Council, full starting XIs for every post-war winner. An intelligentsia formed: polymaths and polyglots, soft of skin and hair (despite the loss of their lotions and balms, their ointments and unguents), in whom it had been embedded that an environment was to be tamed, dominated. Others, the pinch of acquiescent proletarianism still recent (and about whom Dahlmann had written, ungenerously, in *De Telegraaf*: "condemned by circumstance to bruit the hot air of rumour and outrage, ballasted only by degrees of plausibility in the tavern tribunals"), skulked resignedly on the margins.

Little of the teeming jungle and its intense psychedelic syncopations had managed much to perforate the husk of Englishness that clung to these men, men who knew little except football — about which they knew little — and felt that, if they were to remain themselves (a dubious goal), they would need to keep Football close at hand. But the *saudade* was implacable, and from this number crawled the first to be tipped over the edge by the forest's mad cackle and hoot, its nocturnal opera of proximate death, night air refulgent with predatory intent. Others bore the agitated, darting expressions of men weary of the cynical daily blather who realised that defending who they were for grim life was a fate far worse then accepting some psychic recalibration in order, perhaps, to slough off what they had, despite themselves, become. These were not trivial moments in their lives.

Soon the more or less arbitrary origins of the initiates' royal prerogative were forgotten and all settled into the new castes. It was a simple question of survival. For the ex-pros, fame evaporating as quickly as a puddle in

the tropical sun, it was arduous. Savage clung to civilisation by conducting imaginary radio phone-ins, game hacks playing the mad suburban barkers stewing in self-evident truths: "He's claimed his stake in the team, naaah!" they shrieked. Chirà — only on VAR4231 because he was commandeered to make a short feature on Manaus Opera House before jetting back to the Copacabana studio — was already struggling with the storytelling demands when, at his suffrage hearing, he cracked as someone tried prompting him with "wingless wonders" (whether it was the trauma of the plummeting aircraft or the prospect of not getting decent service disappeared with him). "He just ran blind into the jungle, elbowing and trampling the vines out of the way," shuddered Leigh Nixon. "We never saw him alive again."

Memory exhausted, their confabulation shifted to hypothetical games — albeit between real teams: an anachronistic Mundial of Great Losers. Pre-tournament predictions were laboured over (Hungary '54, Netherlands '74, Brazil '82, France or Denmark '86?); each game was the subject of minute debate; a troop of tame marmosets obliged the punctiliousness of the higher primates' reverie by running through attacks while, up in the gods, each movement and pass was meticulously mapped. The arrow-strewn chalkboards became the object of *velliomancy* — divination by arrows — for the need had arisen for some belief to keep the circumambient terrors of the forest at bay. If the pundits hadn't been superstitious when they arrived in Brazil then the decision to show *Castaway* as VAR4231's in-flight movie took on, retroactively, a heavy significance — a significance that told them that, hereafter, they needed to be able to read the signs, the jungle semiology, if ever they were going to make it out alive. So everything, even the pathways travelled by footballers, became pregnant with meaning.

It was in the torrid aftermath of that tournament that this society of wannabe gaffers, these thousand-yard-stare merchants — social media reduced to the crazed gesticulations of the technical area prowlings — suffered fresh upheaval. Mooching in the plane's carcass, Nixon found a ball — a volleyball. An impromptu kickabout started among the plebeian '4-4-2 Crew', yet some thought it sacrilege to play. Before any referendum could take place, however, Michel Cockx confiscated the supernatural orb and placed it in a glass case atop a cairn of Varig crates. They named it Wilson, this apotheosis, then returned — imperceptibly changed — to the old concerns. The quest for formal perfection led them to end the recollected matches and instead run training sessions (while Rodnipp and Nixon cultivated a capoeira-like half-dance, half-football), strutting like martinets after the marmosets. After a while, sloth set in and training was jettisoned; instead, they pondered how to structure hypothetical sessions, what drills to do, what video work, team-talks. Discussing imaginary matches was one thing but conducting imaginary training sessions when they had a real ball was too much for the taciturn, brooding Ray Cain, who followed Chirà into the wilderness, inward into that heart of darkness.

And it was from that darkness that Oswald and Dahlmann emerged, although intellectual fascination (and a certain amount of prurience) saw to it that they soon forgot about any rescue act, happy instead to observe the curious social mechanisms the pundits had elaborated. Dahlmann involved himself where he could, reading nightly from *Ensinamentos*, until, out foraging one afternoon, he discovered, serendipitously, the active ingredient for *yagé*. "This will sort the men from the boys," he chuckled, decocting the sacred vine that evening while Oswald briefed the pundits on its oneiric rigours and (assuming that those who had survived this long were in some way adaptable, supple) asked whether they were ready to follow the exhortations of their id, to leap into the unknown, to become psychonauts charting the uncertain seas in a quest for knowledge.

A new tournament was convoked — true fantasy football. Dahlmann and Oswald were glad Brazil and Holland couldn't be separated in the previous final (over which Tim Hickory and Simeon Kuiper had to be separated) but here there would be no nations — only composite teams from all epochs, all countries, picked for any promiscuous rationale whatever and open to all strata, who would then be obliged to hallucinate passages of the game before each decisive moment (almost every second second, it transpired) would go to tribunal. There would be pre-match disclosure of formations, of the psychological fault lines and breaking points of each player, whose irrationality would be vacuum-packed in the watertight reason of the pundits so that the games could proceed on a purely logical basis (everyone immediately felt they knew for certain precisely what this meant, immediately giving rise to several conceptions). Would this be the moment for a Cruyff turn? Did he try it? Did he succeed? Everything was scrupulously fair, yet laborious.

The night of the first game, Dahlmann, limiting his interventions to the strictly scientific (the brew) and experimental (the *Teachings*, his quest), told these sedentary psychic nomads that the first enemy of the Man of Knowledge is Fear. "We cling to what we think is permanent," he whispered (he didn't want to spook Roy Welkins, then boarding his vessel). "We believe we stand among stable things: identity, values, credos. 'I know what I like,' we gush, not seeing it as the death of potential, of learning, of becoming. *In flight from flight*. What if nations are an obstacle to human freedom? Could we forsake our World Cup fix?"

The *yagé* was to be taken ad nauseam, the games dissected ad infinitum. No matter, for Time had ceased to mean anything: memory was superfluous, the future impossible to conceive as distinct from the present. After a couple of months of this — each step anticipated, each stroke of genius matched, all chaos excised under the unanimous sky — they had conjured five consecutive 0-0 draws. They had wrestled with and cast off the carapace of Fear, bested a formidable, treacherous foe, but in so doing stumbled on the second enemy of the Man of Knowledge: Clarity. Dahlmann again glossed from *Ensinamemtos*: "Fear may be banished, yet this new self-assurance, this special awareness, becomes monomania, righteousness, vehemence, everyone judge and jury." A vulture circled overhead, observing keenly. Where there had been consensus, Dahlmann's words — Don Juan's

words — now perturbed them. Félix Éclair, still *dérangé*, then had the gall to counter (quickly, and with no discernible transition), "Mais oui, but tactics are about finding the perfect balance of attack and defence, non?" Oswald parried: "Yes, but there is balance in 0-0, in 1-1, 2-2, 4-4. Which is optimal?"

Whatever, the obscene and terminal equilibrium was shattered when Wilson — the man of flesh and blood, not the leathery idol — emerged sprightly from the foliage, clapping slowly and sardonically. "Goals are overrated, are they not? These are *perfect* games. Congratulations". Dahlmann recognised him as the man from the plane. "You, the cross..." Wilson wasn't listening, however; instead, he clambered up the zealots' ziggurat and snatched the ball from the jar. "Why the fuck you're not playing a real match when you've got a ball is beyond me!" he rasped, garryowening the totem up into the night and breaking the spell forever. The disenchantment was palpable.

"Goals change games," murmured some heretic, the air thick with tension. Yet Wilson was already addressing the motley punditariat: "You see only tactics, the brute presence of what unfolds before your eyes. But the eyes deceive." He clicked thumb and middle finger and the vulture was transfigured into a Tupi chief. "The game is an infinity of absences. At every moment a great midfield general abandons hundreds of paths of the game's potential unfolding. You have *yagé*. Now open the doors of perception!"

Belatedly, Dahlmann was acknowledged: "You wanted the soul of Brazil. Here." Wilson swept out a hand; the bird-chief juggled a ball awhile as his master related how, having staggered from the wreckage and lacking even basic means to record his thoughts, he went "until the equinox" carving passages from his next four books into the sympathetic bark of some qinchona trees "before cramp set in." After this frenzy of recollection, he ventured upriver with Gábor Markúrtzki and happened upon a tribe with a ball but no structure, so trained them; *quid pro quo*, the tribe fast-tracked him in sorcerery and he became a *shapeshifter*.

"Football is not entertainment, gentlemen," he trumpeted. "So let's play a match. *With the ball... The prize? Life or death: nothing too important!*" Laughing dementedly, he fixed his gaze on Oswald: "Tupi or not Tupi, that is indeed the question".

For five days, under oppressive, heat-trapping clouds, the initiated pundits gathered around the stilt roots of the walking palm (*Socratea exhorriza*) and debated furiously over tactics, style and formation. The two anthropologists persuaded them that Brazil was the country of imagination and improvisation, a football of the unconscious, and it was here, outside time, that such an extemporaneous, eternal football would be rediscovered. They may have arrived as Europeans — Dahlmann's *De Telegraaf* despatch had pinpointed "the fundamental difference between the English and Brazilians: the latter celebrate the start of Lent with a flamboyant week-long carnival while in England they scoff fried batter" — but they would leave as South Americans. The de facto Republic of Punditaria thus played under the Brazilian flag, albeit modified. *Order and Progress*? This was neither better nor worse football, simply different, more exuberant. "History is not linear development," Dahlmann reassured them, a butterfly landing on his shoulder. "It's played between the lines." ("Yeah, they play between the lines in South America, alright," Nixon wisecracked. "Have a line, play, then have another line..."). Snorting with auspicious laughter, they daubed a prefix and accent on the flag to express the liberated imagination, the conditions for chance encounters: *DES-ORDEM É PROGRESSO*. Then they coloured over five stars — the *penta* — so that on the two inverted blue triangles remained 22 stars, symbolising equality, solidarity, collaboration: Corinthian values.

Discussions of the Tupi were just as animated. If they epitomised Brazilian-ness, then Dahlmann was sure they'd adopt a fluid, freestyle approach; Oswald reminded him that they pre-dated 'Brazil' (joking that the Jesuit *bandeirantes* pushing west — breaking in numbers, perhaps overcommitting — past the Tordesillas longitude, the Pope's high line, were offside) and assured them that Wilson would have them organised. He recalled the great anthropologist Nietzsche's description of the founders of the state: "They come like fate, without reason, consideration, or pretext; they appear as lightning, too terrible, too convincing, too sudden... their work is an instinctive creation and imposition of forms." Would the Tupi attain this higher integration? Answers would have to wait until kick-off, for the imperious Wilson failed to attend the mandatory presser. Meanwhile, his former mentor, now long-suffering deputy, Markúrtzki, had died of a broken heart having seen what his errant protégé was doing to the Tupi. His last words

— "The horror! The horror!" a cry that was no more than a breath — conveyed the scorched-earth cultural violence of 4-1-1-3-1, the crucifix schema, new manacles from the old continent.

The day of the game and the din of howler monkeys, brachiating in from far and wide, rumbled across the heavy forest air, transfiguring El Dorado into a bombinating Bombonera of barracked bravado. Dahlmann, a substitute, gave a pep-talk informing the gafferless pundits that the third enemy of the Man of Knowledge is Power: "Fear and Clarity have been conquered, large problems dissolved, the subtle becomes visible, but one doesn't know how to use this power and the two combine in a figure of capriciousness, whim, cruelty…"

Sure enough the Tupi were fiendishly well-drilled — the attacking defensive midfielder covering diligently, the full-backs' metamorphosis into pumas and jaguars rendering wide areas difficult to attack, the tapir a threat up front — but, even with their diabolic coach's sorcery, they lacked technique. The midfield duo became, variously, a black caiman, an anaconda, then, briefly, mistakenly, a headless chicken (corpsing Savage on radio commentary). *Amazonal Marking*, scribbled Barry Slab, grinning with atavistic glee while his compatriots in the press box (those lucky enough not to be playing), reverting to type amidst the lethal pressure, fulminated over Tupi simulation (in a true clash of taboos, the Pundits' brute *physicality* also vexed the Tupi). But the continual transmogrification of your players is exhausting and the English sensed space would open up later on, in the last four hours of the game.

On the other hand, Wilson knew that the rough forest floor disbarred the short game. The pundits needed to change things, and as each took a ladle of half-time *yagé*, Dahlmann, assailed and caressed by the sumptuous phantasmagoria, was tapped on the shoulder by a svelte figure in orange. It was Cruyff. *"Voetballen is heel simpel, maar het moeilijkste wat er is, is simpel voetballen,"* he said, telling the team that the fourth enemy of the Man of Knowledge is Death, the *élan vital* congealed into a thirst for abolition — of oneself and others. "Like Netherlands against Spain in… in Johannesburg. Van Bommel and De Jong, side by side?! Fascist football! Against art — art that the Dutch gave them! No," he trailed off, smiling wanly, "better to have glorious defeat like us in 1974, 1978…"

The pundits — starstruck, tired, hallucinating and unable to get 'their' passing game going — thought awhile about noble defeat, about their tournament of great losers, forgetting, momentarily, the Russian roulette of a game they were playing. Strychnine turned to Dahlmann and queried, "My Portuguese isn't up to much, but your book — is it *The Teachings of Mr Johan…*?" But Dahlmann was firing a blowdart at his philosopher-king (narrowly missing). "He wasn't there in 1978. That's Wilson." (He realised the butterfly was, too.)

The second half was another lengthy stalemate — a purgatory in which death could not be vanquished nor life resumed — and at full-time it was resolved to play until a golden goal. "Sudden death?" mewled Rodnipp. "Literally," Wilson shot back.

By now sceptical of the evidence of their kaleidoscope eyes, the pundits' tenacious empiricism had them scan the Copta charts for a way to break the deadlock, yet they saw only a tactical labyrinth, a garden of forking paths. Bewildered, they turned to Dahlmann on the bench, still hurriedly thumbing through *Ensimamentos*, trying to get to the end before The End. "Which way shall we run, Wim? What does *Don Juan* say?" He considered the *regista*'s thousand abandoned paths, his own forsaken career, and read: "Does this path have a heart? If it does, the path is good; if it doesn't, it is of no use. Both paths lead nowhere; but one has a heart, the other doesn't. One makes for a joyful journey; as long as you follow it, you are one with it. The other will make you curse your life. One makes you strong; the other weakens you. Does this path have a heart? If the answer is no, you will know it, and then you must choose another path. The trouble is nobody asks the question; and when a man finally realises that he has taken a path without a heart, the path is ready to kill him."

In the silence of that momentous epiphany Dahlmann thought about football's history and about evolution, about the deepest truths of survival, about the seedlings straining up, up toward the forest canopy, up toward the light, and deep in the pit of his stomach, as though put there by someone else, came knowledge, insight. Oswald — in whom he saw a summary and cipher of Brazil (his Brazil) — nodded numinously at him, then mouthed the word. "Mixer," Dahlmann ventriloquised, as though Brazil itself had resolved that he should decipher the tactical puzzle. "We need to get it in the mixer. They won't fancy it. I'll go up top." Hedging, Slab scrawled an alternative headline: *Cannibals versus Headhunters.*

If footballing limitations saw to it that Dahlmann entered the field without real hope, he was also without fear. While Wilson twitched in his technical area, the ball was swept out wide, a pass that seemingly defied the laws of physics. The Dutchman attacked the space and, just before the cross came in, two things occurred to him: first, that Wilson's tirade on the plane had been about crosses (*cruzamentos* not *cruzes*); second, that nobody — none of these men marinated in football — had asked who won the 2014 World Cup. None. He understood that transformation is only possible in the wilderness and had the conviction that the pundits were finally escaping the heavy burden of their contexts, finally on the verge of *a breakthrough...*

All this happened in an instant, in the time the truly greats foresee the game. He heard (or imagined) someone bellow, yet softly, as though an echo, "goals don't change games, they change societies," at which point, challenging the Tupi keeper (now some giant poisonous spider, coming to punch everything), he met — fearlessly, judiciously, powerfully — the timeless parabola of that ball fired across no man's land and, as it arrived, the moon on a sixpence, headed it toward El Dorado's frameless goal — never moving, dimensions unaltered — then fell backwards into the everafter. **B**

What is the highlight of the football season?

*According to Fantasy League Pro Managers

2%
FA Cup 3rd Round

3%
Champions League Final

4%
Transfer deadline day

16%
Last day of the season

14%
Opening weekend of the season

61%

Auction Night

Bid for players AGAINST your friends... Fantasy Football as it's meant to be played, since 1991.

175

Greatest Games

"None, though, burned quite so brightly, so briefly, as Igor Protti"

Bari 4 Internazionale 1

Serie A, Stadio San Nicola, Bari, 6 January 1996

By Rory Smith

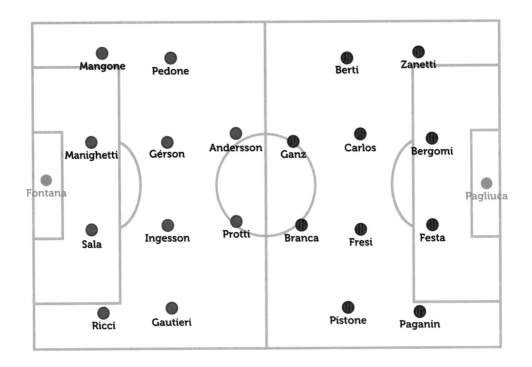

"It's better to live one hour as a tiger than a whole lifetime as a worm."
(The Cat, *Red Dwarf*)

In the mind's eye, every goal is the same. A figure, slightly hunched, hair jet black, shirt untucked, socks rolled around the ankle, standing maybe 30 yards from goal, in the inside-left channel. The ball zips to his feet. He has drifted, almost unconsciously, into that corridor of uncertainty, a little too far from the full-back, out of the orbit of either central defender. He glances up. **Space. The movement starts.**

The ball is brought to heel with his left foot and his body opens up, right arm swinging out, as if holding open a door. He flicks the ball with his right foot and starts to sprint. It is not elegant, like a gazelle, or a horse, but hurried, shuffling, like an adulterer scampering through a garden, clothes clasped in one hand, covering his exposed crotch. One bound. Two. The ball sitting there, invitingly now.

It all happens like that, in the blink of an eye, in a breath. He looks up. The goalkeeper is starting to crouch, poised. He cocks his right leg, a trigger. Now for the poetry. In one motion, he sweeps through the ball, his torso contorting with the force, right arm lifting up, left arm swinging down, a highwayman on the bowling lanes. The ball flies, no spin at all, not into the far corner — as most goalkeepers would expect — but low, flat, inside the near post. He races away, that black hair — slightly mulleted, if we're completely honest with ourselves — flapping against the nape of his neck, mouth gaping in a scream, a roar. In the mind's eye, every single one of the 24 goals he scored in that one golden season is the same.

There is a curiosity to the one-season wonder that exerts a strange sorcery over the imagination. The player who emerges from anonymity, from mediocrity, and then, over the course of nine months, explodes into our consciousness, a flash of light and sound and promise. Anything seems possible. The game's very pantheon shakes at this intruder, this Everyman who might yet rewrite history, who seems suddenly destined to take his seat among the greats. And then? Nothing. He fades into obscurity, ordinarily after moving on to greener, more fertile pastures, and finds himself exiled in Nowheresville once more, forever remembering, wondering, despairing at what might have been, taunted and mocked and jeered and condemned as a waste of talent, of life. He has had his hour as a tiger. He must return to being a worm.

Maybe that is why the one-season wonder appeals so much. It is not just

that its existence hints at life's limitless possibility, that it gives us hope not just that the good-for-nothing makeweights in our team might one day, for one moment, touch the stars; but that we might, too. It is the same sentiment that infuses the narrative of the superhero — the mild-mannered journalist or photographer or whatever who can fly or shoot webs or construct a tool-belt which can contain myriad heavy kit but still, somehow, defy gravity to such an extent that your trousers do not fall down — and that plays into rom-coms, too, those stories of Average Joe getting Katherine Heigl because of the one special trait that he suddenly discovers he possesses. It tells us that our own ordinariness need not be permanent, that it should not hold us back. The one season wonder gives everyone chance to dream.

At first, though, only at first. The inevitable denouement to the story — and it is inevitable, because otherwise they would not be one-season wonders — plays to a different psychological trope. It reminds us that even those who seem to reach to the sky can fall to earth. The one-season wonder is Icarus. It teaches us that perhaps it is OK being a worm, forever, because it means you do not know the pain of what it was to be a tiger. It is hope and it is despair, stirring Wagnerian bombast and muted Radiohead despair. It is life. The one-season wonder is an encapsulation of the human condition.

Everyone will have their favourite. Michael Ricketts, once of Bolton, is probably the purest example. One year of cloudburst, and then an endless desert, a perennial drought. There are more. Marcus Stewart, Francis Jeffers, Chris Armstrong, Matt Jansen, Danny Cadamarteri, Michael Johnson: there are countless domestic examples, increasingly shrouded in the mists of memory. And abroad? Daniel Güiza, maybe, who so cleverly timed his one season in the sun so that he might win the European Championship with Spain. Roque Santa Cruz, too, could be included, for all the rich promise he once boasted and for all that football's most handsome striker has suffered more than his fair share of injuries. You could even make a case for Fernando Torres, if the category were expanded to include those whose excellence endured for two years.

None, though, burned quite so brightly, so briefly, as Igor Protti. In one year, one glorious year, Protti illuminated Serie A. In the 1995-96 season, that was no mean feat. This was a league that was by some distance the finest in the world; it was home to the very best defenders in the world, to the very best teams. Its strike-forces were comprised of Gabriel Batistuta, Roberto Baggio, Oliver Bierhoff, Enrico Chiesa, Pierluigi Casiraghi, the great and the good, and yet they were all left in Protti's wake.

Only Giuseppe Signori, of Lazio, could keep pace with him. Both finished on 24 goals, sharing the prestigious title of *capocannoniere*, but it is a simple measure of Protti's excellence that season that, while Signori was part of a crack Lazio side designed and built at considerable cost to challenge for the title, Bari were relegated. They possessed the league's deadliest striker, but they went down. Protti was not far off a one-man band.

And in the mind's eye, every goal was the same: the cut in, the look up, the searing, fizzing shot and the ecstatic, almost Korybantic, celebration. They were not, of course: he scored headers and tap-ins and free-kicks and chips and, against Atalanta, a brilliant bicycle kick, but sufficient followed the blueprint that it is those that endure most powerfully in the memory. It is those goals that gave him his hour as a tiger.

And in that hour, this was his most tigrine, most predatory moment. The ugly, sprawling monstrosity of the Stadio San Nicola, far from full, but about as full as it ever gets, for the visit in January 1996 of Roy Hodgson's Internazionale, another side with aspirations considerably higher than mere survival.

Looking at the line-ups now, it really was Hodgson's Inter; looking at the line-ups, it becomes clear why Inter did not go on to win the league. He named five full-backs in his two banks of four, one of them, Roberto Carlos, in central midfield. He also named Gianluca Festa in central defence, which rather suggests that the idea of mid-90s Serie A as home of the most impregnable practitioners of *catenaccio* might have been somewhat exaggerated.

And Bari? Well, this was not the Bari of Gianluca Zambrotta — that came later — or the Bari, more recent still, that could call upon a teenage Antonio Cassano. This was Eugenio Fascetti's Bari, with the ponderous Klas Ingesson in midfield, with energetic but limited wingers like Carmine Gautieri and with Kennet Andersson, the Swedish Ian Ormondroyd, upfront. This was not a Bari for the ages. But it was a Bari for Protti. It was the perfect Bari for

Protti, and that year, and that night, Protti was perfect, too.

He would have to be. Even with Hodgson's revolutionary five full-back formation, Inter's class was evident. Roberto Carlos put them ahead just 16 minutes in, a moment worthy of recording, simply because the Brazilian — deployed in midfield —scored with his right foot, crashing in Maurizio Ganz's cut-back from just outside the box.

So far, so regulation. Inter would have been expected to win this game comfortably, in normal circumstances. Bari's approach was unsubtle, predictable: work the ball wide, to Gautieri and Pedone, and try to use Andersson's aerial prowess to expose Festa and Bergomi. Inter, even in such comparatively straitened times, had more than sufficient wit and wisdom to repel their advances.

Not so. Gianluca Pagliuca had not been drawn into a save of note when Bari equalised; in retrospect, perhaps they were profiting from the goalkeeper's boredom. He rushed to meet an inswinging corner, but found himself blocked by Nicola Berti, his own team-mate, and beaten fairly simply to the ball by the leaping Luigi Sala, Bari's rangy 21-year-old central defender. All square.

Suddenly, Bari swarmed all over Inter. Pagliuca redeemed himself, partially, for his mistake just two minutes later, brilliantly tipping over a volley from Protti, then denying Gérson, Bari's pedestrian Brazilian midfield player, from close range. Inter were shaking, crumbling. Who knows: perhaps they did not have enough full-backs on the pitch.

The turning point, though, came when one of those players was forcibly removed, the legendary Giuseppe Bergomi — bafflingly allowed to play while wearing the sort of gold chain you'd expect to see on offer at Elizabeth Duke — dismissed with 20 minutes to play. It was no surprise that his second yellow card came for a foul on Protti. This was Protti's evening. Before then, he had seen two passionate penalty appeals turned down and been denied by Pagliuca once more. He was, in a figurative sense, omnipresent. This was his apotheosis.

It was the moment that he seared that image, contorted limbs and smooth, feline movement, into memory, too. 73 minutes in. Wide left; a touch further out and a touch further across than he would ordinarily like. No matter. Control the ball, drop the shoulder, duck inside Marco Branca's limp, flaccid challenge. Into his stride now, building speed. One touch, two. One pace, two. Open the ball out from his body. Glance up. Shoot.

His entire bodyweight went through that ball, the effort expended lifting him from the ground. He was 30 yards from goal. It was typical Protti. With one exception: the ball did not fly, low and flat, to the near post. It gained altitude, cutting through the air, and seemed somehow to burn not past Pagliuca but through him. It swerved a little, just as he tried to punch it clear, and then it dipped into the net. It was the sort of goal Hotshot Hamish scored. It landed dead centre of the goal. Pagliuca landed on the floor. A wisp of smoke floated from his hair, singed by the speed of the ball.

That was it. Inter faded, melted, slumped. Klas Ingesson scored the third with 10 minutes to go, Gérson nipping to the right touch-line, cutting the ball back, and the Swede, with surprising delicacy of touch, curling round and past the helpless Pagliuca.

The final word, though, was Protti's. Suddenly, grace was flowering in the most unlikely places. Andersson chipped Pagliuca from 35 yards; the ball struck the bar. Protti was there, shirt untucked, socks around his ankles, captain's armband trailing from his bicep, to head the rebound into the corner and wheel away, to receive the ovation of his adoring public. Their night, his night. The night it all worked.

Bari would beat Inter again, three years later, the game in which Antonio Cassano announced himself to the world, controlling Simone Perrotta's long ball with his studs, flicking the ball over his shoulder and scoring the sort of goal most players wait a lifetime to witness, let alone actually perform. That was the start of things for Cassano. He went on to Roma and Real Madrid and Internazionale and AC Milan and he slept with a lot of women and ate a lot of pastries and lived the dream, his dream.

For Protti, though, this season was the end. Before his time at Bari, Protti had toiled away from Italian football's spotlight, at Rimini, Livorno, Messina and the like. He spent four years at Bari, but none of the three that preceded 1995-96 even hinted at what was to come. He scored 46 goals for the club. 24 of them came in that one year.

That was enough to earn him a move to Lazio, and it is here that the narrative of the one-season reasserts its authority. He spent three years in Rome, but was loaned out to Napoli for one of them and Reggiana for much of another. He did not settle. He certainly never looked like he would be able to reproduce the form that had brought him to national attention. He was released from his contract.

And that, really, should have been the end of Protti. He should have faded from view. Maybe, though, he was not quite a one-season wonder. That respectable season on loan at Reggiana attracted the attentions of Livorno, where he had spent three years at the start of his career.

He would end it there, too, helping the standard-bearers of Italy's left — how apt — from Serie C1 to Serie B and then, in 2005, to ninth place in Serie A. They remember him in Livorno, of course. He has been granted the freedom of the city, and he — bizarrely — appeared on stage there in a version of the opera La Bohème in 2012. The club even retired his number 10 shirt, for a time, until he asked them not to.

But it is in Bari where memories burn the brightest. It is to that one glorious year that the mind's eye is drawn, where Protti was perfect, and where all the goals were the same. Ⓑ

181

Eight Bells

"It felt like the carnival
had come to town."

Goalless Draws

A selection of the best 0-0s in history

By Jonathan Wilson

1 Scotland 0 England 0, friendly international, West of Scotland Cricket Ground, Partick, 30 November 1872

There are those who look on goalless draws as a negation of what football should be about but stalemates have always been with us and take a proud place in the history of the game, right from the days when sides would line up with seven or eight forward players. The first game played under the rules codified by the Football Association in 1863, a friendly between Barnes and Richmond in Battersea Park, finished goalless. So too did the first full international fixture.

A match had been played at the Oval on 5 March 1870 between an England representative side and a team made up of Scots living in the London area, and such a success was it that the experiment was repeated four more times in the following two years, England winning three times and drawing twice. It was not, though, a full Scotland team and when the Scottish FA, looking to help popularise the game north of the border, suggested a proper international fixture, the FA were quick to accept.

Their secretary, CW Alcock, who had been born in Sunderland but educated at Harrow, was one of the great early pioneers of the game, establishing the FA Cup and being a prime mover in the five London-based quasi-internationals. He would have captained the England team but for injury and so made do with being their nominated umpire.

More than 2,000 fans turned out in Partick, generating gate receipts of £109, to see Scotland flummox England by adopting the devilish technique of passing. The Scots were just over a stone a man lighter than the English and they had been worried in the build-up to the game that they would be overwhelmed if they indulged in the head-down charging and dribbling that tended to comprise the game then. So they decided they would set out to frustrate England by keeping the ball from them, by passing it, to which end they pulled a forward back to play in midfield, countering England's 1-2-7 with a 2-2-6. They were emphatically successful and changed the nature of the game as a result. "The strong point with the home club," the report in the *Glasgow Herald* noted, "was that they played excellently well together." For a nation new to the game and with far fewer players to draw on than England, a 0-0 draw was regarded as a remarkable triumph.

2 Bury 0 Newcastle United 0, Football League Division One, Gigg Lane, 11 February 1925

The first game and the first international may have finished 0-0, but it was a scoreline that always sat uneasily with the authorities. The first big problem arose in 1898 with the final game in a series of test matches played out between the bottom two in the First Division, Stoke City and Blackburn Rovers and the top two in the Second, Burnley and Newcastle United, to determine promotion and relegation. Going into their final game at the Victoria Ground, Stoke and Burnley were joint top of the table, and knew that a draw would ensure both First Division status; they played out a shameless 0-0 that didn't feature a single shot on goal.

A crowd of 4,000 turned out despite heavy rain and strong winds and seemed to have been disgusted by the way Stoke went about retaining their top-flight status. They booed and jeered and then, in the second half, the crowd on the Boothen Road side of the ground began to amuse themselves by holding onto the ball every time it went into the stand. One ball was punted into the River Trent, another kicked onto the roof of the stand and two simply vanished. At one point a linesman and a policeman, both sprinting to try to prevent another ball ending up on the terrace, smacked into each other and ended up in a heap on the ground. The Football League was so appalled it immediately abandoned test matches and introduced automatic promotion and relegation.

Goals, the League and the FA believed, were the lifeblood of the game, and they regarded the increasing professionalism and pragmatism that followed the First World War with suspicion – in particular the prevalence of the offside trap. Newcastle weren't alone in applying

it, but their full-back pairing of Frank Hudspeth and Bill McCracken were probably the most adept. The goalless draw at Bury, Newcastle's sixth of a season that produced what at the time was an unthinkably low average of 2.58 goals per game, came as the final straw as the authorities sought to combat falling attendances.

At the time, for a forward to be onside, three defending players had to be between him and his opponent's goal, which meant it was relatively simple for one full-back to step up and try to catch a forward offside, knowing the other could still act as cover if he mistimed the trap. The FA came up with two proposed changes: a) require only two players to be in advance of the forward; b) add a line in each half 40 yards from goal behind which a forward could not be offside. A series of exhibition games were arranged to test the two variants, with the first half being played under one proposal, and the second under the other.

At a meeting in London on 15 June 1925, the FA decided they preferred the 'two players' version. The Scottish FA soon adopted the amendment as well, and it was they who presented the proposed rule-change to the International Board, the new variant being adopted ahead of the 1925-26 season. The change was an immediate success, with the average goals per game shooting up to 3.69 the following season. It was adapting to the new rule that led Herbert Chapman to pioneer the development from 2-3-5 to W-M at Arsenal in the latter half of the decade, setting in motion the whole evolution of modern tactics.

3 **Boca Juniors 0 Olimpia 0, Copa Libertadores final**
second leg, La Bombonera, Buenos Aires, 27 July 1979

Not until 1988 did the Copa Libertadores use aggregate score in the final. Until then, if one team won the first leg and the other won the second, the final went to a play-off, no matter what the respective margins of victory. So although goals from Osvaldo Aquino and Miguel Ángel Piazza at the Defensores del Chaco had given Olimpia a 2-0 win in Asunción, that was not quite such a convincing advantage as it may appear to modern eyes. To become the first Paraguayan team to win the Libertadores, they had to go to la Bombonera and avoid defeat against a Boca side seeking a third successive title. Olimpia, despite winning the Paraguayan championship 23 times to earn the nickname 'the King of Cups', had in 12 previous efforts advanced beyond the first phase only once — and that as long ago as 1960.

Any nerves Olimpia may have felt must have been intensified in the first minutes as their goalkeeper Ever Almeida was forced into a sprawling save to push away a ferocious shot from Miguel Ángel Bordón. As the siege continued, Almeida made save after save and Bordón thudded a shot against the crossbar. Boca kept creating chances and they kept on being repulsed, largely by the heroics of Almeida. As Boca grew increasingly desperate, the game became increasingly violent, with the result that each side ended the game with two red cards. More importantly for Olimpia, though, neither finished it with any goals and with a win and a draw they were champions.

"It wasn't just a massive moment for Olimpia fans, it was a massive moment for all supporters of Paraguayan football," Gabriel Cazenave, the sports editor of ABC Color, said. "The event was unique in our history. Everybody can remember where they were that day. I celebrated the victory out on the streets. It felt like the carnival had come to town."

4 **Werder Bremen 0 Bayern Munich 0, Bundesliga,**
Weserstadion, Bremen, 22 April 1986

Even now the former Werder Bremen forward Michael Kutzop changes his phone number every few weeks. The mocking calls have slowed down but they haven't entirely stopped; he remains the man who cost Werder the Bundesliga title in 1986. What made it was worse that it seemed part of an inevitable sequence: Otto Rehhagel's Werder always finished second, they were always pipped by Bayern. When Rehhagel first acquired the nickname King Otto, he was Otto II, always taking silver.

The two sides met in the penultimate game of the season with Werder two points clear of Bayern at the top of the table (the Bundesliga didn't award two points for a win until 1994). Udo Lattek, the Bayern coach, and Rehhagel had been sparring for weeks and extra edge was added by the horrendous foul committed by Bayern's Klaus Augenthaler on Rudi Völler in the sides' first meeting of the season.

Völler had not played since, but was named as a substitute and came off the bench with 12 minutes remaining. 10 minutes later, he was involved in the moment for which the game will always be remembered, as his cross smacked into Søren Lerby's face and bounced down onto his arm. The referee gave a harsh penalty. Bayern protested and a melee broke out. Even after order was restored, several minutes passed before Kutzop could take the penalty, as officials struggled to retrieve the ball from the stands, where it had been kicked by Egon Coordes, the Bayern assistant coach.

Kutzop was a specialist. He had once scored 22 consecutive penalties for Offenbach and had converted eight times from the spot already that season. His secret, it was said, was to wait until he saw the keeper move, and put the ball the other way. Jean-Marie Pfaff, the Bayern goalkeeper, stood still and Kutzop thumped his penalty against the post. It was the only one he missed in six years at the club. "I'll never forget the sound the ball made as it hit the post," he said. Even now, to Germans, a player who hits the post with a penalty is said to have "done a Kutzop".

Shattered, the Werder players trudged off the pitch, past bottles of champagne bought for their title celebrations that would remain forever unopened. The following week they lost to Stuttgart, while Bayern, who had not been top all season, hammered Borussia Mönchengladbach 6-0 to take the title on goal difference.

5 **Steaua Bucharest 0 Barcelona 0, European Cup final, Estadio Ramón Sánchez Pizjuán, Seville, 7 May 1986**

For Steaua Bucharest, the European Cup was an impossible, magnificent dream.

No eastern European side had ever won the trophy and they themselves had never got beyond the first round. When their president, Valentin Ceausescu, the son of the dictator, insisted early in the season they were good enough to do so, he was ridiculed. A magnificent semi-final win over Anderlecht, though, offered compelling evidence of their quality. In the final they faced Terry Venables's Barcelona, another team who had never won the trophy, but one whose sense of its own destiny had been heightened in the semi-final, when they had overcome a 3-0 first-leg deficit to win on penalties. Worse, the game was played in Seville, which meant at least 95% of the stadium would be supporting Barça.

Barça ripped into Steaua from the off, presumably reasoning that an early goal against anxious opponents would settle the game. But with Miodrag Belodedici outstanding, Steaua survived a fraught opening 30 minutes, and as the breakthrough remained elusive, so Barça's doubts began to grow. "After the first half hour," said the Steaua midfielder Lucian Bălan, "the Barcelona players began to lose their confidence and also their nerve."

Central to their concerns was the form of Steve Archibald, who had only just recovered from a hamstring injury to be controversially selected ahead of Pichi Alonso and clearly lacked sharpness. "He ran a lot," said the Steaua defender Adrian Bumbescu. "He was very dangerous, but he wasn't so brave in our physical battles." Archibald was eventually substituted in extra-time, but before that Venables had taken off the brilliant but temperamental Bernd Schuster. Furious, the German stormed not merely off the pitch, but out of the stadium — a clear indication of Barça's shattered morale.

As Barça grew increasing desperate, the Steaua coach Emerich Jenei remained in control, shaping events rather than reacting to them, and, after 73 minutes, he made one of the greatest substitutions ever made in a final. Steaua's assistant coach Anghel Iordănescu had not played in a competitive game all season but he had retained his registration. He came on for Bălan, his composure ensuring calm as the possibility of seeing the game through drew closer. Steaua, though, remained reluctant to press for a winner of their own, and so, after 120 sterile minutes, the match went to penalties. Mihai Majearu, Steaua's usual penalty taker, saw his kick saved by Javier Urruti, but Helmut Ducadam then fisted away José Alexanco's effort. Urruti saved from Laszló Bölni, but Ducadam also kept out Ángel Pedraza's shot.

Having seen four kicks missed, Marius Lăcătuş dispensed with subtleties and belted his kick in off the crossbar. Ducadam, diving to his right for the third time, saved from Pichi Alonso. Gavrila Balint made it 2-0, meaning that Marcos had to score. "Watching it again on television after many years," Ducadam said, "I realise that the fourth taker for Barcelona didn't have a clue what he should do, because I'd saved all the other penalties on the same side. I watched him and had eye-to-eye contact with him. I played a trick on Marcos. I shaped to go to the left and then to the right, then I went left."

He saved it, the last save he ever made for Steaua. "I'd had pains in my right arm for six months before the final," he said. "I got drugs from the doctors to control them, but the medicine wasn't strong enough. One day that summer I was with my friends in my home town and I fell over. I put my hand down to protect myself and the aneurysm went to the artery and blocked the circulation for the whole arm. I had surgery, some kind of bypass. In 1988 I had another operation and [in 2010] I had another operation with modern technology."

Amid rumours Ducadam had been done away with by Ceausescu's henchmen for some unspecified affront, he essentially disappeared, eventually taking up a job as a customs official. "Maybe I was unlucky," he said, "but maybe I was lucky as well. If it had happened just a few weeks earlier..."

6 Netherlands 0 Italy 0, European Championship semi-final, Amsterdam Arena, 29 June 2000

The late nineties saw a surge of wonderful attacking football that culminated at Euro 2000. That was the tournament at which 4-2-3-1 first began to enter the mainstream, when the attacking midfielder, dribblers, wingers and schemers found a new role. It was a tournament in which England and Germany were made to look ponderous and old-fashioned, their three straight lines and antiquated anachronism. It was the tournament of Zinédine Zidane, Youri Djorkaeff, Luis Figo, Manuel Rui Costa, Zlatko Zahović, Raúl and Pavel Nedved, when creators, suddenly revelling in new-found freedom, came out to play. It was also a tournament of one of the greatest goalless draws there has ever been.

The Netherlands had their creators, of course, notably Marc Overmars and Dennis Bergkamp, while Italy had Francesco Totti, but this was a game that came to be defined by national stereotype: as Italy defended magnificently, the Dutch, for all their technical brilliance, imploded.

Bergkamp had already struck a post after jinking past Mark Iuliano when, after 34 minutes, the game seemed to turn decisively favour of Holland. The full-back Gianluca Zambrotta, having been booked for a foul on Boudewijn Zenden earlier in the game, was beaten by a sharp turn from the winger, hacked his legs from under him and was rightly sent off.

Italy reorganised with Alessandro Del Piero tucked into the right side of midfield and dug in, presenting the Netherlands with two banks of four, neither of which was much inclined to leave its own half. Four minutes after the red card, the Dutch were presented with the perfect opportunity to take the lead as Alessandro Nesta impeded Patrick Kluivert to concede a penalty. But Frank de Boer's spot-kick was hit at a comfortable height for the goalkeeper Francesco Toldo, who pushed it away.

At the time it seemed unlikely to matter but with Nesta dogging Kluivert's every step and Fabio Cannavaro outstanding, the expected rush of Dutch chances never materialised. And then, after 62 minutes, came another penalty as Edgar Davids was caught by Iuliano. This time Kluivert took the responsibility, but his firm low shot bounced back off the post.

Reprieved, Italy seemed to find another level as though they sensed fortune was on their side. They could even have won it the first half of extra-time, Marco Delvecchio twice shooting wide after promising counter-attacks, but it finished goalless and went to penalties. Luigi Di Biagio, who had missed against France in the World Cup quarter-final two years earlier, thumped home the first. De Boer, one miss already on his mind, was again denied by Toldo. In four previous attempts in major tournaments, Italy had never won a shoot-out, but as Gianluca Pessotto scored and Jaap Stam blazed a mile over they edged towards the final.

There was a brief wobble as Paolo Maldini missed the fourth kick after Totti and Kluivert had both converted but the Dutch were too set on self-destruction to take advantage. Toldo saved from Paul Bosvelt — a fifth miss out of six in the match for the Dutch — and Italy were through.

- -

7 Barcelona 0 Celtic 0, Uefa Cup fourth round second leg, Nou Camp, Barcelona, 25 March 2004

Under Martin O'Neill, Celtic enjoyed some extraordinary results in European competitions, but none, surely, was so frankly implausible as the rearguard action they mounted in the Camp Nou on the last great European night of his reign. They led 1-0 from Alan Thompson's goal in the first leg, a fractious, enthralling game in which Rab Douglas, Thiago Motta and Javier Saviola were all sent off, but as Barcelona poured forwards in the early stages in the second leg, that advantage looked distinctly flimsy.

With Douglas suspended, Celtic were forced to turn to their 19-year-old reserve goalkeeper David Marshall whose very evident nerves were hardly helped when he skewed an awful Jackie McNamara backpass out for a corner in the second minute. With Ronaldinho to the fore, Barça, coming off the back of nine straight victories in La Liga, put together great fluid passages of passing that at times swept through Celtic's defence: real humiliation was a possibility, and it seemed unlikely they could hold out until the ninth minute, never mind the 90th.

Marshall scrambled away a Gerard header, and Luis Enrique then deflected a goalbound shot against the keeper's extended arm, as somehow Celtic did hold on. Not merely until the ninth minute, but until the 19th, the 29th, half-time. There was no early goal in the second half, and Barcelona's exasperation was palpable — and with it a renewed and agonising sense of Celtic hope.

A Xavi chip set Luis García through against Marshall, but, diving backwards, the 19 year old got enough of a fingertip on his shot to deflect it over the bar. Then, diving to his left, Marshall clawed away a snap-shot from the substitute Sergio García, whose energy and drive had briefly rekindled Barça hopes.

The jitters were gone, and Marshall and Celtic suddenly seemed invincible as Barça's early fluency disappeared to be replaced by a string of frustrated and harmless long-range efforts from Ronaldinho. "He has a terrific presence and calmness, he's not fazed at all," the Celtic manager O'Neill said of his keeper. "He did an interview for TV after the match and was last into the dressing-room. When he came in it was to enormous applause from the rest of his team-mates."

It was richly deserved.

8 Zambia 0 Côte d'Ivoire 0, Stade d'Angondjé, Libreville, 12 February, 2012

There are times when a team's sense of destiny becomes overwhelming. After Zambia had beaten Ghana 1-0 in the semi-final in Bata, the president of their football federation, Kalusha Bwalya, insisted there was no way his side could lose the final against Côte d'Ivoire. "There won't just be 11 players out there," he said, "but also 11 ghosts." It was Zambia's first game in Gabon since a plane carrying their squad from Lusaka to Dakar for a World Cup qualifier in 1993 had crashed shortly after taking off from Libreville where it had stopped to refuel.

Didier Drogba missed a second half-penalty and, with the Ivorians wilting in the face of the Zambians' self-belief, the penalty shoot-out was somehow both nerve-wracking and yet predictable. Seven players from each side scored, then Kolo Touré, stepping forward as Gervinho refused his bench's entreaties to take the eighth kick, was denied by Kennedy Mweene. Rainford Kalaba could have won it, but fired over. Then Gervinho did, at last, go forward —and missed. Stoppilla Sunzu, a centre-back from the DR Congo champions TP Mazembe, lashed home and Zambia — and the ghosts — had their triumph. On the running-track that surrounded the pitch, Bwalya stood silently. On the pitch, the Zambian players knelt in prayer. Zambia's coach, Hervé Renard, wearing the lucky white shirt that gave him the air of a Mills & Boon hero, picked up the injured full-back Joseph Musonda and carried him to join his team-mates in their celebratory devotions. In the press box, journalists openly wept at the emotion of it all.

There were tears too from the Ivorians, their golden generation thwarted for the second time in six years in a penalty shoot-out in the final after a goalless draw. In Cairo in 2006, they had lost to Egypt, poor Drogba both missing a sitter with eight minutes remaining and then failing from the spot.

Their only other appearance in the final, in Dakar in 1992, had also finished 0-0, but that time they had won, to complete a remarkable tournament for their goalkeeper Alain Gouamene, who had gone unbeaten in all five games — a total, given two of the matches went to extra time, of 510 minutes. Côte d'Ivoire drew

0-0 with Cameroon in the semi, then Gouamene saved three penalties in the shoot-out, but what happened in the final against Ghana was even more dramatic.

At the time Ghana were the most successful side in the Cup of Nations' history, and against Côte d'Ivoire, who were looking for their first ever trophy in senior football, they were overwhelming favourites. As in previous rounds, though, Côte d'Ivoire frustrated their opponents, and, after 120 minutes of stalemate, they faced their second penalty shoot-out in successive games. Isaac Asare missed Ghana's fourth-kick, but then Joel Tiehi, with a chance to win it, also failed. And so it went on. And on. After 10 penalties each, it was 9-9. Gouamene scored for the Ivory Coast, but then Edward Ansah, the Ghana keeper, also fired home, so it was back to the start of the list again. Kouame Aka converted for a second time, but Anthony Baffoe saw his effort saved by Gouamene, leaving Côte d'Ivoire as champions and the goalkeeper as an obvious man of the tournament.

Contributors
The Blizzard, Issue Nine

Nick Ames is a journalist for Arsenal. He has also written for *World Soccer* and *Champions*, among others.
Twitter: @NickAmes82

Philippe Auclair is the author of *The Enchanted Kingdom of Tony Blair* (in French) and *Cantona: the Rebel Who Would Be King*, which was named BSBA Football Book of the Year. His biography of Thierry Henry has just been published. He writes for *France Football* and *Offside* and provides analysis and commentary for RMC Sport. He also pursues a parallel career in music under the name 'Louis Philippe'. **Twitter: @PhilippeAuclair**

Anthony Clavane is the author of *Promised Land: A Northern Love Story*, which won Football Book of the Year and Sports Book of the Year at the 2011 British Sports Book Awards. His second book, *Does Your Rabbi Know You're Here?* was shortlisted for Football Book of the Year at this year's awards. He writes about sport for the *Sunday Mirror*.
Website: www.anthony-clavane.com
Twitter: @lufcpromised.

Dan Colasimone is the founder and editor of the Argentina Football World website. After a seven-year stint in Argentina he is now back in his native Australia covering a variety of sports for Sportal. He is currently working on a guide to Argentinian football folklore which is due out later in 2013.
Twitter: @ArgentinaFW

David Conn is the author of *Richer Than God: Manchester City, Modern Football and Growing Up*. It was shortlisted for football book of the year in the British Sports Book Awards. He writes about football for the *Guardian*. His previous books are *The Beautiful Game? Searching for the Soul of Football* (2004) and *The Football Business* (1997).
Twitter: @david_conn

Davidde Corran is a journalist working across TV, radio and print. Originally from Melbourne, Australia he is currently based in England. **Twitter: @Davidde Corran**

James Corbett is a sports correspondent and award-winning author who has reported from 20 countries across five continents for outlets including the BBC, the *Observer*, the *Guardian*, the *Sunday Times* and *FourFourTwo*. His books include the *Everton Encyclopedia* and his collaboration with Neville Southall, *The Binman Chronicles*. He is currently working on a book about football governance. **Twitter: @james_corbett**

Noah Davis is a New York-based freelance writer and deputy editor of AmericanSoccerNow.com
Twitter: @noahedavis

Ian Hawkey is the author of *Feet of the Chameleon, The Story of African Football*, a winner of the National Sporting Club's Football Book of the Year.

Maciej Iwanski is a sports journalist and commentator for Poland's biggest TV station, TVP and has been uefa.com correspondent in Poland for seven years.

Simon Kuper is author of *Football Against the Enemy*, a winner of the William Hill Sports Book of the Year, and *Ajax, The Dutch, The War*. His latest book, *The Football Men*, was published by Simon & Schuster in May 2011. He is a columnist with the *Financial Times*. A new expanded edition of *Soccernomics* (previously called *Why England Lose* in the UK) was published last summer.

Antonis Oikonomidis is a Greek journalist who has worked for *France Football*, *FourFourTwo* and *World Soccer*.

Scott Oliver is an honorary research fellow in Nottingham University's Department of Latin American Studies, where he completed a doctorate on Peronist Argentina. He has written about cricket for the *Guardian*, cricinfo, *Spin* and Wisden India and football for BT and ESPN. **Twitter: @reverse_sweeper**

Gwendolyn Oxenham is the author of *Finding the Game: Three Years, Twenty-Five Countries, and the Search for Pickup Soccer*. She's also the co-director of *Pelada*, a documentary about informal games around the world.

Igor Rabiner is the author of *How Spartak Has Been Killed* (in Russian), winner in the Sports Investigation category at Knizhnoe Obozrenie's Sports Book Awards. His latest book is *Did Russia Buy the 2018 World Cup?* He has been Russian Football Journalist of the Year four times.

Joel Richards is a journalist based in Buenos Aires. He writes about Argentinian football for *World Soccer* and is the author of *Super Clasico*. **Twitter: @joel_richards**

Charlie Robinson teaches philosophy at the Metropolitan University in Prague, and completed his doctorate at the University of Manchester. He writes on the ethics of sport and political philosophy, and has written for *When Saturday Comes* and *The Football Ramble*. Email: robinson@mup.cz

Rory Smith writes about football for *The Times*, as long as someone with a foreign-sounding name is in the news. He has previously worked at all three *Mirror* titles, both of the *Telegraphs* and, briefly, a pair of *Independents*. He ghosted Rafael Benitez's first memoir, *Champions League Dreams*, and moved some commas around on *The Numbers Game*. He was once nearly on *Blockbusters*.

Jon Spurling is an assistant headteacher who contributes to *FourFourTwo* and *When Saturday Comes*. He has written numerous books about Arsenal and *Death or Glory! The Dark History of the World Cup*.

Tim Vickery writes and broadcasts on South American football for the BBC, World Soccer, ESPN, SBS and TalkSport.

Jonathan Wilson is the author of *Inverting the Pyramid*, a winner of the BSBA Football Book of the Year and the Antonio Ghirelli Award, *Behind the Curtain*, *The Anatomy of England* and *Nobody Ever Says Thank You*. His latest book is *The Outsider: A History of the Goalkeeper*. He writes for the *Guardian*, *The National*, *World Soccer*, Foxsoccer, Foxasia and *Sports Illustrated*. **Twitter: @jonawils**

Blizzard Subscriptions

Subscribe to the print version of The Blizzard, *be the first to receive new issues, get exclusive Blizzard offers and access digital versions of all back-issues FREE*

Subscription Options

Set Price for Four Issues

Get a four-issue subscription to *The Blizzard* — for you or as a gift — for a flat fee including postage and packing (P&P):

UK:	£35
Europe:	£45
Non-Euorpe:	£55

Recurring Pay-What-You-Like

Set up a quarterly recurring payment for each edition of *The Blizzard*. The recommended retail price (RRP) is £12, but pay what you like, subject to a minimum fee of £6 plus P&P

See www.theblizzard.co.uk for more

Digital Subscriptions

If the cost of postage is prohibitive, or you just want an excuse to use your new iPad or Kindle, you can set up a subscription to digital versions of *The Blizzard* for just £3 per issue.

See www.theblizzard.co.uk for more

Information for Existing Subscribers

Free Digital Downloads for *Blizzard* Subscribers

Whether you have taken advantage of our set price or pay-what-you-like offer, for the duration of your subscription to *The Blizzard* you are entitled to download every issue FREE.

See www.theblizzard.co.uk for more

We very much value the commitment of our print subscribers and have a policy to make available new issues, special offers and other limited access events and benefits to print subscribers first.

About *The Blizzard*

Distribution & Back Issues
Contact Information
About Issue Nine

Buy *The Blizzard*

We want as many readers as possible for *The Blizzard*. We therefore operate as far as we are able on a pay-what-you-like basis for digital and print versions.

Digital Version (Current & Back Issues)

All issues of *The Blizzard* are available to download for Kindle, Android, iOS and PC/Mac at: *www.theblizzard.co.uk*.

- *RRP: £3*
- *Pay-what-you-like minimum: £0.01*

Printed Version (Current & Back Issues)

Purchase a physical copy of *The Blizzard* in all its luxurious, tactile, sensual glory at: *www.theblizzard.co.uk*. If you haven't felt our rough textured cover-varnish and smelled the inner genius, you haven't properly experienced its awesome true form. Read it, or leave it on your coffee table to wow visitors.

- *RRP: £12* (+P&P)
- *Pay-what-you-like min: £6* (+P&P)

Contact *The Blizzard*

All advertising, sales, press and business communication should be addressed to the Central Publishing Office:

The Blizzard
Ashmore Villa,
1, Ashmore Terrace,
Stockton Road,
Sunderland,
SR27DE

Email: info@theblizzard.co.uk
Telephone: +44 (0) 191 543 8785
Website: www.theblizzard.co.uk
Facebook: www.facebook.com/blzzrd
Twitter: @blzzrd

About Issue Nine

Editor Jonathan Wilson
Publisher The Blizzard Media Ltd
www.theblizzard.co.uk
Design Azure
www.azure-design.com

Copyright

All content is ©Copyright The Blizzard Media Ltd and may not be reproduced without explicit consent. Thanks to Jeanette G Sturis at the Kingsley Motel, Manjimup, for kind use of Warren Walker's original sketches of Dog.

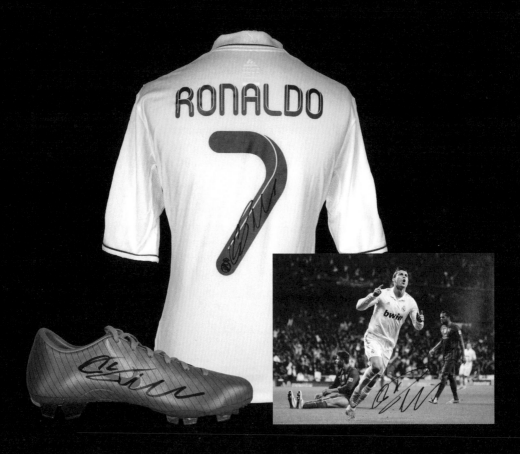